The
Blossoming
Thorn

GEORG TRAKL

The Blossoming Thorn

Georg Trakl's Poetry of Atonement

Erasmo Leiva-Merikakis

Lewisburg
Bucknell University Press
London and Toronto: Associated University Presses

Associated University Presses
440 Forsgate Drive
Cranbury, NJ 08512

Associated University Presses
25 Sicilian Avenue
London WC1A 2QH, England

Associated University Presses
2133 Royal Windsor Drive
Unit 1
Mississauga, Ontario
Canada L5J 1K5

The paper used in this publication meets the requirements
of the American National Standard for Permanence
of Paper for Printed Library Materials Z39.48-1984.

Library of Congress Cataloging-in-Publication Data

Leiva-Merikakis, Erasmo, 1946–
 The blossoming thorn.

 Bibliography: p.
 Includes index.
 1. Trakl, Georg, 1887–1914—Criticism and
interpretation.   2. Trakl, Georg, 1887–1914—Religion.
I. Title.
PT2642.R22Z715   1987   831'.912   85-43246
ISBN 0-8387-5102-4 (alk. paper)

Printed in the United States of America

A
MIREYA

lucero de mis noches

A la frontière du monde invisible, l'angoisse est un sixième sens, et douleur et perception ne font qu'un.

Georges Bernanos

Aufflattert mit trunknem Flügel die Nacht.
So leise blutet Demut,
Tau, der langsam tropft vom blühenden
  Dorn . . .

Georg Trakl

Clamavit Jesus voce magna:
"Eli, Eli, lamma sabachthani?"

Matt. 27:46

Contents

A Note on Sources

Quotations from Georg Trakl's poems, letters, and aphorisms always refer the reader to the first volume of the definitive historical-critical edition of Walter Killy and Hans Szklenar: *Georg Trakl: Dichtungen und Briefe* (Salzburg: Otto Müller Verlag, 1969). The page number in this first volume of Killy-Szklenar will often be followed by the letters *LG* in parentheses, with corresponding page number, when Lucia Getsi's rendition of the poems into English has been used. Absence of a title in both the main text and the note indicates that the poem lacks a title. Absence of a reference to Lucia Getsi's *Georg Trakl: Poems* (Athens, Ohio: Mundus Artium Press, 1973) indicates that the English version is my own. At times I have made slight variations in the Getsi version, where the sense of my interpretation demanded a more literal rendition of the original, particularly in the case of datives and accusatives with nouns, and of tenses with verbs.

Passages of Scripture generally follow the Revised Standard Version. Occasionally, however, when the context called for a more literal rendering, I have translated directly from the Greek. When a Trakl text is being compared to a passage of the Bible, I have employed Luther's version of the Scripture as revised by the Rat der Evangelischen Kirche in Deutschland in the late nineteenth century, the version that Trakl would have used. The source of a scriptural reference is given in parentheses within the text.

Where no translation credit is present for a non-English source, I am responsible for the rendering.

I am very indebted to the Otto Müller Verlag, of Salzburg, for their kind permission to quote the Trakl texts freely from the splendid edition by Walter Killy and Hans Szklenar. I thank Mr. Rainer Schulte of the Mundus Artium Press (now at the University of Texas at Dallas) for permission to use Lucia Getsi's English version of the poems.

Acknowledgments

With great pleasure and gratitude, and without any exaggeration, I can affirm that these pages would not have come to be were it not for my permanent teachers: Fr. Hans Urs von Balthasar, whose "theological aesthetics" provides the very frame of reference that made this study possible; Fr. Louis Bouyer, of the Oratory, who encourages with such intelligence and merriment; and Professor Arthur R. Evans, Jr., who first taught me to read Trakl and who gives of himself with such simplicity.

Very special thanks are due to my friend Antje Lawry for a critical reading of the manuscript that proved enlightening even to the author.

A book on so visual a poet as Trakl would not be complete without images. Thus, readers will surely be grateful to the artist, Gregory Paul Hartnell, for giving their eyes too reason to marvel. While we leave the identification of symbols to the reader's own pursuit, we offer the drawings as a gateway into the mystery of Georg Trakl, who in his life as in his poetry set his face "hard as flint" against the storm of darkness that threatened to engulf him. At the far end of sorrow he was illuminated both by the pyre of the world's conflagration and by the stern light from God's face; by—in his words—a bright "storm of mercy" whose waters make even the thorn of despair blossom.

And I cannot here keep silent the memory of my grandparents: Erasmo Marcelino, Inés, Spyros, and Calliope, whose names I write with honor. By their humble sailing across oceans and their patient plowing of the land they brought me, unbeknownst to them, to this moment of leisure where I may consider the shape of God's mercy within one man's fruitful lament. Αἰωνία ἡ μνήμη!

Introduction
Critical Approaches to Trakl

The life and work of Georg Trakl present us with an abundance of contradictions that account, in great part, for our fascination with the poet and our reaction of hypnotic shock in the face of the poetry. This provincial, undereducated Protestant from arch-Catholic Salzburg, who hardly ever crossed Austrian borders, produced in his short lifetime (1887–1914) a slender body of poems that many critics now rank among the greatest of the century—side by side with those of Rilke, Lorca, and T. S. Eliot. For all the modesty of its bulk, Trakl's work practically explodes before a reader at the mere opening of the volume, and he finds himself involved in events of such symbolic subtlety and power that he will often feel threatened as to the cohesiveness and credibility of *his* own world, so persuasive is the pull of Trakl's resounding vision. Here is no delightful poet, no inspiring bedside companion, but a dramatic lyricist of the first order who draws us into spiritual events of sublime and catastrophic proportions.

Wrenched apart in his heredity, psychic makeup, environment, and spiritual destiny by competing impulses (to achieve oblivion through frantic *dérèglement* in the style of Rimbaud, to attain to purity and holiness of spirit), Trakl wrote a poetry that attempts to mediate between these extreme forces tugging for his life. His poems, however, are neither aesthetic divertissement nor didactic sermonizing. They stake out, in language, the arena where the struggle of the poet's soul with good and evil forces may intensify to the point that total acceptance of the darkness becomes the only light. In such a context, poetic form is no mere "vessel" for a religious message or content. Form, in Trakl, bears the vital function of recognizing and expressing the reality of death, destruction, and decay, thus preparing the way for their possible transformation.

Perhaps no other poet has been more open to misinterpretation or contradictory interpretation in the twentieth century than Georg Trakl. In the late 1950s Walter Muschg did us the considerable service of pointing out the inadequacies of the existing criticism of Trakl's poetry, commenting on both extremes of criticism with equal disappointment. On the one hand, we have the critics of what might be called the "arch-formalist" school, headed by Walter Killy, who refuse to attribute any symbolic or world-critical meaning whatsoever to the aggregate of Trakl's images, seeing in them nothing but "impulses for the imagination of his hearers."[1] This view would make of Trakl a successful artist who shifts his perspective and exchanges images arbitrarily, considering only their aesthetic effect. Muschg observes that this procedure neatly disposes of all the anguish of Trakl's poems and keeps them from causing pain to the reader, since anguish and pain do not normally enter into the categories of the formalist school. We are reminded in this connection of Erich Auerbach's remark that, "without believing in Abraham's sacrifice, it is impossible to put the narrative of it to the use for which it was written."[2] And it is no coincidence that the very critics who "deactivate" Trakl's poetry in the manner described by Muschg are the same ones who emphasize its supposed "hermeticism," by which they may simply mean that they are unable to share the perspective from which the poetry was written. Muschg's conclusion is that the puzzle of Georg Trakl may be better understood only when the "taboo of a purely aesthetic interpretation is broken."[3]

The other extreme of Trakl criticism consists of what I call the "arch-Christian" critics, of which Alfred Focke[4] and Eduard Lachmann[5] are the chief. With considerable contempt Muschg dismisses them as those who "see only a need for hanging a sentimental Catholic mantle around the shoulders of the Protestant from Salzburg who descended into black despair."[6] Along with these arch-Christian critics, Muschg attacks Martin Heidegger, because in his essay *Georg Trakl: Eine Erörterung seines Gedichtes*[7] he shares with them the method of appropriating for his own apologetic use the work of a poet who, according to Muschg, is not to be subsumed under any philosophical or theological persuasion.

Muschg's dissatisfaction with this state of criticism is well founded. While the formalist critics insist on an exclusively aesthetic interpretation of the poems and so busy themselves with endless philological computations of word-frequency and synaesthetic "effects," the religious apologists abuse the poems by reducing them to the poetic expression of an independently existing set of truths, either "poetized dogma" or "dogmatized poetry," in the words of Elisabeth Langgässer.[8] The former, Muschg would say, fail to see the spirit in the letter; the latter see too much.

Lachmann's method of paraphrasing the poems does, in fact, soon become irritating. Rather than showing the function of a given phrase or image within the poem, he either repeats it with slight variations (like certain Sunday preachers commenting on the Gospel reading!) or explains it in terms of something else. Lachmann assumes that each poem is a narrative in poetic form, and so his paraphrase has the function of retelling the hypothetical narration "straight," in prose form, a procedure that, in spite of remonstrances to the contrary, results in an unbearable banalization of the poems. When he does have a genuine insight into key features of the poetry, Lachmann quickly abandons it to return to his paraphrase. For instance, speaking of the last line in the second section of *Helian:*

Ersterbend neigt sich das Haupt im Dunkel des Ölbaums,[9]

Lachmann says: "Here, as throughout, we are struck by the anonymity with which the Lord's apparition is concealed."[10] Rather than asking the important causes of Christ's anonymity here and elsewhere in Trakl, he immediately passes on to his narration.

Between the two poles of Muschg's evaluation of the critical situation with regard to Trakl's work are found a variety of critics, the best of whom combine the insights of both schools. One of the most penetrating and empathetic is Walter Falk, whose *Leid und Verwandlung* examines Trakl, along with Rilke and Kafka, with the goal of establishing the parameters of the Expressionist epoch. Falk asks the question concerning the function of Trakl's poetry and concludes that it achieves a kind of transformation and reintegration; but he does not determine more precisely what the content of this transformation through suffering might be. Part of the problem—and this is typical of most Trakl exegetes—is that Falk does not see the necessity of relating Trakl's poetry to anything outside the Expressionist movement, and certainly not outside of German literature.[11] And Walter Muschg himself is finally a help only partially, in the sense that he points the way to be followed after "breaking the taboo of a purely aesthetic interpretation."[12] Even the phrase concerning Trakl's "descent into black despair" reveals, with its heavy pathos, an excess of pure humanism, apparently Muschg's antidote for "pure aestheticism." It is simply not true to say that Trakl's deepest significance consists in being an extreme paradigm of the chaotic condition of the European spirit at the outbreak of the First World War. A close examination of the poems reveals a pattern of internal transformation of the ugly and the decayed that is closely connected with the all-pervading atmosphere of profound silence and impassivity in the face of cultural and personal collapse. In a fundamental sense, Trakl goes beyond chaos.

A study by Giuseppe Dolei bears a title that seemed very promising in terms of my own concerns: *L'arte come espiazione imperfetta: Saggio su Trakl.* Unfortunately, that promise was not made good in the execution.

The theme of expiation or atonement is nowhere pursued by Dolei in depth as the most revealing motive behind Trakl's creative act. Dolei's book abounds in specific analyses that effectively insert Trakl within the company of Symbolists and Expressionists where he theoretically belongs. His association with the Brenner circle in particular is developed in an enlightening way. But, beyond establishing Trakl's debt to, and differences from, his contemporaries, Dolei's treatment and conclusions remain disappointingly ambiguous. By contrast to the psychoanalytical critics whom we shall see in a moment, however, Dolei does take Trakl seriously as an artist consciously working at his craft and as an ethical person wrestling with the problems of destiny, freedom, and responsibility: "We believe that Trakl's modernity consists in this: he takes his stance at that golden dividing-line between the juvenile impulse toward egocentric closure within the world of images and the mature awareness that he has neither the right nor the possibility of withdrawing from reality—the awareness that he must 'correct himself continuously to give to the truth what belongs to the truth' (Trakl to Buschbeck, fall 1911)."[13]

Mention should be made, in conclusion, of two critics who apply a psychoanalytical method. In a brief monograph simply entitled *Georg Trakl*, Maire J. Kurrik unabashedly identifies Trakl's "schizophrenia" as being the very source of his aesthetic excellence: "The deranged mind cannot create the intelligible symbolic discourse that is the privilege of the authentic indissoluble imagination, but it can without cessation strive to fasten the awfulness of derangement in formal patterns."[14] We are quite wrong then, Kurrik would have us think, in looking for any intelligibility in Trakl's poetry; this search is only the result of our Western mania for intellectual clarity. To read Trakl profitably, in fact, we must first put ourselves in a state of near insanity: "The poem [*Nachtgesang*] can only be interpreted if we try to imagine the alien and bizarre mental states that occur in an extreme schizoid condition."[15] As for any question of Christian faith informing the poetry, any statement that might possibly bear an authentic religious or mystical meaning is denounced by Kurrik as, precisely, proof of Trakl's insanity: "The really pathological element in [Trakl's] identification [with the Christ figure] becomes evident in a reported conversation between Trakl and Dallago, in which Trakl said: 'I am Christ.'"[16]

Clearly such an approach as this is emblematic of a certain academic reductionism because of the manner in which it identifies the foundation of personal reality with quantifiable processes and intentions that are "anterior to consciousness,"[17] and because of its blindness to the existence of the whole spiritual order.

A more recent successor to Kurrik (1974) is Francis M. Sharp, in his book *The Poet's Madness* (1981). In this study Sharp affirms that the "fascination [that Trakl's poetry] continues to elicit . . . hinges on what appears to be the essential otherness of the poet's experience, an otherness rooted in the poet's madness."[18] Sharp appeals to the "antipsychiatry" of R. D. Laing, with whose help he sets out to "activate the human presence in the texts, reinvesting them with a referential density that much of Trakl criticism denies."[19] Sharp makes a laudable attempt not to succumb to the reductive tendencies of the traditional psychological approach, which tries to "peg" a person's identity by leveling everything about him to common denominators. However, one wonders whether he altogether avoids the pitfalls of reduction. One entire section of Sharp's book is entitled "The Enduring Passion," referring, of course, to the all-too-famous incestuous feelings Trakl had for his sister, Grete. Sharp is not content to identify the theme of incest as being relevant to the poetry; it must be *the* theme, and he will not allow any tampering with this clinical triumph. He says that Killy "trivializes [incest] by making it representative of a metaphysical dilemma. In becoming a mere sign for a higher meaning, incest loses its force as a physical and psychological reality that found its way from Trakl's life into his work."[20] Anathema to anyone who would add "metaphysical" or "spiritual" to the dogmatic monopoly of the "physical" and the "psychological"!

Much more level-headed appears to me the observation of Michael Hamburger, whom no one would suspect of being a Christian apologist, when he says with deep simplicity that "incest is [only] one of the many forms of evil that occur in Trakl's work"; for incest in Trakl cannot be understood without reference to the spiritual affinity of his existential faith with that of a Kierkegaard and a Dostoievski.[21] "Evil" and "faith," however, vital as they are to Trakl's vision, are simply beyond the comprehension of the narrow psychologizer. In reenacting lyrically the endless interplay of the phenomena of life, death, decay, and regeneration, Trakl himself, the alleged madman, shows far more breadth of intelligence and lucidity than these diagnostic critics with their pencils and pads, who approach him with no less condescension than they would a laboratory specimen. In this view, every difficult and surprising element, whether of imagery or language, at once becomes coarse grist for the psychoanalytical mill: "The rapid shifts of tenses . . . seem to imitate the outwardly arbitrary shifts from one level of awareness to another in a psychologically labile personality. . . . The very root of the schizophrenic's enigmatic 'word salad' may lie in his inability to set the communicational mode of his fantasy . . . to the listener."[22] Having decided in advance that Trakl is an incestuous schizophrenic, this kind of critic has only to subordinate every utterance in the poetry to a clinical scrutiny that is sure to yield the desired results. The sterility of such an approach is that, while it may expound important principles of psychology, it provides next to no help in understanding poetry as poetry, or a human being as anything more than an unwieldy mass of phobias and guilty desires. In short, it abolishes man as a spiritual being.

To my mind the first significant breakthrough in Trakl criticism has come from Rudolf Schier. Schier suggests that much of the celebrated impenetrability and hermeticism of Trakl's poetry, which has traditionally led critics such as Lachmann to take a very apologetic and noncommittal position with regard to their own interpretation, is the result of a shortsightedness conditioned by the mesmerizing effect of Trakl's style, an effect that has kept critics from determining the nature of Trakl's language by comparing its structure to works of other periods. We shall later have occasion to examine the strengths and weaknesses of Schier's *Die Sprache Georg Trakls;* for the moment, suffice it to say that this analysis has successfully established that Trakl's style is to be seen in the tradition of figural writing. The insight enables Schier, and us, to go beyond the narrow confines of the Killy school and at the same time to avoid the subjectivistic excesses of a Lachmann. A figural interpretation must, by definition, move both within and outside the work being considered, so that the aestheticist illusion is dispelled that the work has no meaning beyond the sensual impressions of its images and, at the same time, the corresponding pietistic assumption is avoided that the poetry is but a transposition of ready-made values and symbols. But in the end Schier insists on so secularistic a conception of the figural method that he violates its essentially religious character; and so his application of it to Trakl's work exhibits the eccentricity that always results from making private use of what has long matured in the keeping of a suprapersonal tradition.

The present study gains its momentum from a dissatisfaction and an enthusiasm. The dissatisfaction coincides with that of Walter Muschg: that none of the existing studies—and he did not even consider the psychoanalytical!—has been able to provide a consistent exegesis that shows the inevitability of its conclusions from the inner structures of the work. In other words, the typical Trakl critic offers either educated guesswork in an attempt to integrate the meaning and ethos of his work into a whole greater than itself, or he abandons all endeavor to make such connections, claiming either that they are simply nonexistent (and that thus Trakl is a unique poetic phenomenon) or that we possess too little or too ambiguous "information" to proceed objectively. The latter group content themselves with linguistic analysis and seek no *logos* manifesting itself in Trakl's poetic utterances.

It is my conviction that the fundamental exegetical principle that must serve as a corrective for this state of affairs is that a critic should strive to understand a poetry as that poetry understands itself, or in the words of

Ignaz Zangerle: ". . . in the exegesis of a poet's work nothing should be left out which was for him of the most urgent reality . . . , precisely with regard to a poet who understood his fundamental experience—man's existence in guilt—in terms of a need for redemption; a poet who, in his desolation, is made paradigmatic by the identity he forged between his own vocation and the destiny of mankind."[23] Indeed, one can hardly read almost any line of Trakl without feeling a deep sense of the urgency and religious passion of his poetry. I cite an example at random:

> Nächtlich tönt der Seele einsames Saitenspiel
> Dunkler Verzückung
> Voll zu den silbernen Füssen der Büsserin
> In der blauen Stille
> Und Versühnung des Ölbaums.[24]

Tremendous demands are made on a reader by such poetry, not only because it wears hard on one's concentration but because it demands an unusual degree of emotional involvement and response. From this perspective we may agree with a critic like Lachmann, who for all his naive apologetics is far closer to the ardent spirit of Trakl's poetry than all the cool detachment of the Killy school. These interpreters forget Plato's remark that a good poet is not so much made by the refinement of his craft (τεχνή) as by the degree of high delirium (ἐνθουσιασμός: "possession by a god") that informs his poetry.[25]

The enthusiasm that propels this inquiry, therefore, derives from the challenge of showing with convincing probability that Lachmann's intuition was correct when he tried to reveal the intimate relation that exists between Trakl's work and the substance of Christianity, an intuition that Lachmann's tendency toward total allegorization of the poetry dissipated into a loss of all distinction and particularity of meaning. In my view, it was not Lachmann's instincts that were misguided; it was his methodology. The work of Rudolf Schier proves essential in this connection. By establishing the figural nature of Trakl's style, Schier provides Lachmann with the methodological corrective necessary, so that the matter of Trakl's place in the Christian tradition may now be pursued from the inside, by reconstructing the interior phenomenal world of the poet's spirit.

By means of an exhaustive analysis of the inner structures of the work, I hope to show that Trakl's poetry forms a continuous whole with his spiritual vision: that the poetry comprises the symbolic aspect, the distillation of his life. The symbolization effected by the poetry, however, is no passive mirroring of static interior realities within the poet. The event of the poem, itself real human act, intertwines vitally with the other activities of the poet's will, intellect, and emotions, both clarifying ongoing spiritual processes and initiating new processes that work their way back into the spiritual and somatic underground where the contours of a human life are forged.

In order to maintain consistently a twin vision on spiritual experience and work, the approach must at the same time be rigorous and flexible. A dialogue must be allowed to flourish between the finished form of the poetry—the objective aesthetic reality—and those more subjective statements of Trakl's concerning the religious ethos of his life, utterances that we find in his letters, aphorisms, and records of conversations. We allow Trakl to become his own exegete. In seeking to "catch" Trakl's work in its perfect flight, at least for the space required to afford some reliable insight into its nature, this study explores the thesis put forward by several critics to the effect that the archetype informing the structure of the poetry is, indeed, the *form of Christ*, his words, deeds, and mystery as described and celebrated in the Gospel and the liturgy of the Christian Church. My method, however, no longer has much in common with that of other interpreters, whose apologetic tone and obsession to "Christianize" the poetry rather obstructs than clarifies the field of vision for the recognition of those theological structures which are present. The comparative approach allows the Christ-form and the form of the poetry to cast much light on each other, and it also prevents them from violating each other's autonomous integrity. Comparison here implements communion in dialogue at an aesthetic and religious level.

The specific task of the study, therefore, is to establish a strict correlation between Trakl's key aphorism concerning the religious ethos of poetic activity, as he views it for himself, and the actual form of individual poems. The aphorism in question conceives the writing of poems as a religious work of atonement. Trakl's exact words are as follows: "Gefühl in den Augenblicken totenähnlichen Seins: alle Menschen sind der Liebe wert. Erwachend fühlst du die Bitternis der Welt; darin ist alle deine ungelöste Schuld; dein Gedicht eine unvollkommene Sühne" [Feeling in the moments of deathlike existence: all men are worthy of love. Awakening, you feel the bitterness of the world; in it is all your unresolved guilt; your poem an imperfect atonement].[26]

An initial chapter examines, at the level of general discussion, the relationship between poetic theory and the dogma of the Incarnation. This introductory survey serves to demarcate the territory that provides the stage for the remainder of the inquiry. The all-important conclusion reached by this first discussion is that an arbitrarily enforced separation of "form" from "content" in poetic criticism is incompatible with an incarnational view of the world, which, in turn, is proposed as the basis for Trakl's poetic creation. A second chapter reviews special moments in what E. Langgässer has called the *Stilgeschichte der Frömmigkeit*, the "history of styles in the Christian faith-experience."[27] With this overview we begin to see Trakl's alleged "hermeticism" in the context of a tradition of visionary poetry and other forms of religious thought that have resulted from the urgent claims made by the belief in the absolute mystery proposed by Christianity. Thus we here examine the "external evidence" of the poetry at a historical level by isolating the "apocalyptic" style that runs from the early Christian pessimists, through the Baroque poets, to the dialectical theologians of the twentieth century.

The third chapter analyzes the poetry at a more exclusively aesthetic level, stressing the Symbolist and Expressionist nature of Trakl's poetics and attempting to relate this poetics to the aesthetic implications of the Incarnation. The *form* of Trakl's christology offers the essential test as to the authenticity of his poetry's transformation in the light of the Christ-form. The thorough way in which Trakl has absorbed and implemented the Symbolist aesthetic (the autonomy of the poetic image) enables him to produce an art in which the poem becomes event. The basic contours of this event constitute a figural realization of the Christ-form. Crucial, however, is the manner in which this Christ-form is realized poetically without the poetic medium becoming a kind of poetized dogmatics. The converging in Trakl of the aesthetic traditions of Symbolism and of Judeo-Christian stylistics makes possible the figural application of the autonomous symbol. Only such a symbolist realization can vouch for the authenticity of transformation—whether of a poem or of a person—in the light of the Christ-form. Only great poetry can embody the whole mystery of the religious event; otherwise we have to do merely with a poetry about religious feelings and opinions.

The fourth and final chapter proceeds on the conviction that the ultimate meaning of a religious phenomenon is found in its finality or eventual end. The deepest question, therefore, that may be put to Trakl's poetry concerns the "internal evidence" of the work at the eth-icoreligious level. By asking whether there exists a fundamental formal correspondence between the intended end of Christ's saving action of atonement and the end to Trakl's poetic activity, we may establish with certainty the degree to which his poetry fully realizes, embodies, repre-sents the Christ-form. In its avowed attempt to realize a work of atone-ment, Trakl's poetry achieves the ontological density as event that is its very identity. The poem must be event, for it conceives of itself as religious act. The reality of guilt may be confronted only with the event of the terrible image.

Beyond its specifc concern for the vitality and accomplishments of Trakl's poetry, this study proceeds from the conviction that the interrela-tionship between literary criticism and theology, or more specifically between poetry and faith, is of paramount consequences for both. From the side of theology, we may affirm that the relevance of literature is nothing less than the concrete demonstration of the fact that the subject of dogma may and must become realized in existence. In a manner that pure theology can approximate but not realize, poetry can be an expression and a dramatic demonstration of incarnate faith; poetry can thus become a testimony for the actual presence of redemptive God-manhood in the world. For, while poetry is actual event, theology must remain description and, to that degree, separation from the object of faith. From the side of literature, the presence of an authentic theological concern liberates poetry from the burden of that "soteriological omnipotence"[28] attributed to art by the Romanticizing idealist tradition. And therefore, in the recognition that "the genuine work of art proceeds only from the awareness of death,"[29] in the recognition, that is, of its own inability to overcome single-handedly mankind's most extreme contradictions in the face of death and abysmal anguish, poetry can rise to its true dignity as the fragile but irreplaceable witness of man's capability of being transformed to an existence beyond the reaches of destruction.

The present study must acknowledge a glaring shortcoming from the outset: the absence of a thorough discussion of *Helian,* perhaps Trakl's most comprehensive and representative single poem. At least two entire books have been devoted to the explication of this one poem.[30] The omission on my part of an analysis of this veritable *Weltgedicht* is founded on two reasons. First, an adequate presentation of *Helian* would easily have required another full-length chapter, which would have extended the text excessively. And, second, I feel that such a discussion would not have added substantially to the results of my other interpretations.

The
Blossoming
Thorn

1

The Poetics of Incarnation

> In the days of his flesh he offered up prayer
> and entreaty to the one who could save him
> from death, not without a piercing cry, not
> without tears; yet with such piety as won
> him a hearing. Son though he was, he
> learned obedience in the school of suffer-
> ing.
>
> Hebrews 5:7–8

From Criticism of Content to Elucidation of Form

It has become fashionable in critical circles to deny with an almost categorical compulsion that the work of any writer considered vitally "modern" could possibly belong within the framework of any tradition, particularly if that tradition is the Christian one. When speaking of the obviously Christian references and symbols contained in *Helian,* for instance, Herbert Lindenberger finds it necessary to say that "Trakl's Christianity, at least as it emerges in his poems, is a distinctly 'literary' Christianity,' one that is neither doctrinal in intent, like the Christianity of George Herbert's *Temple,* nor a direct profession of faith such as one can find even in so Symbolist a poem as T. S. Eliot's *Ash Wednesday.*"[1] Is "literary," then, the only alternative to either "dogmatic" or "apologetic" in matters of religion? "Literary" would seem to be an imprecise category, since the term makes an implicit distinction between the content and form of a poem and thus completely ignores the Symbolist form otherwise so much emphasized by Lindenberger. If Lindenberger points out that the Symbolist nature of the poem makes it impossible to insist on Christian interpretation, how can he then say that "so Symbolist a poem" as *Ash Wednesday* contains a direct confession of faith, since Symbolism presumably excludes confessionalism of any kind? Does Lindenberger grant Eliot room for play that he denies Trakl?

Lachmann's and Focke's deliberately Christian interpretations of Trakl are based on zealous and ingenious guesswork, suggestions that may, in fact, "be the case" or not. The present study asks whether it would be possible to produce one criterion, one clue to the meaning of Trakl's poetry that will not proceed by guesswork leading to a dubious certainty, but will quite objectively demonstrate its adequacy, if not for each detail of Trakl's work, then at least for the general configuration of his mature work. The answer seems to lie in a close analysis of the inner structure and nature of the poetry's *form,* since both the "Christianizers" and the "secularizers" go askew by arguing whether a specific reference is Christian or not. In other words, they are misled by insisting on questions of referential content whereas, owing to the Symbolist nature of Trakl's poetics, his meaning is conveyed in the event of the form itself. Again discussing *Helian,* Lindenberger observes that "it would be tempting to speak of a Christian death-and-rebirth pattern shaping the poem. Yet the problematic quality of the conclusion makes it difficult to postulate any single pattern unequivocally."[2] Aside from the fact that the Christian "pattern" of death and resurrection is neither "tempting" nor "unproblematic," Lindenberger approaches the problem in the wrong manner. By moving back from the immediate confines of the poem we may ask whether the poet, in writing *Helian,* does not *presuppose* such a pattern in the sense that his poem *exists in the world* and is made possible in virtue of that pattern, and further, whether the poem realizes the event of death and resurrection on the aesthetic plane in a particular and unique manner that accounts for the "problematic quality" of the conclusion. In other words, to what extent is the Christian "pattern" a literary motif and, as such, exterior to the structure of the poem, or to what extent is it a structural determinant, that is, the constitutional explanation for the very form of the poem, and not one pattern among many possible ones?

To give an example: the verse from *Helian* previously quoted— "Ersterbend neigt sich das Haupt im Dunkel des Ölbaums"—quite obviously makes use of Luther's translation of the verse from John's Gospel that reads: "Da nun Jesus den Essig genommen hatte, sprach er: Es ist vollendet! und neigte das Haupt und verschied" (19:30). But the question as to whether this is a "Christian reference" or not remains quite sterile until we consider whether Trakl's use of the words of Scripture signals the same gesture on the part of his protagonist as is intended by the evangelist's record of Jesus' attitude. Henri de Lubac writes that "Christ's exegesis does not occur primarily in words: it occurs in action. It *is* Action. Before explaining to his disciples, on the eve of Easter, how the ancient Scripture bears witness to the New Testament and is, therefore, changed into it, Jesus effects this change."[3] In the same manner we must ask whether Trakl's exegesis of Christ's death in his poem imitates Christ's own exegesis of the Old Testament; that is, whether Trakl actualizes within the total structure of *Helian* the radical obedience symbolized in the bending of the head—and to that extent his use of Scripture becomes an "exegesis which is act"—or whether the presence of scriptural language remains foreign to the event of the poem and to that extent constitutes a flaw in the Symbolist aesthetic on which it is based.

The Methodology of Realization

The real issue at stake here seems to be the conception that one formulates concerning the general role of the religious in literature. By suggesting that the religious element be separated from the aesthetic foundation—and this is what Lindenberger does by speaking of a "literary Christianity"—one has already prejudiced the case to the detriment of both elements. Dorothee Sölle, in explicating a Faulkner novel, asks: "Can we regard the biblical dimension as a secondary level which in some way introduces the novel into a religious realm? Such an interpretation would imply a destructive criticism of Faulkner, since it contradicts the aesthetic principle of the functionality of all elements by attributing to religion a merely decorative role."[4] By reducing the religious element to a merely decorative role, the aesthetic integrity of the work is compromised, and no great work of literature results from either compromises or chance. But Sölle explains this aestheticist reduction of the religious as a reaction to the kind of theological criticism Eduard Lachmann represents, to those critics who are "always on the search for something Christian" in literature, Christian objects and Christian contents, and who limit themselves to an "objectified fixation" on the dramatization of Bible stories and the use of religious symbols such as manger, star, cross, and crown of thorns.[5] Such a procedure totally overlooks the specific manner in which religious language is used and thus quickly absorbs the uniqueness of the work into the omnivorous religious concern of the critic. Sölle adds that good theological reasons also censure such a method, since "the Judeo-Christian understanding of the Absolute prohibits precisely the objectified fixation on *one* of its forms."[6]

A religious methodology that is thus "objectively fixated" is, in fact, a rather inferior manifestation of theological concerns, since it seeks only "the repetition of what is already known at a level which is termed the 'aesthetic,' although nothing new is actually *perceived*."[7] An "objectively fixated" methodology suffers from a literalism that is foreign to the most traditional Christian exegesis. Commenting on Origen, de Lubac says that "the spiritual understanding is interior and discovers 'internal causes,' while the literal sense remains exterior, on the surface."[8] And Sölle concludes: "The criterion of the theological interest in literature is never objectified, but is conceived functionally."[9] The endeavor of the secularizing critics may, then, be understood in terms of an interest in safeguarding the uniqueness and particularity of a given work in the face of a not-too-scrupulous theologizing onslaught. The inadequacies of both these extremes instruct us to seek the total relevance of theological concerns within the total unity of the work of art. For if the "objectively fixated" religious mentality must be overcome, so must the corresponding aesthetic positivism that insists on a strictly immanent interpretation of literature, and thus seals the work of art off from the fact that it exists within a living tradition and within the reality of its author's life. The consistent presence of religious language in poetry—and by this I mean, primarily, explicit or implicit biblical citations—is the most obvious indication that the work understands itself as existing within a given religious tradition.[10]

Dorothee Sölle provides Rudolf Schier with the corrective needed if the concept of figural language is to produce, with regard to Trakl's work, the far-reaching consequences that it should. In a manner that I have previously called "eccentric," Schier insists on a very negative application of the idea of figural language. Basing his view on statements of Trakl to the effect that in his poetry he strives for a constant depersonalization of the image in order to subordinate himself to the truth,[11] Schier concludes that "a figural conception must seek the destruction of the natural world, since the natural world stands in the way of a supernatural, divine order."[12] This interpretation takes no heed of the intrinsically Christian character of the figural tradition, whose existence in Trakl's poetry Schier has so well established. De Lubac stresses the fact that nothing remotely approaching the figural mentality can be found outside of the Christian faith, since here we have to do with "a theory which, in its very form, owes everything to this faith and which, in its context, wishes to express it totally."[13] The application of Schier's thesis is based on an arbitrary separation of the order of nature from the divine order, which he claims are mutually exclusive. The use of figural language would then be an attempt to "destroy" nature in order that God may speak through the poet's work all the more clearly. Furthermore, Schier identifies the Neoplatonic view of nature-as-divine-emanation with the Christian view, "especially because of the Incarnation." Figural language becomes a tool against both nature and Christianity, and finally against the poetic consciousness itself, which strives for self-examination.[14] The confusions of this theological muddle are too intricate to unravel here. It is evident, however, that Schier violates the essence of figural language as being a promise of fulfillment by turning it against both man and nature. The very use of figural language already implies belief in the *pro me* of Scripture.

In order to apply to literature the essence of the figural method of scriptural interpretation, Dorothee Sölle has developed the concept of *realization,* which she defines as the "worldly concretion of what is 'given' or promised in the language of religion."[15] Realization belongs in the tradition of figural language because it presupposes that what is meant by the mythico-religious language of Scripture requires, by its very nature, that it be concretized in existence.[16] Hence realization consists of the making actual, in a particular situation, of what Scripture proclaims absolutely. Corresponding to the prefiguration of Christ's advent in the Old Testament, the concept of postfigural transformation means essentially that salvation history is not yet complete, and that in this sense Scripture continues to be written in the lives of those who are transfigured according to the likeness of Christ, particularly as this transfiguration is expressed in a work of literature.[17] The radically Christian character of postfigural interpretation is that it occurs solely on the incarnational model of God's presence in the world, and thus it sharply contrasts with, without contradicting it, the prefigural expectation of the Hebraic dispensation. The attitude of the postfigural imagination has perhaps not been better summarized than in Peter Damian's terse aphorism: "Mea grammatica Christus est,"[18] in which both the literary and the mystical components of the *figura* are intimately united.

We must be careful with what we mean by "realizing the promises of Scripture," for, as de Lubac points out, the Christian does not seek to "actualize" Scripture in the sense of updating it or making it relevant, since the promises of the Old Testament have been actualized, once and for all, by Christ himself.[19] For this reason we speak of postfigural transformation, the permanent and irreplaceable source of the transformation being precisely the reality of the form of Christ as depicted in the New Testament. Dorothee Sölle's concept of realization, far from being a modern invention, is but the application to literature of the New Testament's understanding of what it means to be a Christian. St. Paul was the first to use the term κάνων to refer to the manner in which the event of salvation is proclaimed by Scripture: the fact that Christ was crucified and died for the world and, by his rising from the dead, effected a new creation (Gal. 6:16).[20] This κάνων requires not so much that it be believed as that it be incarnated in the lives of those who call themselves Christians.

"The whole of Scripture has a Christian form," writes Hans Urs von Balthasar, "and, as Scripture powerfully impresses itself upon the history of the Church and of mankind, it molds lives in the shape of the Christ-form [christusförmige Lebensgestalten]."[21] In a text of paramount importance, St. Paul establishes the new principle of postfiguration or metamorphosis *(Umgestaltung)* in con-formity with the form of Christ: Ἡμεῖς δέ πάντες ἀνακεκαλυμμένῳ προσώπῳ τήν δόξαν Κυρίου κατοπτριζόμενοι τήν αὐτήν εἰκόνα μεταμορφούμεθα ἀπό δόξης εἰς δόξαν, καθάπερ ἀπό Κυρίου πνεύματος. ("All of us, reflecting with unveiled face the glory of the Lord for us as in a mirror, are being transformed into the same likeness, from his glory into our glory, and this through the Spirit of the Lord" [2 Cor. 3:18]). Ontological metamorphosis in Christ is the essence of Christianity and the full explanation of what Peter Damian meant when he said that Christ was his "grammar": that the believer's life-form con-forms in the endings of its every declension and conjugation with the unique and exclusive paradigm of Christ's reality. Later on we shall have occasion to examine at length how an event such as occurs in the last section of *Helian*—

> Da Helians Seele sich im rosigen Spiegel beschaut
> Und Schnee und Aussatz von seiner Stirne sinken[22]—

expresses the same kind of healing reintegration as that which Paul calls for in describing individual transformation according to the glory of Christ, which is seen as "in a mirror." For the time being, however, it must suffice to say that our inquiry is based on a doctrine of spiritual perception the structure of whose noetic processes is conditioned by the ontological reality of the Christ-event, existentially (that is, mystically) realized and appropriated by faith.[23]

Erich Auerbach explains the (pre)figural mentality in the following terms:

> Figural interpretation establishes a connection between two events and persons in such a way that the first signifies not only itself but also the second, while the second involves or fulfills the first. The two poles of a figure are separated in time, but both, being real entities or persons, are within temporality. They are both contained in the flowing stream which is historical life, and only the comprehension, the *intellectus spiritualis,* of their interdependence is a spiritual act.[24]

The use of a figural method, following this explanation, is a manifestation of a theological memory which is forever endeavoring to actualize the promises of faith by discerning their spiritual presence. But with the advent of the Christian dispensation, Auerbach's description accounts for only half of the reality; for, after Christ, we must speak of the era of postfiguration in Paul's sense of metamorphosis. More than its being a matter of the "literary influence" of the tradition, we have here the real shaping principle of Christian literature: the experience of being transformed by God in Christ in the present, so that the dominance of historical time recedes into the background in the face of the existential contemporaneity of the believer with Christ. It is the experience of Christ's action in the present that perpetuates in a living manner the figural tradition by realizing postfigurally Christ's Incarnation, Passion, and Resurrection at each moment of history. Thus, the meaning of postfiguration is that the individual in time is himself fulfilled—and to that extent receives a new existence outside historical time—by being conformed to the likeness of Christ, in the same manner that Christ fulfilled once and for all the expectations of the Hebraic dispensation. The essence of understanding one's reality within the scope of postfiguration is whether or not "the form of one's own existence becomes undecipherable except as a function of the Christ-form."[25]

In this context, the general thesis of this inquiry is that the discovery of the christological form of Trakl's poetry is *the* essential insight into the total meaning of the poetry. The method of demonstration of this thesis will be a comparison of the Christ-form of Scripture, dogmatic theology, and liturgy with the composite protagonist-form of the poems, with particular attention being given to the figural nature of Trakl's language. The manner of making such a comparison will be governed by several aesthetic and theological principles that must be clarified at this time.

Christ-Form and the Form of the Poem

$$\text{Μέχρις οὗ μορφωθῇ Χριστός ἐν ὑμῖν.}$$
Gal. 4:19

The first of these principles is that the act of Christian faith is a transformative experience of the whole person, rather than a mere mental process; it entails a new creation that radically (ontologically) modifies the subject's perception of the world and of himself. Because the whole person is thus affected by the experience of rebirth in Christ, so, too, the creative intellect (imagination), all the more so since the act of faith itself requires the cooperation of the creative intellect, without which collaboration the human being is unable to appropriate any form from outside himself, including the Christ-form as presented by Scripture and the Church's teaching. What may be descriptively distinguished as the "creative" and the "believing" intellects actually coexist in a tight subliminal and unreflected unity in the existing subject, so that there is a strict interdependence between faith and aesthetics. In a masterful way Hans Urs von Balthasar describes the effect of the "appropriation of the

Christ-form," this being his theologico-aesthetic definition of the act of faith:

> If Christ is the image of all images, then it is impossible that he not affect all images of the world through his presence, ordering them around himself. There is no such thing as an isolated image. Every image makes its appearance before a background of "fellow-images." Every image expands and impresses itself upon the world, manifesting by its interior form that it belongs to a "community of forms" and that it has the creative power to shape the world around itself. Through Christ's form, the things in the world acquire their correct distance from him and one another and their correct proximity to him and to one another. The believer does not "believe" all of this; he *sees* it. This sensual world in which he lives and in which he apparently feels at home is determined through and through by Christ as central image and event. The believer clings in faith to what he is given to see: the displacement and magnetic readjustment of the world's images by the image of God in their midst.[26]

The precision of this passage greatly clarifies our future discussion. If the appropriation of the Christ-form by a believer so radically modifies his perception of the sense-world in general, since that central form or figure organizes all other forms around it as by crystallization, then this "law of crystallization" holds *a fortiori* for the artist, who leaves imprinted upon his art his expression of the structure of the world. Because of the thoroughness of the believer's modification by faith, and because of the primary unity of the creative and the believing intellect, the act of aesthetic creation will inevitably confer on its product the plastic imprint of its creator's ontological reality as modified by the act of faith.

Commenting on St. Thomas's dictum that "operatio artis fundatur super operationem naturae,"[27] Jacques Maritain writes that "in the same way that God's trace and image appear in his creatures, the human mark is imprinted upon the work of art—the full mark, both sensual and spiritual, not only the mark of the hands, but that of the whole soul."[28] Since the operation of art is a virtue or "habit" of the soul, the art of a Christian soul will be Christian art, not necessarily by intent, but un-avoidably, following the principle of *operatio sequitur esse*[29]: "Christian art is defined by the subject in whom it is found and by the spirit from which it proceeds. We say 'Christian art' or 'art of the Christian' as we say 'art of the bee' or 'human art.' It is the art of ransomed mankind."[30]

We recall at this point Herbert Lindenberger's remark that "Trakl's Christianity, at least as it emerges in his poems, is a distinctly 'literary' Christianity."[31] In the light of the principle just established, I must emphasize the fallacy of such an attempt to separate forcibly what by nature cannot be kept apart. Owing to the dynamism of the Christian event of transformation, we must agree that, if Trakl organized his world around the Christ-form, then his subjective life-form cannot but in-form the shape of his art. "Do not attempt the absurdity of dissociating the artist from the Christian," Maritain concludes. "They are one, provided one *is* truly a Christian and provided one's art is not isolated from one's soul by some system of aesthetics."[32] Not only was Trakl's art not isolated from his soul by "some system of aesthetics," but, as I shall endeavor to show, his particular use of Symbolist aesthetics coincides with the Christian ascesis of transformation in Christ.

There is a very precise analogy between the Pauline doctrine of transformation in Christ, as expressed in 2 Corinthians 3:18, whereby the believer is conformed (*umgestaltet*, metamorphosed) to Christ by contemplation of His likeness, and that philosophical axiom which we have just reviewed (*operatio sequitur esse*), which requires that the structure of a work of art carry the imprint of its creator—that is to say, a transformation of the art-material in conformity with the living reality of the poet. We have here a schema of two originals and two likenesses, a pair each in the realms of mystical theology and of poetics. Now, our objective evidence for the reality of Christ is the Christ-form of Scripture, which is the literary record of revelation, while the evidence for the reality of the poet is, naturally, his poetry. If we are able to establish an objective correlation between the form of a poetic work and the form of the Christ-reality as presented in Scripture—and this is possible, given the aesthetic nature of the evidence in each case—then we may draw decisive conclusions regarding the kind of spiritual substance that constitutes both a poet's life and his work. In the event the question of the correlation between work-form and Christ-form is answered affirmatively, then we may take the further step of identifying the "original" of which the work of art is a likeness (i.e., the poet) with the likeness of which the Christ-form is the original (i.e., the believer). In other words, we may identify poet and believer, so that the four terms of our schema:

are now reduced to three, and the art work can be viewed in a constellation along with the Christ-form of revelation and its subjective appropriation (*Nachgestaltung*) by faith. As a result of this passing over from a parallel foursome to the triangular threesome:

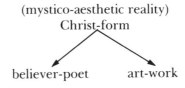

(mystico-aesthetic reality)
Christ-form

believer-poet   art-work

we may reach a fundamental insight by seeing the work of art itself as an act of faith that reveals the Christ-form to a specific historical time even as it reveals the reality of the poet. The poet will then be seen as one who in his life and work mediates for his time the eternal reality of the theandric act of redemption, not so much in the sense that he evokes that reality in poetry as that he again incarnates, repeats, and actualizes it. In this sense the poet, sharing in the reality of the redemption, "fills up in his flesh what is lacking of Christ's afflictions for his body, which is the Church" (ἀνταναπληρῶ τά ὑστερήματα τῶν θλίψεων τοῦ Χριστοῦ ἐν τῇ σαρκί μου ὑπέρ τοῦ σώματος αὐτοῦ, ὅ ἐστιν ἡ ἐκκλησία. [Col. 1 : 24]). The compound prefix αντανα- of the original for "filling up" is important, for it conveys both the sense of repetition (ἀνά) and the specification that the believer's action does not replace, but occurs in answer to (ἀντί) Christ's one-time deed. Such an action transforms any given moment of historical time into a *kairos* of salvation history.

The question of Georg Trakl's existential Christianity must remain a working hypothesis in this study, since at any rate this could not be the matter of our inquiry nor of *any* inquiry. As previously stated, our concern is the demonstration of the conformity of the event of Trakl's poetry with the event of the evangelical Christ-form. The subjective identity of a person's soul is not available as such for anyone's investigation; but the perceivable form that reflects that identity, belonging to the modality of communication, requires interpretation in order even to exist.

Form as Event: Menschheit

Up to this point I have been using the word *form* a great deal without explicitly specifying what is intended. There are several reasons for my insisting on the question of form. From the point of view of our immediate subject matter, we must attribute the great impact produced by reading even a few lines of Trakl's poetry to the extreme purification of its form, not only in the sense of the perfect balance achieved by its rhythms, sounds, and evocations, but also because of the sovereign freedom with which individual words stand in relation to one another. More than in any other poetry known to me—except perhaps Mallarmé's, but here the artifice of deliberate mystification is all too apparent—the word, as Trakl uses it, is so removed from its usual role of communicating a meaning beyond itself (the role of sign), that word becomes event (the role of symbol). It is quite useless, one would almost say iconoclastic, to ask "what is being described" with regard to a strophe such as:

> In blauem Kristall
> Wohnt der bleiche Mensch, die Wang' an seine Sterne gelehnt;
> Oder er neigt das Haupt in purpurnem Schlaf.[33]

The absoluteness of the events described is breathtaking, and yet we are quite uncertain as to what the actual "content" of these events might be. In other words, we are deliberately denied an object foreign to the poem itself and are therefore thwarted in our instinctive need for some equivalent to which to reduce the mystery before us. The poet is telling us: "There is no equivalent. Live with the mystery before you."

This quality of being "fraught with mystery" is not unique to Trakl's poetry or to poetry like his; mystery is the fundamental property of any form that is contemplated for its own sake and is not reduced to a conceptual description. St. Thomas defined beauty as *splendor formae,* and Maritain explains why this is a precise and fitting definition: "'Form,' which is to say the principle that makes for the perfection of everything that is; that constitutes and completes things in their essence and in their qualities; which is, finally, the ontological secret which things carry within themselves, their spiritual reality, their operative mystery, and above all the proper principle of intelligibility, the splendor proper to every thing. . . ."[34] The definition surprises us by the degree to which it demonstrates the impoverishment of the modern concept of form, which, when applied to poetry, connotes little more than mechanical matters having to do with rhyme and meter. In this way, we cannot grasp the true function of material tools such as rhyme and meter even when we understand their technical operations well. Traditional exegesis quickly passes on to the "content," to see whether "what the poet intended to say" has been cast in an adequate "form."

According to the Thomistic view, however, form is the very appearance or shining forth of reality, and, as such, a dynamic event fraught with mystery and irreducible to any other category. "To affirm with the scholastics that the form of things is the proper principle of intelligibility, is to affirm by the same token that form is the supreme principle of mystery. To define the beautiful as 'the splendor of form' is to define it at the same time as 'the splendor of mystery.'"[35] The intelligibility of a thing, therefore, is not so much *our* ability to explain it (away!) by abstract categories, as it is *its* property of radiating the mystery of its being. We have been calling this radiance of form (whether of the

Christ-form or of the form of a Trakl poem) an event because it is only events that enter the horizon of consciousness unannounced and resist all attempts on our part at abstract reduction. The perception of a form is an event within the horizon of our consciousness.

As previously stated, this study endeavors to compare two forms in their possible relation to one another as original model *(Urbild, Vorbild)* and likeness *(Nachbild)*, these being respectively the Christ-form of Scripture and the form of Trakl's poetry. Concerning the form-problem of Christian literature, Wilhelm Hoffmann has written that "many Christians, of course, compose Christian contents, but not by far in a Christian way [*christlich*]."[36] The problem, so stated, probes the nature of the living form of existence as opposed to the content of doctrinal language. My thesis examines the possibility of Trakl's poetry exhibiting one possible form of Christian *art*, which is vastly different from a question about Christian poetry in general. Maritain distinguishes well when he radically separates church or sacred art from Christian art, the latter being defined not by its destined use, but solely from its character and inspiration. He makes the point emphatically clear when he adds that "what is most wanting in our days in a great number of works of sacred art is precisely a truly religious character."[37] The distinction is vital, for the difference between a Christian content and a Christian form is exactly that between decorative religiosity and its existential reality. For: *form is being in existence.* The exterior, explicit (referential or "literary") use of traditional Christian symbolism in Trakl's poetry, so emphasized by some as supporting evidence, so discredited by others as mere atmospheric décor, is actually in a secondary relationship to the "interior" evidence of the form. If the form did not consistently support the explicit symbolism, when this is present, the latter would indeed be an artificial device external to the meaning of the poetry. If the form does support the symbolism, then the symbolism is but the jutting tip of the iceberg. Furthermore, and this is most important of all, it is possible to recognize a Christian form by its intrinsic qualities even in the absence of all traditional symbolism. In fact, as we shall see later, the religious pregnancy of Trakl's mature poetry intensifies as the more external religious symbolism recedes. The question we ask, then, is one concerning the possibility of verifying in the case of Trakl's poetry the realization of St. Paul's exhortation to the Galatians, over whom he suffered birthpains "until Christ gain form within you" (μέχρις οὗ μορφωθῇ Χριστός ἐν ὑμῖν [Gal. 4:19]).

For the sake of clarity, I shall here illustrate the procedure of form-analysis envisaged. I choose the poem *Menschheit* because of its brevity:

Menschheit

Menschheit vor Feuerschlünden aufgestellt,
Ein Trommelwirbel, dunkler Krieger Stirnen,
Schritte durch Blutnebel; schwarzes Eisen schellt,
Verzweiflung, Nacht in traurigen Gehirnen:
Hier Evas Schatten, Jagd und rotes Geld.
Gewölk, das Licht durchbricht, das Abendmahl.
Es wohnt in Brot und Wein ein sanftes Schweigen
Und jene sind versammelt zwölf an Zahl.
Nachts schrein im Schlaf sie unter Ölbaumzweigen;
Sankt Thomas taucht die Hand ins Wundenmal.[38]

The poem falls naturally into equal halves of five lines each. The balance we might expect from this exterior arrangement is indeed ratified by the interior events of the poem, events that are unified without exception by the transfiguration of the chaos of the first part into the order of the second. The first five lines unfurl a panorama of war and hatred, which are made present in the images of drumbeat, blood-fog, and black iron. With the words *Hier Evas Schatten* the poet attributes the reign of evil to the fallen state of human nature, or "original sin." This first scriptural reference is the indication of the poem's figural nature, and, in the light of what follows, we may resume the first half as belonging to the Old Testament dispensation of condemnation under the Law.

The word *Gewölk* marks the transition to the second half of the poem, but there is no separation into strophes and the transition is not sudden. One realizes that a change has occurred after it has already taken place. The breaking through of the light activates a series of transformations that leave no element of the first part unaffected. Here all the effects of chaos are found again, but now transfigured: abstract "humanity," face to face with imminent destruction, reappears in the "Twelve" (the order of definite number), who are gathered to share a meal. War yields to communion. The meal consists of the sacramental signs, indicating the presence of him who said: "I am the living bread which came down from heaven . . ." (cf. the breaking through of the light). "He who eats my flesh and drinks my blood abides in me, and I in him" (John 6:51, 56). The grating iron and drumbeats yield to the gentle and profound silence that radiates from the bread and wine, so that the sense of being in-dwelled by a life-giving presence takes the place of the sense of total abandonment to chaos (Heidegger would say *das Ausgesetztsein*) of the first half. The blood-fog becomes clouds shot through with light, the blood itself being transfigured into wine. The despair now emerges as the tranquil and surprised recognition of the triumph of peace over chaos, so that the *Verzweiflung* is healed by the *anagnōrisis*.

Although in this poem the division into chaos and order is rather explicit, yet it is by no means an automatic or mechanical one, since the Christ indirectly presented in the last line is not a *deus ex machina* who magically resolves a hopeless situation, but the God who authoritatively transfigures by himself bearing the effect of sin in his own body. Christ, in fact, is made present solely by the naming of the wounds, so that Trakl interprets the essence of this transfiguration as being the bearing of glorious wounds. By the exclusive token of the wounds, which, like the bread and wine, radiate a profound silence, Christ now reveals himself as one of those whose "brains had been sad with night" in the first half, and line 9 witnesses to the disciples' own share in the suffering of being delivered over to chaos. It is in probing with his own hand the hole of the wounds that Thomas recognizes the authenticity of Christ's deed of peace.

Because the scriptural references to Eve and to the apparition after the Resurrection are perfectly integrated in the poem's structure of transformation, we may say not only that Trakl's language here is figural, but that he realizes in the form of the poem Christ's promise of peace to those who choose to have their reality within the unique form of his redemption: "Truly, I say to you, unless you eat the flesh of the Son of Man and drink his blood, you have no life in you" (John 6:53). The poem promises peace to those who commune or share in the fate of the Lord in every detail of its "grammar." The mention of the apostle Thomas in line 10 corresponds to the mention of Eve in line 5, so that, in Thomas's recognition of the glorious wounds, the penalty imposed on Eve in Genesis 3 is paid, and the poem completes its figural mode by realizing God's promise to the serpent in Eden: "I will put enmity between you and the woman, and between your seed and her seed; he shall bruise your head, and you shall bruise his heel" (Gen. 3:15). The "bruising" of the serpent's "head" is the overcoming of chaos by resurrection; the bruise of the heel of Eve's seed is precisely Christ's permanent though triumphant wounds.

Even this (for Trakl) rather "referential" poem nowhere mentions the name of Christ, since the form of the transformation has made his presence so vibrant that any further explicitness would violate the force of the recognition through the effects. Many other things could be said about this poem. For instance, we could remark on the manner in which biblical events and recent history are presented as contemporaneous. But for the moment we must conclude that Trakl understands Christ as the one who transforms chaos by bearing it and overcoming it in his own flesh. With this understanding Trakl reveals the solid theology that undergirds his poetry. The poem *Menschheit* is such a perfect parallel of the phrase that opens the collect prayer of the Second Sunday after Easter in the Roman Missal: "Deus, qui in Filii tui humilitate jacentem mundum erexisti . . .,"[39] and such a precise exemplification of the paradoxical phrase of the *Victimae paschali:* "Dux vitae mortuus regnat vivus,"[40] that we may, in passing, consider the poem as itself a liturgical prayer in the manner of scriptural glosses and responsories that operate according to the theological principle that the *lex orandi* dictates the *lex credendi,* or that the form of prayer determines the matter of dogma. This view of the poem as prayer finally gives us the basic insight into the poem and the real reason why there is no arbitrary transition from darkness to light. Because there is only one verb, and that in a subordinate position *(schellt),* in the first half of the poem, that half acts as a kind of preamble or relative clause to what follows. In other words, the first half sets the scenario for the transformation of the second half, so that war and despair are not the primary subject of the poem, but rather their being already transfigured is mirrored by the very form of their presentation. Likewise, no one begins to pray explicitly who is not already praying.

The question concerning *form* in the poetry of Georg Trakl, then, has to do with identity rather than with chance expression. The transcendental form of a thing *is* its identity. And so the question concerning the form of a poetry is, at the same time, a question about the identity of its maker. This inquiry, far from leading us to Lachmann's question of determining "what the poet wanted to say,"[41] brings us to the critical encounter with the actual event of the poems. Lachmann's question derives from a Platonizing mentality that has traditionally been as prevalent in literary criticism as it has been an obstacle to the perception of the form of poetry. Rudolf Schier expresses himself in the following terms, for instance, and he here reveals the reasons why, in my opinion, his figural analysis of Trakl's poetry finally fails:

> The search in Trakl's poetry for a hypothetical point where all motifs of his work converge *(Fluchtpunkt)* presupposes a dualism of nature and super-nature, of divinity and world created through emanation, of spirit and matter. The "point of convergence" is likewise the spiritual component of which the images are an emanation. Just as we could understand the world if we found God, so, too, would we understand Trakl's language of images if we could determine the point of convergence of which it is an emanation.[42]

Such a Neoplatonic understanding of both God's and man's creation fails to make the necessary distinction between maker and thing made, viewing the one as an "emanation" or extension of the other. The Platonizing aesthetic derived from it seeks the "spirit" that hides behind the "appearance" perceived by the senses and thus radically devalues the intrinsic importance of the perceptible form.

Schier overlooks the crucial fact that a doctrine of emanation is totally incompatible, both on the theological and the aesthetic planes, with the use of figural language. The *Fluchtpunkt* for which it searches is actually not something outside of the poet and behind the images, but the unity of the creative and the believing intellect. Being able to conceive of the world only as an emanation from God, Schier concludes that Trakl uses a figural as opposed to a metaphorical language because, for him, the world is no longer epiphanic of the divine. Schier betrays a typically modern theistic conception of God and the world that is incompatible with the Judeo-Christian doctrines of creation and incarnation. With his usual eloquence, Pascal corrects the theistic misinterpretation of the Christian tradition:

> Si le monde subsistait pour instruire l'homme de Dieu, sa divinité y reluirait de toutes parts d'une manière incontestable; mais, comme il ne subsiste que par Jésus-Christ et pour Jésus-Christ, et pour instruire les hommes et de leur corruption et de leur redemption, tout y éclate des preuves de ces deux vérités. Ce qui y paraît ne marque ni une exclusion totale, ni une présence manifeste de divinité, mais la présence d'un Dieu qui se cache. Tout porte ce caractère.[43]

The mystery that the world reveals a *hidden God* and thereby instructs man concerning both his corrupt state and his redemption far more closely describes the God of Trakl's poetry, the God whose mighty silence is ubiquitous, than does the more facile eudaemonistic scheme of nature as divine emanation. The last strophe of the untitled poem that begins *Ein Teppich, darein . . .* portrays salvation as resulting precisely from the recognition *(Spiegel)* of the presence of the divine *(Engel)* in the midst of putrefaction and death. The opening image of the "blind children of the Passion" already contains the promise of the conclusion:

> Charfreitagskinder blind an Zäunen stehen
> Im Spiegel dunkler Gossen voll Verwesung
> Der Sterbenden hinseufzende Genesung
> Und Engel die durch weisse Augen gehen
> Von Lidern düstert goldene Erlösung.[44]

Such poetry is not so much the external expression of an invisible intention as the symbolic manifestation of an intellect that has ordered reality according to a definite form. Since only the Christian imagination can conceive of divinity as compatible with decay, not in a relationship of identification but in a total process of transfiguring mercy, it is my claim that this definite form is the Christ-form of Scripture as appropriated by Trakl in the contemplation of faith.

Nor is this structure of mercy-transfiguring-decay to be discovered solely where motifs of redemption are explicitly named. We may recognize the same basic structure as it reappears in the following lines, in which integrity triumphs through destruction and in which a hidden power reveals itself in utter helplessness:

> Die Nacht ist über der zerwühlten Stirne aufgegangen
> Mit schönen Sternen
> Über dem schmerzversteinerten Antlitz,
> Ein wildes Tier frass des Liebenden Herz
> Ein feuriger Engel
> Stürzt mit zerbrochener Brust auf steinigen Acker,
> Wiederaufflatternd ein Geier.
> Weh in unendlicher Klage
> Mischt sich Feuer, Erde und blauer Quell.[45]

At every step the poet lets a silent indestructibility shine forth through the forces of violence: the racked brow and the countenance rigid ("petrified") with pain are illuminated by the stars of the night; the loving heart, devoured by the wild beast, persists as a fiery angel with a crushed breast; the eternal lament intermixes the cosmic and primordial elements of fire, earth, and water.

At this point I must again emphasize the radically modifying effect that existential contemplation of the Christ-form has on the believer. Von Balthasar writes:

> Christian contemplation is the opposite of a distancing consideration of images. As Paul says, it is the metamorphosis of the seer into the image he sees (2 Cor. 3:18), the "realization" of what the image expresses (Newman). This is possible only by giving up one's own standards in order to conform oneself to the proportions of the image. . . . The image unfolds itself into the contemplator; it extends its consequences into his life. It is not I who draw my consequences for myself from what I have seen. What I have seen, if it has really been seen in itself, draws its own consequences *in me*.[46]

This process of the beholder's coming to resemble the contemplated image ever more faithfully is not only the basis of Christian mysticism; it explains as well the reason for the impact of the faith-experience on the creative intellect. The object of contemplation has a form that con-forms the believer to itself and which, therefore, in-forms (i.e., shapes) the work of the believer as poet. But because the Christian is both trans-formed in the image of Christ and retains his identity as a person, or better, because he gains his unique identity as person in being transformed in the image of Christ, Trakl's poetry is an analogue or icon not primarily of a dogmatically objective Christ-form, but of the Christ-form as appropriated by Trakl subjectively. That is to say, his poetry is not imitative *Nachdichtung* of Scripture, but *Nachvollzug* or realization of the event proclaimed in Scripture. The poetry is an objective correlative or an adequate semblance of Trakl's subjectivity as a Christian; but as an objectively existing entity it exhibits an aesthetic structure of its own.

The Function of Trakl's Poetry

It is in the very structure of this aesthetic form that we are to identify the shaping presence of the Christ-form of Incarnation, Passion, and Resurrection. We have already seen with the example of *Menschheit* how the transformation of chaos into order determines the structure of the poem, and this "order" was seen to be no mathematical or utopian construct, but, rather, the presence of a person who has the authority and power to confer peace. For the conclusion of this chapter, it should now be asked whether there exists a similar structure in the self-understanding of Trakl's poetry as a whole with regard to its function. In other words, is the particular structure of the poems reflected in Trakl's conception of the function of the poet's craft?

On departing for the Russian front in July 1914, Trakl handed Ludwig von Ficker a note containing the aphorism already quoted in the introduction, which I consider the fundamental explanation of Trakl's understanding of his poetic activity:

> Gefühl in den Augenblicken totenähnlichen Seins: alle Menschen sind der Liebe wert. Erwachend fühlst du die Bitternis der Welt; darin ist alle deine ungelöste Schuld; dein Gedicht eine unvollkommene Sühne.[47]

These words are important because, for one thing, they bring all of Trakl's main themes into functional unity: death, man, love, guilt, atonement. Moreover, the fragment itself shows the structure already emphasized: the passage from death and guilt to atonement through the mediation of both love and bitterness. Most important is Trakl's explanation of the writing of poetry in terms of an "imperfect atonement." When art was called by Maritain a "virtue of the practical intellect" and I suggested that the artist produces an artifact, the stage remained set for the next logical question: What is the use or function of such activity and of such an artifact? Although this question cannot be answered univocally for art is general, nevertheless it is possible to search for the individual artist's finality in creating his art work. Trakl tells us that he understands the function of his activity to be atonement or expiation for the unresolved (unredeemed) guilt of the world, his own included. Now, the statement is fully in keeping with the structure of at least the paradigmatic poem *Menschheit,* so that we see that the craft's finality is adequately borne out in this case by the nature of the proximate art object.

Trakl's understanding of the function of his poetic activity as atonement explains the figural nature of his language as being more than a mannerism. In a passage from a letter to his friend Erhard Buschbeck, concerning the second draft of a poem, Trakl writes:

> Ich bin überzeugt, dass es Dir in dieser universellen Form und Art mehr sagen und bedeuten wird, denn in der begrenzt persönlichen des ersten Entwurfes. Du magst mir glauben, dass es mir nicht leicht fällt und niemals leicht fallen wird, mich bedingungslos dem Darzustellenden unterzuordnen und ich werde mich immer und immer wieder berichtigen müssen, um der Wahrheit zu geben, was der Wahrheit ist.[48]

Far from its being a merely technical statement concerning Trakl's manner of composition, the passage reveals Trakl's aesthetic application of his religious understanding of poetry as atonement. The use of figural language signals the insertion of its user into a salvation history that both transcends and contains one's personal history and the temporal history of the world. Postfigural language in particular requires, as we have seen, the con-formity of the believer to the Christ-form, which is the fulfilment of figural expectation. In the total figural scheme we see more than a system of literary correspondences; these, rather, convey "the radically new re-creation of all meaning through the death of God's Logos."[49] For Trakl, the poetical ascesis that is the implementation of the pure impersonalism of Symbolist aesthetics has as cause the death and resurrection of the human word, which dies as a natural sign and rises as a resonant symbol, following step by step the "grammar" of the divine Logos.

Ferdinand Ebner, who anticipated Martin Buber in the revolutionary rediscovery of a "thou" in theology, who was a contemporary fellow-Austrian of Trakl's and, like him, a contributor to von Ficker's metaphysical journal *Der Brenner,* writes in his *Das Wort und die geistigen Realitäten:*

> Only when the recognition of sin becomes word and avowal does man emerge without reservations out of his ego-isolation and into a relationship to God, who is the true "thou" of his "I." Through the word man is delivered from the curse of sin and of the Law.[50]

There is an intimate connection between atonement and word. The purified word delivers the self from the "limited personal form" that

Ebner calls *Icheinsamkeit:* the isolation of the self-enclosed ego. Atonement occurs through the word because "recognition of sin is already the 'breakthrough' to life in the Spirit,"[51] and it is the purified word which alone acknowledges guilt as guilt. The purified word is already a word of love in that it seeks a healing of the fragmentation brought about by sin. "Only love and the word can deliver man out of his ego-isolation."[52] Figural language is more than unparticipating reference to the Logos' death and resurrection; insofar as it is the transition from letter to spirit it is participation in the event of salvation.[53] In the light of postfiguration, Trakl's description of the function of his poetry and his goal of giving a universal form to his art may be understood to mean the *Geistwerdung des Buchstabens,* the letter's becoming spirit, which is the essence of figural realization.

Fundamental to Trakl's understanding of guilt and the need for atonement is his prophetic presence in the decadence of the dying Austro-Hungarian monarchy. In visionary fashion he writes:

> Ich sah viel Städte als Flammenraub
> Und Greuel auf Greuel häufen die Zeiten,
> Und sah viel Völker verwesen zu Staub,
> Und alles in Vergessenheit gleiten.[54]

The relationship of prophet to decadence is less that of one who condemns than of one who transfigures. In this respect, Trakl is as different from the other Expressionists in their vitriolic anger as Dostoievski, the underground man, was from Tolstoy, the rationalist utopian. Although seeing decay and corruption everywhere, Trakl never makes himself a force for their destruction, but for their atonement. Rather than separating himself as justified saint over against the bleak reality of his era, Trakl identifies himself so fully with it, rather in the manner of Hosea, the prophet who fornicates with a prostitute, that at times he appears himself to be a demonic visionary. In *Das Grauen* he portrays himself as follows:

> Dumpfe Fieberglut
> Lässt giftige Blumen blühn aus meinem Munde . . .
>
> Aus eines Spiegels trügerischer Leere
> Hebt langsam sich, und wie ins Ungefähre
> Aus Graun und Finsternis ein Antlitz: Kain!
>
> . . . .
>
> Da bin mit meinem Mörder ich allein.[55]

Trakl's demonism is indicative of the extent to which a fated victim can exhibit in his own torment the traits of its persecutor. Walter Muschg observes in this connection that "in Trakl compassion for the victims of an unjust social order is the unspoken presupposition for his poetic activity."[56] The demonic aspect of Georg Trakl's character is but a measure of the extreme to which, in purifying his word to give it a universal form, he made himself transparent to the spiritual plight of his time. In this sense, the religious import of his quest for aesthetic objectification becomes comprehensible, according to which he strives to give expression, not to a private vision, but to an objective truth beyond himself. In its postfiguration of Christ's saving deed, poetic transformation is the medium that restores the wholeness of a decaying world, and this work, in turn, is the content of Trakl's "atonement."

Von Balthasar writes concerning the Incarnation of the Logos a theological elucidation that is important for our understanding of the christological form of Trakl's poetry and its function as explained in Trakl's aphorism:

> The Word of God becomes a Word which speaks through Christ's flesh, which is expressed in it, and which resounds all the louder precisely when it must grow mute within the density of flesh. It grows mute to the point that the whole man, having become God's language, not only *speaks* the Word of God with his body and soul, but *is* that Word. This does not result in a language that muteness has made to be hermetically sealed off and incomprehensible, but in the universally understood language of suffering and death, events which occur not by force, but out of love, not by compulsion, but out of obedience.[57]

Rudolf Schier claims that the two aspects of Trakl's aphorism—love and guilt—contradict each other, since the feeling of every man's love-worthiness belongs to a metaphorical "unity with nature," and the feeling of guilt derives from a break with this natural unity.[58] In the light of von Balthasar's meditation on God's self-expression in the humanized Logos, we may conclude, however, that Trakl's striving for poetic impersonalism and objectification corresponds to the *ekstasis* of the Logos from his form as God (cf. Phil. 2:5–8) in order to "objectify" himself in the Incarnation. Love is the motor-force of the Redeemer in becoming man, and it is shared by Trakl when he writes his objectified poetry as atonement; in both cases the goal, in Trakl's words, is "um der Wahrheit zu geben, was der Wahrheit ist." Again, Pascal indicates the primordial unity that exists between love and truth in the Christian understanding, and it is in this manner that we should understand the continuity between the feeling of love and the feeling of guilt in Trakl's aphorism, both of which together create the ethos of poetry as atonement: "On se fait une idole de la vérité même; car la vérité hors de la charité n'est pas Dieu, et est son image et une idole, qu'il ne faut point aimer, ni adorer."[59] Atonement is the believer's manner of participating in Christ's Passion, since it is precisely this participation which in the creature completes the act of redemption. In this context I may say that the final purpose of this study is to establish a strict correlation between Trakl's aphorism concerning the religious ethos of his poetic activity and the actual form of the work as we encounter it.

2

Trakl and the Apocalyptic Tradition

Tu dici: "Io veggio l'acqua, io veggio il foco,
l'aere e la terra e tutte lor misture
venire a corruzione, e durar poco . . ."

Ma vostra *vita* sanza mezzo spira
la somma beninanza, e la innamora
di sè sì che poi sempre la disira.

Dante[1]

In a letter to Ludwig von Ficker written a year before his death, Trakl gives expression to an awesome experience taking place in his spirit:

Es haben sich in den letzten Tagen für mich so furchtbare Dinge ereignet, dass ich deren Schatten mein Lebtag nicht mehr loswerden kann. Ja, verehrter Freund, mein Leben ist in wenigen Tagen unsäglich zerbrochen worden und es bleibt nur mehr ein sprachloser Schmerz, dem selbst die Bitternis versagt ist . . . Vielleicht schreiben Sie mir zwei Worte; ich weiss nicht mehr ein und aus. Es ist ein so namenloses Unglück, wenn einem die Welt entzweibricht. *O mein Gott, welch ein Gericht ist über mich hereingebrochen.* Sagen Sie mir, dass ich die Kraft haben muss noch zu leben und das Wahre zu tun. Sagen Sie mir, dass ich nicht irre bin. Es ist ein steinernes Dunkel hereingebrochen. O mein Freund, wie klein und unglücklich bin ich geworden.[2]

The passage is deeply moving and important for an understanding of the archetypical situation that the poet assigns to his life and to his work. The anonymity of the immediate causes for this crushing experience points to the fact that Trakl's spiritual condition in November 1913, as he wrote this letter, is but an extreme instance of the mood that dominates the whole of his work. Trakl experienced the world in terms of its dynamic and catastrophic breaking asunder. At its most subdued, this vision constantly informs his images of gradual decay and gliding into death:

Am Fenster welken Blumen warm und rot,
Die man dem schönen Knaben heute brachte.
Wie er die Hände hob und leise lachte.
Man betet dort. Vielleicht liegt einer tot.[3]

At its most violent, the critical state of the world is embodied in a poem such as *Das Gewitter:*

Traumhaft erschüttern des Wildbachs
Dunkle Geister das Herz,
Finsternis,
Die über die Schluchten hereinbricht![4]

In the passage from his letter, as in this poem, Trakl conveys the thorough nature of his experience of distintegration by using a form of the verb *brechen* ("to break") four times in three variations: *zerbrochen, entzweibricht,* and *hereingebrochen.*

The experience of the shattering of the world, however, exhibits in Trakl two aspects that qualify its destructiveness by providing it with a religious context. The speechless and unutterable pain *(sprachloser Schmerz)* experienced is described in terms of an event *(ereignet)* that has irrupted from outside the sphere of its occurrence *(hereingebrochen),* and that Trakl names a judgment or sentence *(Gericht).* We have already seen that it is a feature of the figural imagination to think of the world, not as an encapsulated realm in which cause and effect succeed each other with relentless horizontality, but rather to conceive of existence in time as an open-ended situation that may at any moment (and does, indeed, at *all* moments, although not always perceptibly) undergo a sudden incursion of God's free action. Trakl's description of his painful experience is, then, in keeping with his figural view of the world as embodied in his poems. The devastating event, furthermore, leads the poet to formulate a desire for persevering in the "doing of the truth," an expression pregnant with scriptural associations concerning those who are doers and not mere hearers of the Word. We must conclude that, in some manner, Trakl regards his frightful experience as occurring within a context that determines, but is not to be equated with, the immediate phenomena of namelessness, painfulness, and unremitting darkness *(steinernes Dunkel).*

The same Ludwig von Ficker to whom the letter was addressed provides us with a commentary on the epochal significance of Trakl's experience of the world in crisis. According to him, Trakl personified in an extreme manner "the exposure *(Ausgesetztheit)* of all human creatures as they are caught in the fate of their existence."[5] Erwin Mahrholdt comments in similar manner that, "in the lucidity of his consciousness, Trakl's personal destiny became for him the destiny of his age."[6] The anonymity of Trakl's experience of the self as standing under a severe judgment thus stems from the fact that Trakl felt to a particularly intense degree the coincidence of his personal life with the situation of the contemporary world in which he lived. Here Trakl's aesthetic striving for the objectification of his images and for submission to the truth of what is to be represented *(das Darzustellende)* receives an added dimension. The aesthetic criterion of a universal image is seen to derive from an ethical awareness of the unity of the self and the world.

The present chapter approaches the demonstration of the christological form of Trakl's poetry by proposing that Trakl may be best understood in the context of a particular tradition within Christianity, which I call the "apocalyptic tradition." The term *apocalyptic* is here understood to denote a vision of the world that is characterized by a sense of the ephemeral nature of human accomplishments and by an awareness of the permanently critical state of existence within historical time. I shall limit myself to juxtaposing Trakl's awareness of the world with that view of existence exemplified in chosen moments of what Elisabeth Langgässer has called the "history of Christian styles" *(Stilgeschichte der Frömmigkeit).* In this case we are concerned with the tradition of the apocalyptic style, in which we note a progressive inte-riorization of the actual "revelation" experienced.

If the early Christian apocalypticists, living in the *inclinata res publica* of the Roman Empire, sought a verification of God's judgment of the age in the external calamities they observed, later heirs of the tradition re-garded the interior crises of individuals as the arena in which the battle of self and world was to be waged. Consequently, during the Baroque period, we observe an extreme concentration on the theme of the Passion of Christ and conclude that, at this time, the figure of the suffering Savior became the archetype for the condition of man in the world. During the course of the nineteenth century, Søren Kierkegaard (1813–55) accelerated the interiorization of the crisis of man in the world by proclaiming not only that suffering is *the* expression of religious man in his relationship to God, but that the authenticity of such a relationship is to be found in its total anonymity.[7] Early in the twentieth century, finally, and contemporary with the movement of German Expressionism to which Trakl is generally held to belong, we encounter an upsurge of apocalyptic fervor at the heart of that revitalization of religious life for which the so-called "dialectical theologians" were responsible. The Prot-estants Karl Barth (1886–1968) and Paul Tillich (1886–1965), among others, and Catholics such as Ferdinand Ebner (1882–1931) and Theodor Haecker (1879–1945), were responsible for the theological *prise de con-science* that again became keenly aware of the fundamental difference between God and man and between Good and Evil, and they awakened the lethargic European soul to the critical situation of man in the world.

In spite of the many differences that might be noted even among the few instances of the "apocalyptic style of piety" I have just surveyed, one feature unites them all. This is the uncompromising passion that, in Kierkegaard's words, sees the Christian life as a religious relationship to an absolute *telos*. Here other noble names crowd the memory, modern "pilgrims of the absolute" such as Gerard M. Hopkins, Léon Bloy, Simone Weil, and Georges Bernanos. The very absoluteness of their apocalyptic experience of God requires that the world be regarded as radically ephemeral, an assertion that already goes a long way in explaining Trakl's almost obsessive insistence on death and decay.

The present chapter will provide the more external or historical points of reference necessary for an understanding of the identity of Georg Trakl's poetry. It will be seen that if, on one level, Trakl's ubiquitous concern with death and all its attributes stems from what William Johnston describes as the Austrian cultivation of a "Baroque vision of death as the fulfillment of life,"[8] on another and much more fundamental level Trakl's experience of the world in crisis is to be regarded as an expression of his Christian apocalypticism. A comparison of Trakl's style with other manifestations of the same basic vision of the world will contribute considerably to our demonstration of the christological form of his art, since it will finally emerge as a common and essential element of this tradition that the passing of the world already contains in a concealed manner the promise of its resurrection into a mode of imperishability. The intensity of apocalyptic longing, particularly in the context of the Passion of Christ, has no other adequate explanation than its being regarded as an ardent desire for the glorification of the Son of God, and also of the self and of the world in him who had previously identified himself with them in his own incarnation, bruising, and death.

Trakl and the Early Christian Apocalypticists

> It is a fearful thing to fall into the hands of the living God.
>
> Heb. 10:31

In his biography of Georg Trakl, Otto Basil has pointed out the similarity of function shared, on the one hand, by Trakl as a prophet of decay and *Untergang,* writing in the last days of the Austro-Hungarian monarchy, and, on the other, those writers of the first centuries of the Christian era who depicted the degeneration and moral collapse of the late Roman Empire. Striking is not only the similar content of their moral invective, but also the fact that both Trakl and these Christian pessimists communicate their vision in a fantastic and "surrealist" manner. Writes Basil:

> The pre-eminence had in Trakl by everything having to do with "corruption," the phantomlike and ruinous state of his natural and urban landscapes, are already a foreboding of the ideological and, particularly, the sociopolitical revolution which begins with the European catastrophe of 1914. In Trakl's poetry we encounter the accursed generation, which vegetates in deceptive well-being and which is rotting both spiritually and morally. . . . In *Helian* we read: "Awesome is the generation's decline," and it remains in the dark whether here a particular generation (that of the fathers) is mourned for as it collapses, or whether the downfall of the entire human race—the *humanitas*—is meant.[9]

The answer to this ambiguity noted by Basil is, of course, that Trakl gives expression to the decline both of his own generation and of mankind in general, since the particular historical instance is representative of the intrinsically fallen and corrupt state of man as such. Historical prophecy derives in the case of Trakl from metaphysical clairvoyance, a lucidity that rests primarily on his personal experience of the self as standing under the law of decay.

In the third strophe of the poem *Abendland* we find portrayed the initial or catastrophic moment of the apocalyptic imagination:

> Ihr grossen Städte
> Steinern aufgebaut
> In der Ebene!
> So sprachlos folgt
> Der Heimatlose
> Mit dunkler Stirne dem Wind,
> Kahlen Bäumen am Hügel.
> Ihr weithin dämmernden Ströme!
> Gewaltig ängstet
> Schaurige Abendröte
> Im Sturmgewölk.
> Ihr sterbenden Völker!
> Bleiche Woge
> Zerschellend am Strande der Nacht,
> Fallende Sterne.[10]

In similar apostrophic style the poet Commodian (3d cent.) addresses his contemporaries:

> Heu doleo, cives, sic vos hebetari de mundo!
> Excurrit alius ad sortes, aves aspicit alter,
> Belantum cruore fuso malus inspicit alter
> Et cupit audire responsa bona crudelis.[11]

The awareness of the spiritual decay of the times leads Commodian to a visionary description of the end of the world that corresponds to Trakl's panorama of ominous clouds and stars falling over the dying peoples:

> Dat tuba caelo signum sublato leone
> Et fiunt desubito tenebrae cum caeli fragore.
>
> Summittit oculos Dominus, ut terra tremescat,
> Adclamat etiam, ut audiant omnes, in orbem:
> Ecce diu tacui sufferens tanto tempore vestra!
> Conclamant pariter plangentes sero gementes,
> Ululatur, ploratur, nec spatium datur iniquis.
> Lactanti quid faciet mater, cum ipsa crematur?
> In flamma ignis Dominus iudicabit iniquos.[12]

"God shall judge the wicked in the flame of fire." However, in both Commodian and Trakl this catastrophic judgment is understood as not only sparing the just, but as fully revealing them to the world in their justice. At the conclusion of his *Carmen apologeticum,* Commodian says that the ruination of the world and the falling of the stars will be as dew to those known to Christ:

> Stellae cadunt caeli, iudicantur astra nobiscum:
> Turbantur caelicolae, agitur dum saecli ruina . . .
> His tantum proficiet, qui fuerint Christo notati;
> Ros ad illos erit, nam caeteris poena laetalis.[13]

In the final strophe of *Abendländisches Lied,* Trakl similarly makes the hour of general collapse coincide with the eschatological glorification of the just, here called "those who love":

> O die bittere Stunde des Untergangs,
> Da wir ein steinernes Antlitz in schwarzen Wassern beschaun.
> Aber strahlend heben die silbernen Lider die Liebenden:
> *Ein* Geschlecht. Weihrauch strömt von rosigen Kissen
> Und der süsse Gesang der Auferstandenen.[14]

The catastrophic or external moment of the apocalyptic vision has as complement an ethical or internal moment that contemplates what the individual's right attitude ought to be in the face of the world's judgment. In Commodian, as in Trakl, we discover what might be called an "ethos of melancholy," which is above all informed by the figure of the suffering Christ. Commodian reflects as follows on the advisable spiritual attitude to be assumed by man in the present life:

> Tormentum est totum, quod vivimus isto sub aevo;
> Hinc adeo nobis est spes in futuro quaerenda:
> Hoc Deus hortatur, hoc lex, hoc passio Christi,
> Ut resurrecturos nos credamus in novo saeclo.
> Sic Dei lex clamat: fieret cum humilis Altus,
> Cederet infernus, ut Adam levaretur a morte,
> Descendit in tumulum Dominus suae plasmae misertus.
> Et sic per occulta inanivit fortia mortis.[15]

The life of the believer is here seen to be an *imitatio Christi* and, as such, no one can attain to resurrection in Christ who has not suffered the Passion of Christ. Commodian's injunction for the ideal Christian is, thus, to live in sorrow:

> Cum Dominus dicat, in gemitum edere panem,
> Hic ut quid nunc agis, qui cupis vivere laetus? . . .
> Tu qui iocundaris, ergo iam exter es illi . . .
> Esto ergo talis, qualem vult esse te Christus:
> Mitis et in illo hilaris, nam saeculo tristis.[16]

Trakl could have drawn the motto of his poetry from this phrase of Commodian's that "he who is merry is already alien to the Lord." In Trakl we may even speak of a celebration of melancholy, such as in this apostrophe of the poem *In ein altes Stammbuch:*

> Immer wieder kehrst du Melancholie,
> O Sanftmut der einsamen Seele.
> Zu Ende glüht ein goldener Tag.
>
> Demutsvoll beugt sich dem Schmerz der Geduldige
> Tönend von Wohllaut und weichem Wahnsinn.
> Siehe! Es dämmert schon.[17]

Essential as the experience of sorrow may be in Trakl, however, we are ultimately kept from speaking of a "cult of suffering" in his regard because he nowhere exhibits a will to generate melancholy, but rather is always found in the attitude of obedience and patience in the face of what inevitably descends on him from without.

   Another writer of the third century, Dionysius of Alexandria, in a letter to Hierax, a fellow-bishop in Egypt, provides us with a description of recent bloodshed in his city that is comparable to Trakl's expression in his late poems of the doom impending over Europe in the early twentieth century:

The river flows onward, polluted with blood and slaughters and the drowning struggles of men. . . . And what other liquid could cleanse water, which itself cleanses all things? How could that ocean, so vast and impassable for men, though poured out on it, ever purge this bitter sea? . . . When will the air, befouled as it is by noxious exhalations which rise in every direction, become pure again? For there are such vapors sent forth from the earth, and such blasts from the sea, and breezes from the rivers, and reeking mists from the harbors, that for dew we might suppose ourselves to have the impure fluids of the corpses which are rotting in all the underlying elements.

Dionysius concludes this "expressionistic" account of the involvement of the cosmos in the evil wrought by human hands with the decisive turning to the ethical implications of the events described:

And yet, after all this, men are amazed, and are at a loss to understand whence come these constant pestilences, whence these terrible diseases, whence these many kinds of fatal inflictions, whence all this large and multiform destruction of human life.[18]

To this passage we compare the first half of Trakl's last poem, *Grodek,* written at the front in Galicia in 1914:

> Am Abend tönen die herbstlichen Wälder
> Von tödlichen Waffen, die goldnen Ebenen
> Und blauen Seen, darüber die Sonne
> Düstrer hinrollt; umfängt die Nacht
> Sterbende Krieger, die wilde Klage
> Ihrer zerbrochenen Münder.
> Doch stille sammelt im Weidengrund
> Rotes Gewölk, darin ein zürnender Gott wohnt
> Das vergossne Blut sich, mondne Kühle;
> Alle Strassen münden in schwarze Verwesung.[19]

We note here, as in Dionysius, the same summoning up of natural elements—forest, lakes, sun, clouds—as a means to express the destruction effected by man. The last line—"all roads lead to black putrefaction"—closely corresponds in its strong hyperbole to Dionysius's river, made putrid with human blood, and to the "fluids from the rotting corpses," which are seen as the only "dew" possible in the context of such catastrophe. At the same time, both passages contain a moral reflection on the meaning of the crisis. Dionysius implies with the repetition of the rhetorical "whence" that the epidemics raging in Alexandria are the just result of man's violence and hatred. Trakl, for his part, says explicitly that it is a "wrathful God" who presides over the destruction that man has brought on himself. We are reminded of the words of the Psalmist, who prays, in Luther's translation:

> Steh auf, Herr, in deinem Zorn!
> So werden die Völker sich um dich sammeln;
> > du aber throne über ihnen in der Höhe!
>
> Gott ist ein gerechter Richter
> > und ein Gott, der täglich strafen kann.
> > > > (Ps. 7 : 7–8, 12)

These lines bear a striking similarity to Trakl's scenario, both in the physical location of God, hovering over the apocalypse as in the *shekinah* (cf. 2 Chron. 5:13), and in the moral identification of God's wrath with his justice. In this sense we may see Trakl's poetry as a form of historical interpretation that, again, is an essential feature of the figural imagination.[20] Contrary to the assertion made by some that every Trakl poem gives "ciphered" expression to a concrete event of his biography,[21] it may be affirmed that Trakl's figural method creates a poetry that judges the world from a religious perspective and is nowhere concerned with providing a mimetic reproduction of experience in any realist sense.

In Dionysius, as in Commodian, we witness the turning from a catastrophic to an interior apocalypse, again keynoted by a dwelling on Christ's Passion. Commenting on the passage of St. Luke that says that in agony Jesus "prayed more earnestly; and his sweat became like great drops of blood falling down upon the ground" (22:44), Dionysius reflects that "those drops of sweat flowed from him in a marvellous way like great drops of blood, in order that he might, as it were, drain off and empty the fountain of fear which is proper to our nature."[22] In the same way, Trakl concludes the apocalyptic poem *Das Gewitter,* quoted at the beginning of this chapter, with a strophe that shows fear banished as a consequence of the catastrophe, here experienced as purification:

> Angst, du giftige Schlange,
> Schwarze, stirb im Gestein!
> Da stürzen der Tränen
> Wilde Ströme herab,
> Sturm-Erbarmen,
> Hallen in drohenden Donnern
> Die schneeigen Gipfel rings.
> Feuer
> Läutert zerrissene Nacht.[23]

Fear, described by Dionysius as proper to our (fallen) nature, is here identified by Trakl with the serpent of the Garden of Eden, and the apocalyptic destruction that fell upon Christ could fittingly be juxtaposed to Trakl's *Sturm-Erbarmen:* this "storm of mercy" in which Christ receives in his flesh the full weight of the divine wrath because of his compassion for those who had stirred up God's anger. The christological moment of interiority, which is the indispensable counterpart of the initial moment of violent judgment, enables us to assert that, in the tradition of Christian apocalypticism, "the drama of the human downfall becomes in its entirety an expression of divine love."[24]

The most significant characteristic of the Christian view of God's judgment of the world is thus that even in its severest extremity this judgment is understood to coincide with God's love for man. The decisive proof of this identity is the fact that God delivered his own Son to the most catastrophic of sentences for the life of the world. Federico Garcia Lorca, who could be considered Trakl's Spanish counterpart in the revitalization of Baroque sensitivity and imagery, expresses this paradoxical mystery as follows:

> Vivo estabas, Dios mío, dentro del ostensorio.
> Punzado por tu Padre con aguja de lumbre.
> Latiendo como el pobre corazón de la rana
> que los médicos ponen en el frasco de vidrio.[25]

Tertullian, in his treatise *On the Flesh of Christ,* goes so far in his devotion to Christ's state of humiliation as to affirm categorically that "his body did not reach even to human beauty. . . . Would any man have dared to touch even with his little finger the body of Christ, if it had been made of the stars; or to smear his face with spitting, if it had not invited it by its abjectness?"[26] Tertullian inaugurates a tradition that locates holiness and grace precisely within what is ugly and contemptible by worldly standards. In his zeal for the absolute hiddenness of the divine presence among men, he even dares speculate, in the face of Marcion's angelism, that Christ might have chosen to be incarnated as an animal in order to preach the kingdom of heaven,[27] a statement whose metaphorical energy is approximated by Lorca's likening of the Eucharistic Christ to the "poor heart of a frog, pierced by the Father with a needle of light."

Tertullian's insistence on the Christ who must of necessity appear deformed, as a consequence of his willing self-identification with condemned humanity, is of great importance for the particular christological modality of Trakl's poetry. There is a late untitled poem that may be seen as a representation of the crushed *Ecce homo:*

> Rosiger Spiegel: ein hässliches Bild,
> Das im schwarzen Rücken erscheint,
> Blut aus brochenen Augen weint
> Lästernd mit toten Schlangen spielt.
>
> Schnee rinnt durch das starrende Hemd
> Purpurn über das schwarze Gesicht,

> Das in schwere Stücken zerbricht
> Von Planeten, verstorben und fremd.
>
> Spinne im schwarzen Rücken erscheint
> Wollust, dein Antlitz verstorben und fremd.
> Blut rinnt durch das starrende Hemd
> Schnee aus brochenen Augen weint.[28]

This poem bears close iconic resemblance to the famous passage in Isaiah concerning the appearance of the suffering servant: "He had no form or comeliness that we should look at him, and no beauty that we should desire him" (53:2). Typical, however, of Trakl's images of the destruction of his protagonists (whether they are anonymous, as here, or whether they bear the names of Helian, Elis, or Sebastian) is the moral or spiritual beauty that is gradually revealed precisely as the physical devastation becomes more total. In the poem just quoted what emerges as true protagonist is a quiet obedience to what is being inflicted, so that the moral integrity, preserved in spite of the violence, reflects an ultimate indestructibility, which is conveyed by the return of the refrain:

> Blut aus brochenen Augen weint . . .
> Schnee aus brochenen Augen weint.

The source of these tears of blood and snow seems inexhaustible. Similarly, only Christ Jesus, the God-man, can, in Pascal's words, "be in agony until the end of time." The Christian God reflects his omnipotence by his perseverance in suffering.

The coincidence, in Christ, of extreme love with extreme humiliation reveals the most essential aspect of Christian apocalyptic thought. Methodius of Olympus, a writer of the late third century, declares that Christ's flesh—and, with it, all flesh—was crucified to draw forth its immortality,[29] and elsewhere he adds that Christ's "soul was separated from the flesh, that sin might perish by death, not being able to live any longer in one dead."[30] These statements convey succinctly the belief that suffering and death are necessary stages on the way to regeneration. The christocentric origin of the process emphatically distinguishes its dynamism from any kind of Platonizing speculation on the transmigration of souls: it is the flesh that yields its immortality. Early Christian pessimism, deriving from the unstable nature of the present world and the corruption of men's morals, inevitably comes to rest in the contemplation of the Passion of the Lord. Here all apocalyptic fears experience a transformation enjoined by the divine identity of the one suffering the calamity of the world. The ugly formlessness of the suffering servant is seen by the eyes of faith to be a temporal mode of his glory: it is love which, in utter abjection, reveals an eternal majesty, in deformity *(Ungestalt)* the mystery of transcendental form *(Übergestalt).* Christ's bearing of the world's sin (cf. John 1:29) and his being made sin itself for our sake (cf. 2 Cor. 5:21) are understandable only as functions of the majesty of love.[31]

The unheard-of proclamation that God has so identified himself with the world as to become the least regarded among men is the essence of the Gospel. This *kerygma* radically sabotages every stable human aesthetic. Nikolai Berdyaev observed long ago that "a perfect classicism, one capable of extracting from nature a wholly content and satisfying harmony, is impossible ever since Christ's agony and crucifixion."[32] And Amos Wilder remarks with specific reference to language that "the Gospel arose out of that kind of radical break in human affairs when old customs and continuities are undermined; it reflected that level of experience in which men and the world are made and unmade, and in which language will inevitably have a dynamic character and inevitably take on symbolic and surreal expression."[33]

The language of apocalypticism stands in a particularly impressive manner under the sign of the Passion of Christ. No longer is any mere jeremiad feasible that would simply envision the wrath of God destroying a generation. The full thrust of the "wages of sin" has been endured by him who was made sin for our sake, and henceforth destruction is possible only in the sense of transformation in the direction of healing.

St. Jerome offers a striking instance of the connection between external, temporal ruin and the implications that such a calamity should have for the interior life of faith. Bemoaning the capture of Rome by Alaric in 410, Jerome writes:

> Pro nefas, orbis terrarum ruit et in nobis peccata non corruunt . . . Vivimus quasi altera die morituri et aedificamus quasi semper in hoc victuri saeculo. Auro parietes, auro laquearia, auro fulgent capita columnarum et nudus atque esuriens ante foras nostras in paupere Christus moritur.[34]

In a poem aptly entitled *Unterwegs,* Trakl conveys a comparable sense of the vanity and stupidity of the world in the face of its own ephemeral nature. With this sense of apocalyptic judgment Trakl, like Jerome, couples a deep compassion for the neglected and downtrodden, who in both cases emerge as the locus of divine epiphanies, in keeping with the structure of the Christ-form of the Passion already examined:

> Im Finstern trippelt puppenhaft ein Greis
> Und lüstern lacht ein Klimperklang von Geld.
> Ein Heiligenschein auf jene Kleine fällt,
> Die vorm Kaffeehaus wartet, sanft und weiss.
>
> .   .   .   .

Karrossen abends durch Gewitter ziehn.
Durchs Dunkel stürzt ein Leichnam, leer und fahl.
Ein heller Dampfer landet am Kanal,
Ein Mohrenmädchen ruft im wilden Grün.

Schlafwandler treten vor ein Kerzenlicht,
In eine Spinne fährt des Bösen Geist.
Ein Herd von Seuchen Trinkende umkreist;
Ein Eichenwald in kahle Stuben bricht.

Im Plan erscheint ein altes Opernhaus,
Aus Gassen fluten Masken ungeahnt
Und irgendwo loht wütend noch ein Brand.
Die Fledermäuse schrein im Windgebraus.

Quartiere dräun voll Elend und Gestank.
Violenfarben und Akkorde ziehn
Vor Hungrigen an Kellerlöchern hin.
Ein süsses Kind sitzt tot auf einer Bank.[35]

A passage from the *Ecclesiastical History* of Eusebius Pamphilus (265–341) shows a sensibility similar to that of *Unterwegs* in its portrayal of famine and pestilence:

Some, wasted away to mere skeletons, stumbled hither and thither like dead shadows, trembling and tottering from excessive weakness and inability to stand; they fell down in the midst of the streets, where they lay stretched out, and only earnestly begged someone to hand them a little morsel of bread, then drawing in their breath, with their last gasp they cried out "Hunger!" having only strength sufficient for this most painful cry . . . Now in the midst of the streets and lanes, the dead and naked bodies, cast out and lying for many days, presented a most painful spectacle to the beholders. Some, indeed, were already the food of dogs, on which account, especially, the survivors began to slay the dogs, lest growing mad they should devour men. . . . All places, therefore, were filled with lamentation, in all streets, lanes, market-places and highways. Nothing was to be seen but tears, with the accustomed flutes, and funeral dirge. In this manner death waged a desolating war with these two weapons, famine and pestilence.[36]

The affinity between Trakl's poem and these passages from Jerome and Eusebius is twofold. There is, first, an obvious external similarity derived from the events described. In each case we witness a public calamity that destroys the routine pace of life. We have here a style of crisis that accounts for the quasi-obsessive fixation on images of death and decay. More important still, however, is the common tenor of elegiac lament for the state of mankind, which intertwines observations of a physical with those of a moral order. While Eusebius concludes his account by directly attributing the calamities just described to God's "indignation and anger,"[37] Jerome and Trakl emphasize the commiseration they feel with suffering humanity. Jerome's image of the poor man in whom Christ dies of hunger at the threshold of palaces decked with gold is expanded by Trakl to the images of the scurrying old man, the girl waiting in front of the coffeehouse, and the child sitting dead on the bench. Trakl consistently combines these images that elicit compassion with more apocalyptic ones: the clinking money, the falling corpse, the plagues, the flood of masks, and the conflagration. The judgment passed on the times, as in Jerome and Eusebius, takes in Trakl the form of a silent invective against the absence of mercy.

As has already been affirmed, the central christological mystery that reveals God's love in the form of human humiliation revolutionizes all aesthetic concepts. Moral harmony—the ascendancy of spiritual truths—takes precedence over a systematic balancing of aesthetic symbols. The aesthetic medium will henceforth bear evidence of an apparent discontinuity, which at a deeper level is seen to be the expression of God's radical intervention in human affairs. Scripture itself is the model of all aesthetic witnessing to the reality of God's dynamic presence, and it is the Bible which establishes that "style fraught with background" (Auerbach) which will serve as foundation and constant reference for the figural imagination. The Bible, as literary record of God's intervention in history, exhibits that radical end of a worldly aesthetic which coincides with the definitive emergence of the divine aesthetic. This end and this emergence are events uniquely symbolized by the Cross.[38] An aesthetic of worldly triumphalism and exterior harmony gives way to an aesthetic that must portray the triumph of life over death by affirming the indestructibility of life in death. Scripture refuses to define man systematically, which means he cannot be grasped essentially outside of his steady process of becoming. Scripture "defines" man dynamically, as being always engaged in an "act of living," an act that is not totally to be grasped by thought. Man is, therefore, seen to exist on an open-ended plane, and this awareness of incompleteness is what gives rise to a discontinuous style "fraught with background." Karl Barth sees in the unsystematic and broken style of Scripture not only its strength, but the evidence itself of its truth.[39]

By comparing Trakl with the early Christian apocalypticists we have seen that his style, too, stands radically under the sign of the Cross, in the sense that his poetry represents the death of a worldly aesthetic of fixed harmonies and its transfiguration into a divine aesthetic of incarnation and passion, which alone opens the way to truly incorruptible harmonies. We have discovered in Trakl's poetry the same ethical sentence passed on the times, the same commiseration with the fallen state of mankind, the same discontinuity of style that witnesses to an understanding of existence in the world as essentially characterized by its incompleteness and openness to transformation through apocalyptic judgment.

Trakl and Baroque Apocalyptic Poetry

> **Confige timore tuo carnes meas;**
> **a judiciis enim tuis timui.**
>
> Ps. 118:120

When Ludwig von Ficker visited Trakl in a field hospital near Cracow in October 1914, only a few days before the poet's death, part of their conversation consisted in Trakl's reading to von Ficker from the work of the Baroque poet Johann Christian Günther (1695–1723). Like Günther, Trakl would die at the age of twenty-seven. One of the strophes from the poem *Bussgedanken,* cited by von Ficker in his account of the visit, and which he says had particularly struck Trakl, is as representative of the Baroque sense of the passing of temporal things as it is of Trakl's manner of closely associating guilt, decay, and spiritual renewal. Addressing death, Günther had written:

> Komm nun und wie du willst, die Erbschuld abzufodern,
> Der Leib, das schwere Kleid, mag reissen und vermodern,
> Weil dies Verwesen ihn mit neuer Klarheit schmückt.
> Ich will ihm zum voraus mit freudenreichem Sehnen
> Auf Gräbern nach und nach den Schlummer angewöhnen,
> In welchem ihn hinfort kein eitler Traum mehr drückt.[40]

With evident enthusiasm, Trakl praised Günther's poem to von Ficker as "die bittersten Verse, die ein deutscher Dichter geschrieben hat."[41]

A comparison of Trakl's poetry with that of the Baroque period reveals certain common elements of style and imagery that are conditioned by a similar view of the world. The similarities, as I hope to show, are too immediately apparent to be dismissed by Gisela Luther's conclusion that there is no ultimate compatibility between the Expressionist and the Baroque styles.[42] I shall continue this survey of the Christian apocalyptic imagination with particular regard to the Baroque poetry of the world's end and that of the Passion of Christ, which occupy us respectively in this and the next sections.

It is no coincidence, as we shall see, that a Baroque poet of Günther's temperament, who could write lines such as

> Mein junges Feldgeschrei bringt stumme Klagelieder,
> Es keimt, es gärt bereits durch alle meine Glieder
> Der Same und das Gift geerbter Sterblichkeit,[43]

should be one of the very few writers we know to have moved Trakl deeply. The subject of Christ's Passion, furthermore, provides us with a useful point of continuity between the early Christian apocalypticists and the Baroque poets. As we have seen, a sense of apocalyptic judgment was closely linked with the figure of the suffering Christ in the early period, to the extent that one could speak of this figure as constituting a second apocalyptic moment of interiority. In the contemplation of faith, the panorama of cosmic catastrophe becomes contracted to the personal fate of Jesus, who once and for all receives upon his flesh the sentence of the Father's wrath. Not only do we here explore an important aspect of the Christ-form of Scripture, but we see emanating from it the pervasive mood of melancholy that characterizes so much of the Baroque poets' and Trakl's own work. In the present comparison, therefore, I endeavor to clarify three levels of Trakl's work simultaneously: (1) its apocalyptic sense of the world in crisis, which generates (2) a ground tone of melancholy in the face of the decay of the temporal, both of which aspects become "incarnated," as it were, in (3) the form of the suffering Christ.

The last judgment is a frequent subject of Baroque poetry. Johannes Khuen (1606–75) sees the entire cosmos in a final bidding of farewell, and demands a conversion to God not only from man, but from all beings:

> Ach unerhörts Getümmel:
> Was fliegt und schwimbt, heut abschid nimbt,
> Fewr, Wasser, Lufft, und Erdten;
> Weh denen die sich nit allhie
> Vorher, zu Gott bekehrten.[44]

Justus Georg Schottel (1612–76) emphasizes the event of transformation that turns the corruptible into incorruptibility:

> Unser Leib und Fleisch und Blut, voller Unart dieser Zeiten,
> Ungeschickt zum Ewig-seyn wegen der Vergänglichkeiten,
> Fähig wird der Ewigkeit, unvergänglich, neu und jung,
> Wundersamst durch Gottes Macht, mittels dieser Wandelung.[45]

Like Schottel, Trakl sees a transformation in death, a metamorphosis that bears the indelible stamp of a final intensification of both torment and bliss. The apocalyptic sense in the following strophes is conveyed primarily by the communal *wir* and other peculiar plurals, which hint at the cosmic scale of the transformation:

> Im hellen Spiegel der geklärten Fluten
> Sehn wir die tote Zeit sich fremd beleben
> Und unsre Leidenschaften im Verbluten,
> Zu ferner'n Himmeln unsre Seelen heben.
>
> Wir gehen durch die Tode neugestaltet
> Zu tiefern Foltern ein und tiefern Wonnen,
> Darin die unbekannte Gottheit waltet—
> Und uns vollenden ewig neue Sonnen.[46]

But it is Andreas Gryphius (1616–64) who, in his unique manner, sees the apocalypse as a personal moral judgment. He dramatizes the impending doom of the recalcitrant in the galoping dactyls of *Die Hölle:*

> Diss ist die Flamme der grimmigen Rache, die der erhitzete Zorn
>   angeblasen:
> Hier ist der Fluch der unendlichen Straffen, hier ist das immerdar
>   wachsende Rasen:
>   O Mensch! verdirb, um hier nicht zu verderben.[47]

The change of meter from the dactyls to the iambs of the last verse—a change from a falling to a rising rhythm—signals that total *metanoia* which the didactic framework of the poem intends to effect and whose pivot is the elegiac *O!* The paradox contained in the injunction *Verdirb!* may be regarded as representative of the apocalyptic vision, which sees the disintegration of the temporal as necessary for the corresponding ascent of the eternal.[48] The resolution to decay demanded by this imperative provides us with a solid bridge to Trakl, who in *Gesang zur Nacht* welcomes the suffering that, although destroying him in the present, simultaneously acts as a means to the attainment of the great peace, the definite article here bearing the important function of indicating the finality of the state envisioned:

> Dass sich die letzte Qual an mir erfülle,
> Ich wehr' euch nicht, ihr feindlich dunklen Mächte.
> Ihr seid die Strasse hin zur grossen Stille,
> Darauf wir schreiten in die kühlsten Nächte.[49]

The attitude at once of challenge and deliberate passivity—"Ich wehr' euch nicht"—provides us, furthermore, with a clear parallel to Christ's word to Peter in the Garden of Gethsemani, as the rabble approached with Judas to arrest him: "Do you think that I cannot appeal to my Father, and he will at once send me more than twelve legions of angels?" And Christ's reason for his deliberate passivity corresponds to Trakl's, both being understandable only in the light of the figural imagination: "*Wie würde aber die Schrift* erfüllet?" (Matt. 26:53–54); "*dass sich die letzte Qual an mir* erfülle. . . ."

The dominant sense of the impending end of the world has as a logical result the radical devaluation of the purely temporal and a tending toward almost violent melancholy. Examples from Baroque poetry illustrating the world as judged consistently *sub specie aeternitatis* could be multiplied endlessly. While Günther directs his lament to his own heart as final refuge in his extremity—

> So ist's, bedrängtes Herz, aufs eusserste gekommen;
> Das Elend hat den Lenz des Alters mitgenommen,
> Schmach, Armuth, Schmerz and Müh gebiert noch keine Ruh . . .
> Und wo mein Jammer klopft, da schlägt die Thüre zu[50]—

the young Trakl experiences the loss of his vain hopes, and his heart knows only the rhythm of despair:

> Nun schlägt es nach dem Takt verklungner Tänze
> Zu der Verzweiflung trüben Melodien,
> Indes der alten Hoffnung Sternenkränze
> An längst entgöttertem Altar verblühn.[51]

And expanding on Trakl's *verblühn,* Johannes Plavius (fl. 1636) gives the following warning:

> Diese welt mit ihrer lust
> Ist nur lauter koth und wust
> Gegen das was ewig ist . . . :
> Diese welt mit ihren lüsten
> Wird vergehen, liebe Christen.[52]

Gryphius, for his part, is quick to expose the "dream of life":

> Was frag ich nach der Welt! sie wird in Flammen stehn . . .
> Die Schönheit ist wie Schnee, diss Leben ist der Tod.[53]

His favorite landscapes are those which produce a sober *prise de conscience* by reminding him of the nearness of death and God's severe judgment:

> Schrecken, und Stille, und dunckeles Grausen, finstere Kälte
>   bedecket das Land . . .
> Dort, wenn der plötzliche Tag wird anbrechen, wird was geredet,
>   gewürcket, gemeynt,
> Sonder vermänteln eröffnet sich finden vor des erschrecklichen
>   Gottes Gerichte.[54]

In similar manner, Trakl experiences the intense melancholy that pervades creation in the following landscape:

> Ein Stoppelfeld. Ein schwarzer Wind gewittert.
> Aufblühn der Traurigkeit Violenfarben,
> Gedankenkreis, der trüb das Hirn umwittert . . .
> Da schweigt die Seele grauenvoll erschüttert
> Entlang an Zimmern, leer und dunkelfarben.[55]

The soul's silence is the anchor of this poem, for its astonishment subsumes the elements of decay and thereby gives a hint of their transformation. Only the soul's silence remains.

In the poem *Thränen des Vaterlandes, anno 1636,* Gryphius displays before us in apocalyptic images a panorama of death and destruction that closely parallels Dionysius of Alexandria's description of the war in his city and Eusebius's account of the plague:

> Die Thürme stehn in Glut, die Kirch ist umgekehret.
> Das Rathhaus liegt im Grauss, die Starcken sind zerhaun,
> Die Jungfern sind geschänd't, und wo wir hin nur schaun
> Ist Feuer, Pest, und Tod, der Hertz und Geist durchfähret.
> Hier durch die Schantz und Stadt, rinnt allzeit frisches Blut.
> Dreymal sind schon sechs Jahr, als unser Ströme Flut,
> Von Leichen fast verstopfft, sich langsam fort gedrungen.[56]

Common to all these reports is their excess of hyperbolic expression. Blood drenches the ground and corpses obstruct the rivers. Gryphius makes fire, pestilence, and death inhabit not only the cities, but also the hearts and the spirits. Such hyperbole may be attributed to a fundamentally apocalyptic imagination that instinctively equates historical catastrophe with eschatological judgment and seeks to develop a fantastic imagery that will convey a sense of moral horror.

We discover the same procedure in Trakl, although with the difference that this poet needs no actual historical calamity to activate his apocalyptic vision. Trakl sees apocalypse in the commonplace; his eschaton occurs on a silent afternoon by the Salzach River:

> Am Kehricht pfeift verliebt ein Rattenchor.
> In Körben tragen Frauen Eingeweide,
> Ein ekelhafter Zug voll Schmutz und Räude,
> Kommen sie aus der Dämmerung hervor.
>
> Und ein Kanal speit plötzlich feistes Blut
> Vom Schlachthaus in den stillen Fluss hinunter.
> Die Föhne färben karge Stauden bunter
> Und langsam kriecht die Röte durch die Flut.[57]

At this point Gryphius and Trakl vie with one another in their use of grotesque images. While Trakl has made the earth's surface the stage where rats, garbage, entrails, and thickened blood contend for attention, Gryphius confines his visions of violence and decay to the graveyard, that "school in which the highest art is taught us mortals":

> Der Därmer Wust reist durch die Haut,
> So von den Maden gantz durchbissen;
> Ich schau die Därmer (ach mir graut!)
> In Eiter, Blut und Wasser flissen!
> Das Fleisch, dass nicht die Zeit verletzt,
> Wird unter Schlangen-blauem Schimmel
> Von unersättlichem Gewimmel
> Vielfalter Würmer abgefresst.[58]

Now, while these images are entirely appropriate in a cemetery, Trakl imposes the same kind of sensibility on life in general:

> Wie scheint doch alles Werdende so krank!
> Ein Fieberhauch um einen Weiler kreist. . . .[59]

Trakl's conviction that the deepest truth of earthly life was to be located in its character of decay led him to formulate an aphorism that renounces all striving after happiness as a delusion, and instead seeks the kind of knowledge afforded by melancholy: "Nur dem, der das Glück verachtet, wird Erkenntnis," wrote Trakl.[60] This viewpoint may, at the same time, be regarded as characteristic of the Baroque poets, and it is again Johann Christian Günther who, in the poem *Auf das Glück,* launches a scathing attack on the tyranny that happiness attempts to impose on mankind. After calling happiness an "idol of low-lying minds," Günther goes on to expose it as a cruel despot:

> So, so, verdopple Schlag und Eifer!
> Schlag schärfer und begreif dich nicht!
> Der Schmerz erregt mir Jäscht und Geifer,
> Den spei ich dir ins Angesicht.

And he concludes with an image worthy of any Expressionist:

> Und könte mir mein Wuntsch geschehn,
> Dass jede Wunde Lippen hätte,
> So wolt ich dich recht grausam schmähn.[61]

In a much gentler manner, Trakl's poem *Nachtlied* likewise invites pain and suffering to bring him to perfection. Günther's grotesque wound-with-lips is transformed in Trakl into a sublime image that indicates the extent to which he has reconciled suffering and beauty, a harmony never achieved by Günther:

> Triff mich, Schmerz! Die Wunde glüht.
> Dieser Qual hab' ich nicht acht!
> Sieh aus meinen Wunden blüht
> Rätselvoll ein Stern zur Nacht!
> Triff mich, Tod! Ich bin vollbracht.[62]

This complex image of a wound from which, in the night, a star blossoms forth brings us to the specifically christological part of this discussion. We shall presently see how the oxymoronic juxtaposition and near-identification of death and life, darkness and light, corruption and transformation, which we have seen to be characteristic of Baroque poetry, will now gain in concreteness and explicitness when explored with reference to the poetry of the Passion.

Trakl and the Baroque Poetry of the Passion

> **Para el asesinato del ruiseñor, venían tres mil hombres armados de lucientes cuchillos.[63]**
>
> **Lorca**

The Baroque poetry of the Passion achieves an extreme intensification of the elements of world judgment and radical melancholy that we have been exploring. Such density of expression gives form to concurrent emotions of anguish and of joy, and the poets concerned compete with one another in accomplishing a poetic fusion of these opposed tendencies. The identification of opposites in the contemplation of the suffering Christ gives this poetry an ecstatic pitch that raises it to the level of great religious and erotic poetry. The intensity conveyed by these verses is to be attributed to the successful integration of a deeply thankful love for the suffering Savior with a super-realistic representation of the physical afflictions endured by him. Such description, always bordering on the gruesome, is employed as a function of the devotion and interior conversion it is supposed to arouse. Paul Fleming (1609–1640) apostrophizes the Lord's wounds directly as follows:

> Ihr Zuflucht meiner Angst, ihr aufgethanen Ritze,
> darin ich sicher bin, wenn der erzürnte Gott
> ümm meine Sünde schilt . . .

He goes on to develop the image of the open gashes into a conceit:

> Wie seelig bin ich doch, wenn ich Erlöster sitze
> in eurer Hölen Schoss.[64]

The topos of wound as sheltering cave is one of the most constant in the Baroque poetry of the Passion. Thus, in his *Ein Charfreytagsgesang*, Johannes Rist (1607–67) expands Fleming's conceit as follows:

> Wach' auff mein Geist, erhebe dich
> Wach' auff, hie sind fünf Todestich'
>   Und Wunden deines Herren,
> Wach' auff, lass Welt und Wollust seyn,
> Ich wil dich in die Höhl hinein
>   Immanuels versperren . . .
>
> Fünff Höhlen zeigt uns dieser Ort,
> Die trägt an sich des Vaters Wohrt . . .

Just as beasts and birds seek a place of refuge during a storm, so too the soul inside Christ's wounds:

> Auch du mein Geist verzage nicht
> Im Fall' ein starcker Donner bricht
>   Die Wolken grosser Gnade.
> Kriech' in des Herren Wunden ein. . . ,
> Da trifft dich weder Blitz noch Zorn.[65]

Trakl likewise uses the image of a cave as a sinner's refuge from God's wrath:

> Ein Orgelchoral erfüllte ihn mit Gottes Schauern.
> Aber in dunkler Höhle verbrachte er seine Tage,
> log und stahl und verbarg sich.[66]

More significant still is the following explicitly christological use of the image, again in connection with God's anger:

> Rasend peitscht Gottes Zorn die Stirne des Besessenen . . .
>
> Aber stille blutet in dunkler Höhle stummere Menschheit,
> Fügt aus harten Metallen das erlösende Haupt.[67]

These examples enable us to draw at least a tentative conclusion concerning the similarity of world views of the Baroque poets and Trakl, who envision a situation in which the opposition of man's sin and God's wrath is mediated by a sheltering figure who himself incarnates simultaneously divine wrath *(rasend peitscht)* and divine mercy *(aber stille blutet)*, symbolized by the blood and the cave.

The oxymoronic structure of much Baroque poetry and of Trakl's work, to which I have alluded, has its origin in this theological identification of wrath and mercy, divinity and humanity, in the Christ-form. In the poem quoted, Rist concludes his rhapsody to Christ's five wounds by seeing them, successively, as five pearls, five stars, and five jewels:

> Hie findest Du das Freudenöl,
> Hie gläntzen güldne Sterne,
> Hie steckt ein Kleinod solcher Art,
> Dessgleichen nie gesehen ward . . .
>
> Des Herren Wunden nem' ich mir,
> Den besten Schmuck auf Erden,
> Wer den nicht hat, kan nimmermehr
> Zu dieses Lämleins Hochzeit Ehr'
> Hinein gelassen werden,
> Nur der, den dieses Kleinod ziert,
> Wird auff diss grosse Mahl geführt.[68]

In a late untitled poem of Trakl's we find an application of this same imagery of wound, star, jewel, and bridegroom, in a configuration that is particularly striking because of its similarity to the Rist poem:

> Unter dem Dornenbogen lagst du und es grub der Stachel
> Sich tief in den kristallenen Leib   '
> Dass feuriger sich die Seele der Nacht vermähle.
>
> Es hat mit Sternen sich die Braut geziert,
> Die reine Myrthe
> Die sich über des Toten anbetendes Antlitz neigt.[69]

Far beyond making mere use of a "Christ-figure," this poem is christological in a specifically ecclesiological sense. The stars, which in the poem correspond to the wound in the protagonist's body, are precisely the jewels with which the bride decks herself. This instantaneous shrinkage of a cosmic emblem (star) to the confines of human proportions (jewels) can be seen to be made possible only through the mediation of the figure whose body shared with the stars their crystalline nature. The emphatic purpose clause: "lagst du und es grub der Stachel . . . dass. . . ," can only be explained christologically in terms of a deliberate laying down of life in order that the bride might enter the wedding feast. The center around which this poem gyrates is not so much the destruction of the protagonist as it is the deliberate willfulness with which he accedes to his demise and his resulting unification with a

"bride" that has been transferred here figurally from the Canticle of
Canticles.

In a poem that offers us perhaps the most excellent instance of that
peculiar fusion of gruesome imagery and elegiac joy in the Passion of
Christ, Daniel Casper von Lohenstein (1635–83) creates a scenario in
which the *dramatis personae* stand in a configuration that corresponds to
that of Trakl's poem just analyzed. The poem is a gloss on the 53d
chapter of Isaiah, that scriptural passage to which may be traced Tertullian's aesthetic of the "ugly Christ." The subtitle of the poem is: *weil
seine Gestalt hesslicher ist, denn andere Leute,* and it begins with the following
invitation:

> Auf Seele! die du dich so hässlich hast beflecket,
> Die du das Ebenbild des Höchsten hast entweyht . . .
> Geh aus der Eitelkeit verführerischen Schrancken
> Halt deinen Bräutigam den Glaubens-Augen für . . .
> Sih von der Scheitel an den Heyland bis zun Füssen,
> Und schaue: welch ein Mensch, ja welch ein Wurm er ist!

The soul, in the feminine, is urged to look upon her bridegroom, whom
her sins have made ugly, in the same manner that in Trakl's poem the
bride, now made pure as myrtle as a result of the bridegroom's receiving
in his flesh the penetrating spike, bends down over his dead countenance, rigid with adoration. There follows a succession of greatly moving images that release a riot of emotions. All of these images have in
common the terrible lyrical awe that arises at seeing the greatest beauty
identified with the uttermost defilement and physical injury:

> Sein Haupt von feinstem Gold' ist eytricht und voll Beulen,
> Die Tauben-Augen sind mit Speichel zugeklebt . . .
> Sein Raben-schwartzes Haar, von dem stets Tau getroffen,
> Bäckt durch geronnen Blutt itzt an einander an . . .
> Aus seiner Nase trift geronnen schwarz Geblütte,
> Die vor wie Äpfel roch, und Narden Öl stach weg;
> Die Lippen, die vor Myrrh- und Rosen theilten mitte,
> Sind braun und blau zerschwolln, zerkerbet und voll Fleck.
> Der Glieder Helffenbein mit Türck'ssen eingeleget
> Ist ein viel strömicht Brunn, wo eitel Bluttschaum kwilt.

The anaphoric juxtaposition of physical beauty and ugliness is followed
by metaphysical considerations on the identification, in Christ, of essential might with utmost weakness:

> Die Händ' und Füsse sind mit Nägeln angepflöcket,
> Damit er Erd und Meer hat in die Luft gehenckt . . .
> Der Engel um sich hat, und Sterne zu den Füssen,

> Mus krümmen Rück und Hals für seines Kreutzes Last . . .
> Der Richter kniet verdammt, der alles Fleisch wird richten,
> Und der ist Fingernackt, der allen Kleider gibt,
> Die Wahrheit mus auf sich Verleumdung lassen tichten,
> Und Gott, des Vaters Lust, ist bis in Tod betrübt.

The death of God: von Lohenstein finally reveals the theological kernel of faith that has made his meditation possible. The range of lyrical effusions that he has brought into play radiates from this hard fact as the sensual manifestation itself of the mystery of faith. He concludes his poem on a moral note, which only lends a final intensity to this total interfusion of things human and divine that we have been experiencing, a veritable erotic experience of faith:

> Wir richen Gott itzt wol die wir für Sünden stincken,
> Denn Jesus balsamet mit seinem Blutt' uns ein;
> Dass unsre Seele könn' ihr hesslich Antlitz schmincken,
> Muss sein faul Eyter uns die reinste Salbe seyn.[70]

In this conclusion we find the same purpose clause with *dass* as in Trakl: "Dass feuriger sich die Seele der Nacht vermähle," and this structural similarity supports the parallelism of the events expressed: "Es hat mit Sternen sich die Braut geziert, / die reine Myrthe."

Trakl's most typical imagery offers the same juxtaposition of ugliness and beauty we find in the Christ of von Lohenstein—the same simultaneity of power and helplessness:

> In Kühle eines Baums und ohne Schmerz
> Atmet das Vollkommene
> Und bedarf der herbstlichen Sterne nicht.

This strophe, indicating a consciousness where perfect peace, self-sufficiency, and "centeredness" prevail, is immediately followed by an expression of utter weakness, signaled by the ever-present christological motif of the thorns:

> Dornen, darüber jener fällt.
> Seinem traurigen Fall
> Sinnen lange Liebende nach.[71]

This congruence of perfection and loss of self is, as in our Baroque poem, framed by the *anamnēsis* of the lovers, who have been summoned to commemorate the bridegroom's deed of self-emptying. What is more, these votaries are constituted in their very identity as lovers precisely by this previous deed. And Trakl elsewhere uses a characterization of his protagonist that is in keeping with the lyrico-theological function of all the Oriental preciosity of von Lohenstein's images of myrrh, aloes, balm, and turquoises. Trakl writes:

> O! ihr stillen Spiegel der Wahrheit.
> An des Einsamen elfenbeinerner Schläfe
> Erscheint der Abglanz gefallener Engel.[72]

Ivory: the same attribute given by the Baroque poet to Christ's limbs is applied by Trakl to his protagonist's temples, which at the same time act as mirrors of truth (and von Lohenstein has already described Christ as "the truth who must let himself be sentenced for calumny") in reminding the contemplative soul of its pristine beauty and radiance. The soul *is restored* to its former glory through the humiliation of the Savior: "Die du das Ebenbild des Höchsten hast entweyht . . . / Muss sein faul Eyter uns die reinste Salbe seyn."

Many variations accrue to this central theme of the redemptive identification of might and helplessness. Primary among them is Christ's motive of obedience to the will of his Father. Andreas Scultetus (1622–47), in his *Blutschwitzend-Todsringender Jesus,* has Christ direct a monologue to the heavenly Father, with deep silence as the only answer to the pathos of the forsaken Son:

> Mein Vater, wiltu nicht nach deinem Kinde fragen?
> Bistu dann, sagt dein Mund, O Zorn-Gott, unbewegt? . . .
> Dein Willen sey vollbracht.[73]

Trakl correspondingly shows the protagonist of his *Sebastian im Traum* being led to Calvary by his Father:

> Oder wenn er an der Hand des Vaters
> Stille den finstern Kalvarienberg hinanstieg
> Und in dämmernden Felsennischen
> Die blaue Gestalt des Menschen durch seine Legende ging,
> Aus der Wunde unter dem Herzen purpurn das Blut rann.
> O wie leise stand in dunkler Seele das Kreuz auf.[74]

This "wound under the heart," in its hieratic enthronement, belongs explicitly to the Baroque devotion to the Sacred Heart of Jesus, a cult that Max Jacob, the French surrealist poet and Jewish convert to Catholicism, has said was symbolic of that physiological knowledge of the world which alone makes for great poetry.[75] Here Trakl anchors in sound theology his doloristic images of wound and blood, by interpreting them as the effects of Christ's essential obedience. Such a frame of reference consistently keeps his work from lapsing into a decadent exploitation of the grotesque:

Demutsvoll beugt sich dem Schmerz der Geduldige
Tönend von Wohllaut und weichem Wahnsinn . . .

Schaudernd unter herbstlichen Sternen
Neigt sich jährlich tiefer das Haupt.[76]

The paradoxical nature of Christ's obedience as expressive of God's
love receives dazzling lyrical form in Gryphius:

O Schmerz! das Leben stirbt! O Wunder! Gott muss leiden!
    Der alles trägt fällt hin, die Ehre wird veracht,
    Der alles deckt ist nackt, der Tröster ist verschmacht,
Der Lufft und Wälder schuff, muss Lufft und Wälder meiden![77]

The logical contradictions involved in the christological mystery are
echoed by Trakl by the simultaneity of integrity and decline:

Ein feuriger Engel
Liegst du mit zerbrochener Brust auf steinigem Acker.[78]

But God is pierced that the food of life may flow forth. Johannes Rist
sings in the poem we have seen:

Fünff Keller blicken hie herfür,
Die stehen gantz voll Weins vor dir,
    Mit welchem wird geträncket.[79]

And Trakl answers:

Blaue Tauben
Trinken nachts den eisigen Schweiss,
Der von Elis' kristallener Stirne rinnt,[80]

whereby Elis parallels the eucharistic aspect of Rist's Christ by providing
nourishment through suffering. The extreme delicacy with which Trakl
here represents the passion of an intrinsically noble and innocent protagonist closely follows the procedure of Philipp Zesen's (1619–89) portrayal of the utterly ravaged Christ:

Ach seht der Glieder Auen
Wie sie verwelcket seyn! War nicht das Angesicht
Ein rechtes Rosenthal? Wie ist es zugericht?
Es haben Ihm durchwühlt Cocytus wilde Schweine
Das haaselbraune Haar, die unzerbrochnen Beine.[81]

The wilting of the valley of roses and the devastation by wild pigs are
intensified in Trakl through the fusion of realms that in Zesen remain
separate:

Jener aber ward ein schneeiger Baum
Am Beinerhügel,
Ein Wild äugend aus eiternder Wunde,
Wieder ein schweigender Stein.[82]

This survey of Baroque poetry has enabled us to establish its basic similarity to Trakl's work. The various elements of world-in-crisis, radical melancholy in the face of decay, and the apocalypse as it descends on Christ with a highly distilled and, for that reason, almost atomic violence, may all be resumed under the category of total presence. Both the Baroque poets and Trakl burst all temporal-historical confinement in order to elevate the present moment to its primordially revealed status as judgment and transformation. In this they are faithful heirs of the figural tradition. The heavy emphasis given to decay proceeds from a stance taken within the absolute and the eternal. "In the structure of Trakl's verses," writes Walter Muschg, "there is at work an irrepressible, explosive energy which imposes itself so relentlessly that Trakl himself cannot withstand its pressure and consequently shatters as its vessel. His melancholy is not conditioned merely by the time in which he lived."[83] The sacramental reality of Christ's continuing life in the believer explodes the limitations of time and space and makes historical time irrelevant at this level by establishing a mystical contemporaneity with the *kairos* of revelation. The death of the believer who has been crucified with Christ effects an awakening to a new life and consciousness that knows the reality of the present exclusively. In this manner, poetry's quasi-sacramental character anticipates eternity.[84]

Trakl in the Context of Dialectical Theology: The Expressionist Style

In order to safeguard the absolute distinction that exists between God and man—a distinction that lies at the heart of the apocalyptic imagination—contemporaneity with eternity receives a largely negative expression. The language of man is, after all, an earthly tool, itself subject to the laws of decay and ephemerality. With the radical distinction between God's actions and man's deeds we come to the final phase of the present comparison of Trakl's poetry with chosen moments in the history of styles of Christian piety.

Theological thinking at the beginning of the twentieth century, especially among Protestants, is marked by a radical break with the harmonious cultural Protestantism of the nineteenth century. This revolution of the spirit was impelled by a profound awe before God's simultaneous distance and presence with regard to man. Thus Paul Tillich (1886–

1965) gives us the following definition of Protestantism, important for its emphasis on God's aseity and man's intrinsic destitution: "The Protestant principle . . . emphasizes man's finitude, his subjection to death, but above all, his estrangement from his true being and his bondage to demonic forces—forces of self-destruction. . . . It is man in anxiety, guilt, and despair who is the object of God's unconditional acceptance."[85] In the light of this definition, we are in a better position to understand the meaning of the *wrath of God,* the judgment that we have seen to be so much a part of the tradition under examination here. In his famous *Commentary on the Epistle to the Romans,* Karl Barth gives us an explanation of God's wrath that reveals the metaphysical content of that mythological term:

> The wrath of God is the judgment under which we stand in so far as we do not love the Judge; it is the "No" which meets us when we do not affirm it; it is the protest pronounced always and everywhere against the course of the world in so far as we do not accept the protest as our own; it is the questionableness of life in so far as we do not apprehend it; it is our boundedness and corruptibility in so far as we do not acknowledge their necessity.[86]

Like Tillich and Barth, the Catholic writer Ferdinand Ebner, whom I shall often refer to in these pages as providing a conceptual explanation for many levels of Trakl's poetry, sees the "word" as being the *primum agens* of theology.[87] In the reality of the word, Ebner sees the matrix of man's dynamic relationship with God:

> In the act itself of being expressed, the word presupposes the Thou. Now, since the Thou in the last analysis can only be God, this means that man's existence as spirit has God's existence as its presupposition. In other words: Man was created by God.[88]

Man's fundamental identity as corruptible creature that comes into existence by being addressed as a "thou" by the God whose existence alone is absolute fact: this conviction accounts for a great many of those features which we have come to consider most characteristic of Trakl's poetry. His consistent obsession with the workings of evil in man and nature conveys his experience that grace and transformation must come from outside the sphere of man, or not at all. This, I think, is the meaning of his constant images of decay and destruction. The dramatization of human guilt, likewise, is neither the consequence of a loss of faith nor the expression of an inherent cynicism concerning human nature, but rather a confession of the reality of one's fallen state, an imploring admission that already invites the appearance of mercy from beyond the self.[89] "The eternal recollection of guilt which characterizes the hidden inwardness is anything but despair," writes Kierkegaard in his dialectical manner. The awareness of guilt, rather, is "the mark indicative of the relationship to an eternal happiness . . . , always sufficient to prevent the leaping aside of despair."[90] It is no wonder that Kierkegaard, with his emphasis on negative religiosity, was one of the moving forces behind the revolution of dialectical theology. And another heir of Kierkegaard, the Catholic Gabriel Marcel, speaks of the *recours absolu,* the "absolute recourse or appeal bellowed out from the depths of my indigence *ad summam altitudinem,*" which presupposes "a radical humility on the part of the subject, a humility polarized by the very transcendence of the one it invokes."[91]

At the heart of Trakl's melody of decline, "a moral melodiousness that assumes a natural harmony between the evening landscape and the 'fallen' figure of man,"[92] we always perceive Marcel's *recours absolu;* and for this reason we note that Trakl's poetry everywhere shows a character of dialogue radically opposed to, say, Rilke's poetry of the solipsistic "I." Decay in Trakl is everywhere met with an enfolding receptiveness, and his lament is characteristically directed to a silent but present Thou:

> Die Bläue meiner Augen ist erloschen in dieser Nacht,
> Das rote Gold meines Herzens. O! wie stille brannte das Licht.
> Dein blauer Mantel umfing den Sinkenden;
> Dein roter Mund besiegelte des Freundes Umnachtung.[93]

Here we note the typical structure of transformation, whereby the blue and the red that are extinguished in the subject reappear in the receptive Thou whom he addresses. The dialogical situation, conveyed more by gesture than by word, is supported here, as often throughout Trakl's poetry, by the word *um* ("about," "around") both as preposition and as prefix, which, especially in conjunction with the verb *fangen* ("catch," "take up"), as in this example, is one of Trakl's favorite indications of relationship.

Self-evident though the following statement may appear, I must emphasize the fact that the dialogical relationship between God and man is the *sine qua non* of both the apocalyptic imagination and of the possibility of man's transformation. In this sense, we can see the continuity that has led from the early Christian apocalypticists, through the Baroque poets, and finally to the dialectical theology of the early twentieth century. I now conclude this chapter with some consideration of the style of "Expressionism," that epochal nexus to which Trakl is usually said to belong.

In all discussions about the relationship between Christian faith and art, the constant caveat must be the necessity of abstaining from any final identification of the Christian experience of the world with any one particular style of expression. The very existence of a "history of Christian styles" should bear witness to the fact that the expression of Christian faith is not reducible to a particular mode of discourse. For one thing, the *kerygma* of the Church is multi-facetted; and, although a unity of the moments of death and resurrection is of the essence of this proclamation, one or the other of these can gain ascendancy in the light of the historicocultural state of the world at a given moment. Thus we may speak of a style of resurrection and a style of passion. At times these have been equated with a Catholic and a Protestant style, respectively. Karl Hammer, for instance, has produced a theological interpretation of Mozart's music that sees in the harmonic microcosm of this genius an aesthetic counterpart to God's creation in all its intrinsic goodness: "The harmony of the world is not haphazard; it is cosmic harmony, that is to say, total harmony; and the world is not an indifferent, merely aesthetic cosmos, but precisely a harmonic cosmos. In the same way, the harmony of Mozart's music is not arbitrary. It is the order itself of the world in which we live, just as God has created it and wished for it to be."[94] Paul Tillich, on the other hand, is of the opinion that the eruptive, "broken" character of the Expressionist style makes it most adequate to express religious meaning directly.[95]

Christian theology has always felt the tension between a strong view of the goodness of creation and the radical emphasis on the redemptive deed of Christ, who delivered the world from its corruption. Mozart, composing music in a century that cultivated reason, light, and stability, was able to give adequate expression to the first of these theological poles. Between Mozart and Trakl, however, there intervenes a century of dissociation, which carves out an abyss between the works of God and the works of man; but this time the separation is man-made; it is a destructive and ominous dichotomy, the opposite of the essential distinction between divinity and creation that is a source of healing.

The first twenty years of our century bring to a public and catastrophic culmination all the centrifugal elements of dissolution that had long fermented. "Between soul and world," writes Stefan George (1868–1933) about this time, "there is no longer found a creative unity. Historicism, the comforts brought by technology, faith in progress that abolishes all responsibility for the moment—all this is so much 'rotten fruit.' "[96] Along with a generation of Expressionists, Trakl experiences "an interiority which loses the world in a world which has lost interiority. . . . They had to cope with an era in which a frightful activism and a brutal kind of reality ruled the day."[97]

Because Christianity is not an abstract ideology whose tenets remain untouched by the most calamitous crises of an era, and because the God of Christianity so identified himself with the temporal destiny of mankind that he is said to have "suffered at the hands of sinners," Christian styles are an *imitatio Christi* by successively incarnating aesthetic modalities congruous with the spiritual condition of the times. The Christian style must proclaim its convictions in such a way that it is understood; and "style," in this connection with the epithet "Christian," necessarily signifies a style of life that is continuous with a style of expression. The sublime intensity of Trakl's style is a function of this continuity between life and work. The poetry presents an adequate semblance of the poet's existential reality, which is the reality of one condemned by the very sickness of the time in which he lived, condemned because choosing to show forth in his own person the awesome judgment that descends upon a time that confounds good and evil and that dismisses all conviction as irrelevant: "The dissolution of the poetry—the apparently disconnected series of impressions and expressions—itself symbolizes the dissolution of the world in its entirety. The disintegration of one epoch, in the War and in Trakl's soul, comes to symbolize eternal disintegration as such. The eschaton of one circle is transformed into a supratemporal eschaton. The uncanniness *(Unheimlichkeit)* of one era makes manifest the homelessness *(Heimatlosigkeit)* of all temporal things."[98]

3
The Traklian Grammar of Being

Il dramma umano è di necessità morale, impegnato nel contrasto e nella lotta con la passione viziosa e delittuosa. E, quando questa lotta si esprime puramente e poeticamente, non ha più il linguaggio che era dell' agitazione, del convellimento e dello strazio, ma una nuova voce che sa le tempeste, conosce l'orrore e la vergogna, vede le cose in nuova prospettiva e con nuove proporzioni, e risponde col pudore delle imagini e delle parole al pudore che si è assiso nel cuore.

Benedetto Croce[1]

Spiritus ipsius litterae, Christus.

John Scotus[2]

The apocalyptic style of Christian literature and theology has now provided us with a context in the history of Christian styles that might throw light on the alleged uniqueness of Trakl as a "religious phenomenon."[3] This brings us to the point where we must begin to explore the inner structures and logic of the poetry itself. The comparative method proved valuable when I was attempting to show that Trakl, for all his uniqueness and hermeticism, nevertheless partakes at various essential levels of the tradition of Christian apocalypticism. But such comparison must at best remain an external approximation which, although making credible enough the possibility of the existence of a dominant Christ-form in Trakl's poetry, does not finally offer sufficient demonstration that this is necessarily so.

In the opening chapter I emphasized the fact that, if Trakl's work has the Christ-form of revelation as its most constant and indispensable shaping principle, the *Urbild* without which the poetry must indeed remain inaccessibly hermetic, then this Christ-form is not present in the manner of a theme or of a subject matter for poetic elaboration, but as the very form of the poetry. A preliminary task in approaching the demonstration of the interior structure of the work must therefore be to answer the question concerning the nature of Trakl's poetics. We must explore the kind of language we have before us. For if the Christ-form possesses the essential role in this poetry that I have assigned to it, it is because the Christ-form becomes figurally realized in the form of the poetry, which is to claim that Christ-form and language are here one. In this connection, it is helpful to recall the aesthetic premises of my thesis, which require a strict correspondence and near-identity between the *Urbild,* which is the Christ-form of Scripture, and the *Nachbild,* which has it as its indispensable presupposition. The first premise says that, because the act of faith ontologically modifies the subject's perception of the world, so also will it modify his expression, in art, of the structure of the world. An expansion of this premise requires that, because of the primary unity between the creative and the believing intellect, the act of aesthetic creation will confer on its product the plastic imprint of the creator's ontological reality as modified by the act of faith. Both of these premises finally rest on the axiom *operatio sequitur esse,* which here specifically means that the form of art follows the form of faith.

Romantic-Symbolist Background of Expressionism

Although the question concerning the nature of Trakl's poetics is not the ultimate question that may be asked of his work, yet it does constitute a central pivotal point without which we can proceed no further. The necessity of asking, and answering, this question derives from the paramount importance held in Trakl's work by its form. Perhaps more than with any other poet, understanding the nature of the form of Trakl's poetry is tantamount to understanding its meaning. Even Paul Tillich, speaking from an emphatically theological perspective, calls style the key to understanding cultural creations,[4] and form their "ontologically decisive element."[5] It is the form that conveys an author's ultimate concerns. If a poem is to encounter a reader, not in the manner of a rational discourse, but as an event *(ereignishaft),* then its "how" and its "what" must be fused as perfectly as possible.[6] Form is not something merely physical, although it is that too, of course. Total form *(Gestalt),* according to Romano Guardini, implies "a law of proportions, an essential image, a delineation of value *(Proportionsgesetz, Wesensbild, Wertfigur)*—and all of this spiritually as well as materially."[7]

If theologians such as Tillich and Guardini have come to gain such insight into the decisive importance of the form of art, they owe it in no small measure to the literary movement, begun in the latter half of the nineteenth century, loosely known as "Symbolism." For all their numerous excesses, the French Symbolists recovered a fresh sense of the autonomy of the work of art, a new awareness that revitalized poetry and salvaged it from the fumes of Romantic languor. Baudelaire, who stands permanently at the heart of Symbolism, transformed what had been a very diffuse Romantic nostalgia into *émerveillement* before the well-chosen, well-constructed poetic symbol. A nostalgia turned inward comes about in both the poet and his reader by mediation of the symbol's compressed magnetic power. Nostalgia for the ideal becomes concretized in Baudelaire as the experience of the beauty of a particular symbol, which incites to reverie and lifts one above the world by virtue of its quasi-magical use of correspondences. Hence is born the properly magical aesthetics of the *poétisation du prosaïque,* whereby the subject matter is not so important as the state of mind created in the reader— what Ricoeur and others call the difference between explanation and interpretation.

Mallarmé was later to emphasize Baudelaire's insistence on the autonomy of art to the point of creating a metaphysical system based on that creed. But far more numerous are those heirs of Baudelaire who combine in varying proportions the two terms of his poetic theory: emotion and form. Although, as we shall see in a moment, exclusive emphasis on the autonomy of art finally led to a withering of the artistic vitality itself, the fundamental dogma of the Symbolists changed the course of poetry in Western culture. Symbolism provided a seed that was to come to mature fruition not in the Symbolists' own art, but in the rediscovery of the substance of form not only by artists but also by theologians and philosophers one generation later. And so we find the Neo-Thomist philosopher Jacques Maritain writing in 1918 that "art as such does not consist in imitating, but in making, composing, or constructing, and this according to the laws of the object which is to be brought into being."[8] Thus art is raised from the level of social and religious functionalism to the status of ontological autonomy. Elsewhere Maritain even affirms that art, in its own way, "continues the labor of divine creation."[9]

More recently, Susanne Langer developed a theory of art which, through Cassirer, is highly indebted to the Symbolists' emphasis on the primacy of form. "The form is built up out of relations peculiar to the qualities of a work of art," she writes. "They are formal elements in the structure, not contents."[10] Langer's reasoning attempts to show the inadequacy of a theory of art based on a distinction between form and content, and in this effort she comes to term that quality by which a form is itself, and yet more than itself, the artistic import. By speaking of "vital import" and not of "meaning" where nondiscursive symbols are concerned, the temptation is somewhat obviated to look past the "external form" in order to discover the "real significance" of a given poem.

Before proceeding to examine the effects of French Symbolism on Trakl's poetics, we shall follow the development of Baudelaire's seminal theories to their conclusion. By doing this we shall be able to determine the extent to which Trakl made positive use of Symbolist innovations, and also the manner in which he reacted against the self-defeating rationale of pure Symbolist aesthetics.

Baudelaire's theory of correspondences seeks to give particular application to the fundamental Romantic conviction that all things are cosmically interrelated and that the material world is, in its own right, divine. Transposing categories from the sensual realm, Baudelaire attributes number, color, and scent to the spiritual in an effort to give it a specific identity and locus. But, in consequence, he also effects the inextricable confusion of the two realms. While Baudelaire still possessed the kind of moral dynamism and conscience to make out of this confusion a source of creative tension, his epigones were soon to tilt the balance in favor of the purely natural aesthetic symbol, by now endowed with an inalienable (pseudo-)spiritual identity and established in its own right against any "extraneous" claims from the direction of morality or sheer, unbeautified "life."

At this point we enter the Symbolist decadence proper, which made an idol out of art and severed it from any contextual concern. Decadence, in fact, may be defined as the total absence of such a realistic context, resulting in the fragmentation of life in the name of artistic wholeness. Thus the pure, ideal beauty that the Symbolists were convinced could be realized through art turns out ultimately to be an artificial and impotent thing.[11] Nikolai Berdyaev remarks, quite incisively, I think, that, for all its cult of beauty, "aestheticism does not believe in the real transformation and transfiguration of this world, which lies in deformity, into the true world of beauty, into beauty as essential thing. In the religion of aestheticism beauty is contrasted with what is; beauty is outside being. Aestheticism is incapable of creating beauty as the final and truest reality of the world."[12] We shall finally see, in a detailed analysis later on in this chapter, that the power of Trakl's poetry is founded on the fact that, for him, beauty coincides precisely with this transformation of the world as it lies in deformity. From this fidelity to reality derives the incarnational character of his poetics.

Of Baudelaire's many followers, only one rose to the rank of truly great poet: Stéphane Mallarmé. While most of the Symbolists may be said to have fallen prey in various ways to a self-indulging decadence, the matter is much more complicated with Mallarmé. The reason, however, is not that Mallarmé did not share in the others' most profound excesses, but precisely that he was more extreme than any of them, and this in a highly intellectual way. In a word, Mallarmé "was all in one, the priest without temple who has projected all and himself in his song, in his music, rising from nowhere to nowhere; he has become God."[13]

With Mallarmé's absolute Symbolism, saved from manifest decadence by its intellectual rigor, we arrive at the end of the nineteenth century. The time is ripe for the brief but revolutionary interlude of German Expressionism, a movement to which Trakl is generally held to belong. This classification can prove misleading in several important respects. For instance, although Trakl shows superficial similarities of form with other Expressionist poets, such as Georg Heym and Else Lasker-Schüler, nevertheless his passion for the religious absolute is far removed from their pamphleteering agitation and much closer to the great religious art of a Dostoievski and a Bernanos or to the *philosophie engagée* of a Kierkegaard or a Pascal. But for the moment we may include Trakl in the following comments on the relationship of Expressionism to Symbolism.

As far as Expressionism is concerned, there is one feature common to the vast majority of poetic theory and practice in the nineteenth century, from Goethe and Lamartine to Mallarmé and Stefan George, a feature that radically divides the period from everything Expressionism represents: this is that incurable and hereditary Romantic affliction, present even in proto-Expressionists such as Nerval, Lautréamont, and Büchner—poetic egocentrism. At its most general, but also at its most profound, the Expressionist "aesthetics," if indeed we may speak of one, is based upon the total and even violent rejection of the self-centered sensibility. In this sense, all of the mainstream poets had been Romantics. In most of them the Expressionist condemns the solipsistic direction of creative energy from the poet back to the poet himself. Expressionist reaction to Romantic solipsism is at the root, for instance, of the extreme manner in which Trakl extinguishes the presence of an ego from most of his mature poems. Objectification of feelings and states of mind reflects a basic concern to remain faithful to a transpersonal reality. The simplest way of formulating the Expressionist's position is to say that his aesthetics derives from his practice, because for him art is a function of life; artistic creation is secondary to human essence; individual person, to community; nation, to world.

The Expressionist movement is foremost a movement of moral and metaphysical revolt, which took a very particular form in the literary medium; but the aesthetic medium always remained coincidental to the spiritual attitude. Most particularly, the Expressionists were reacting against the (to them) decadent Neo-Romantic Symbolism of contemporary poets such as George, Rilke, and Hofmannsthal. They rejected these poets' aristocratism, their self-idolization, their lack of effective compassion for human suffering (Rilke's *Stundenbuch* contained enough aesthetic compassion!), their ironical detachment, and their search for their own perfection as artists. The phenomenon of Expressionism was a part of Europe's spiritual renewal at the turn of the century, a purification that was to receive apocalyptic proportions in the bath of fire that was the First World War. "The best spirits of many lands confronted each other in their common rejection of a world given over to death, a world that had sold itself to the deification of matter and of power. . . . The radicalism of their endeavor corresponded to the fantastic proportions of the forces threatening mankind. The spiritual center of the Expressionist movement is to be located in this historical context and, therefore, beyond aesthetic concerns."[14]

Thus much said concerning the spontaneous, conscious attitude of the Expressionists toward decadent Romanticism and Symbolism in any form, we must go on to explore how, in practice, Expressionism presupposes the aesthetic canons of the very poets whose world-view it rejects. We shall eventually see how the formula that yields the clue to the nature of Trakl's poetics may be described in terms of the conjunction of Symbolist aesthetics with an Expressionist ethos, which means that Trakl's poetics is wholly identifiable with neither of these, and yet that the identity of his own poetry derives from both. This apparent contradiction is explained by the fact that the Expressionists put the kind of autonomous image that had been hard won by Baudelaire, in particular, to a very different kind of use. By mediation of the despised Symbolists, Expressionism inherited in spite of itself a purified concept of symbol: the autonomous, self-significant metaphor and image, liberated from the necessity of autobiographical, confessional, and moralistic effusions. The particular merit of Expressionism, however, is that, granted the Symbolist accomplishment, the symbol is again returned to its relationship with extra-aesthetic realities. Thus Bertold Brecht, in his early Expressionist phase, can assert that art is autonomous but not autarchic.[15] The symbol receives an ethical function from within. No longer can it be used decoratively or coincidentally with didactic-moralistic utterances or confessional vignettes, as in pre-Symbolist days, or in the solipsistic and autotelic manner of the Symbolists themselves.

The poetry of Georg Trakl is, to my mind, the finest product of such a long gestation of the aesthetic symbol. Trakl, and only Trakl, is able to implement all of the extreme purification of the image demanded by Symbolism while at the same time imbuing his image with an instinctive sense of ethical commitment and clairvoyance. Trakl conveys, often in a single image, an abyss of metaphysical horror at the state of man's being:

> Nachhallen die purpurnen Flüche
> Des Hungers in faulendem Dunkel,
> Die schwarzen Schwerter der Lüge,
> Als schlüge zusammen ein ehernes Tor.[16]

The image is replete with Baudelairian correspondences and musicality, and is as pure as even Mallarmé could have hoped for. Yet it contains something that is nowhere found in either Baudelaire or Mallarmé: the prophetic, totally altruistic and virile howl of a conscience stricken with grief at the falsification of man's spiritual identity and dignity in the contemporary world. The instantaneous psychological effect of shock and fearful transport produced generally by Trakl may be attributed precisely to the vitality of an elemental conscience. Paul Ricoeur observes that "consciousness of self seems to become constituted in its depths by the mediation of symbolism. Such consciousness elaborates an abstract idiom only as second instance by means of a spontaneous hermeneutic of its primary symbols."[17] In a way achieved by very few artists, Trakl was able to persevere consistently at a level where these "primary symbols of consciousness" were constantly available to him in his aesthetic activity, so that his poems possess a character of inevitability that does not at all appear to derive from artistic deliberateness and abstract rationality. Rather, there is an authenticity about them that Ricoeur explains in these terms: "The symbolism of the stain still holds on to cosmic sacralizations by the rich tresses of its roots. The symbol of the stain adheres to everything that is unheard-of and terrifying in the world, to everything which at once attracts and repulses. For these reasons, the symbolism of the stain is finally both inexhaustible and ineradicable."[18]

Two Kinds of Symbolism

With Trakl and the Expressionists we witness the emergence of a different kind of Symbolism. Joseph Chiari distinguishes between a first and a second "wave" of Symbolist poets. The first of these includes the poets from Baudelaire to Mallarmé, who formulated the Symbolist aesthetics but eventually fell prey to its excesses, and the second refers to the work of poets such as Valéry, Yeats, Claudel, and Eliot, who bring "a reborn sensibility and a fresh approach to reality. The sense of mystery remains, music is still an important prerequisite for poetry, but the poet has reassumed his pristine role in society; he wishes to warn his fellow-beings and to testify to the existence of forces which might crush or save man; he is fully aware that the phenomenal world is the only way to approach the ideal and that eternity is reached through time."[19] The existence of this kind of Symbolism is essential for an understanding of Trakl's own position.

In one of those brief but penetrating articles which see and meet the need to clarify terminological muddles, G. Ingli James carries Chiari's distinction between the two waves of Symbolists to a more general and essential level. James identifies the insistence on the autonomy of the work of art and its symbols—and, by extension, of the artist—as the fundamental insight of the Symbolist movement. However, by reference to fourth-century trinitarian controversies, James shows that the concept of the autonomy of the individual is not a new one. He demonstrates not only that the possibility of Symbolism itself rests on a patristic understanding of the nature of the Persons of the Trinity, but that the extreme "decadent" Symbolist elaborations represent a heterodox reinterpretation of the Christian understanding of personhood. This understanding of person is specifically termed "Christian" not so much because it was developed by the Fathers of the Church as because it resulted from theological considerations of the nature of the Trinity.

In the classical Greek view of the world, the individual was "dismissed as something incapable of becoming the object of knowledge, save as a particular instance of a universal rule."[20] In trying to penetrate the logical paradox posed by the dogma of the Trinity, the Fathers came to distinguish between the divine *ousia* ("essence" or "substance"), on the one hand, in which the three Persons fully participate, and, on the other hand, the unique individuality of each of these Persons, in Greek called *hypostasis* and in Latin *persona*. " 'Hypostasis' now represented the individual considered, at last, as capable of being known."[21] But, in analyzing the nature of divine personality, these theologians "had illuminated, though without fully realizing it, the nature not only of human personality, but of all the individual entities of earthly experience and the manner in which they are known."[22]

I believe that James performs his greatest service to our understanding of the issues at stake in Symbolism and, eventually, in Trakl, when he now makes the connection between the Christian view of both divine and human personhood and our manner of thinking of works of art. If we think of a poem as autonomous, says James, it is because the Christian tradition has taught us to think of a person as autonomous.[23] Thus we see the great relevance of the seemingly far-fetched comparison between a fourth-century theologian's manner of thinking about the divine Persons and the nineteenth-century Symbolist's way of conceiving his own person and work.

But it is not without good reason that the comparison appears far-fetched. For these two understandings of autonomy relate to one another as do orthodox dogma and its heresy. The extreme Symbolist teaching of a Mallarmé is the equivalent of a trinitarian teaching that would collapse the community of Persons in the Trinity to a monolithic divine consciousness in the style of Plotinus, in which the tension of uniqueness within community has been abolished for the benefit of the absolutely noncommunicating individual essence. The *tertium comparationis* of these two related but essentially incompatible doctrines of autonomy, as they are reflected in the two corresponding views of art, is that they are both "reactions against a rationalistic view of life and art, and both conceive of poetry as the embodiment of our experience of what transcends definition and classification."[24] Here the similarity ends, however, and James finally makes a radical distinction between the two mutually exclusive kinds of Symbolism, one based upon the analogy of the Trinity, which is the Symbolism based on the Christian idea of autonomy *(symbolisme engagé)*, the other likewise taking its departure from the Christian understanding of the individual as knowable, but developing a notion of the absolute freedom of the individual person or symbol, of which the Sartrian concept of autonomy is representative *(symbolisme pur)*. "Pure Symbolism" is the brand of autonomy glorified by the French Symbolists, for whom "isolation is something to be embraced. The artist must recoil from the intractable naturalistic world into the depths of his self-consciousness. . . ."[25] "Art is to be the embodied experience of the isolated individual who communicates only with himself."[26] The logical conclusion of this extremist position reveals to us the central reason behind the process of artistic decadence: "To demand that art should be autonomous in the Symbolist sense is to require that it should be meaningless, since what is totally unique is by its very nature unintelligible."[27]

The poetic movement that Chiari has described as the "second wave of Symbolists" and the German Expressionists, with whom we are concerned because of their epochal connection with Trakl, have this in common: that, realizing intuitively something of the situation that G. Ingli James has described historically, they strove to salvage the most valid and perennial insights of pure Symbolism and integrate them within a holistic view of man in the world, including man's ethical aspect as responsible agent.

Significantly enough, the aesthetic technique that these revolutionaries of sensibility adapted from Symbolism, and transformed, may again be expressed with reference to the trinitarian analogy: "Metaphor, analogy and paradox are verbal devices which, because of the ambiguity they involve, had seemed to the Greek philosophical mind to be a dangerous perversion and failing of language. In the doctrine of the Trinity, with its paradoxical insistence on one yet not one but three, three yet not three but one, such linguistic techniques presented themselves more obviously perhaps than ever before as the means of arriving at and recording insights incapable of being expressed in literal, conceptual terms."[28] What the Expressionists take over from the Symbolists, in other words, is a linguistic technique rather than a doctrine of art, a poetics rather than an aesthetics. In their understanding of the role of the work of art, the Expressionists display an attitude that I have termed *symbolisme engagé*, which is to say that the poetic symbol as used by them has the implicit ethical function of moving its receiver deeply with regard to some absolute beyond art, whether this be an absolute of the metaphysical, religious, or social order.

Trakl's Use of Symbolism

Put on the Lord Jesus Christ.
Rom. 13 : 14

In Trakl's kind of Expressionism the most extremely spiritual elements are found alongside the most sensual; and, although Trakl often exhibits the same tortured obsession with suffering of many decadent Symbolists, yet there is even in his most seemingly hermetic and "purely autonomous" passages a connection with reality. His Symbolist technique becomes all the more impressive precisely for speaking out of an existential context.[29] The whole impulse of Trakl's poetic practice may be seen as spurred by a desire for clarification of sentiment and ordering of reality. For this reason, Trakl nowhere gives evidence of a Symbolism in the style of Mallarmé, who sought to disengage poetry from all "extraneous" connections with meanings and realities beyond itself. The basic tendency of the Expressionist movement was to confront man in his entirety, an aspiration which, in art, manifests itself in a profusion of multi-media techniques. Not only do we encounter Expressionists who are poets, musicians, painters, and sculptors, but a poet such as Trakl gives such full play to color and musicality even within his own medium that we have before us a poetry that seems to be more than poetry as it invades the several senses at once.

The technique of the compressed image that Trakl inherited from Symbolism, which we will have occasion to examine later on in this chapter, allows him to achieve a "maximum range of reference with a minimum amount of explicatory statement."[30] Because this procedure has basically to do with the manner in which language is fashioned, and not with a world view, in itself it is neutral. It may be put to any use a poet chooses, or to no use at all. Much has been made of the influence of Rimbaud's Symbolism on Trakl; and yet Bernhard Böschenstein has shown how the Symbolist poetics itself makes possible perhaps for the first time in literary history a "pure" influence of one writer on another, by which is meant an influence in form but not necessarily in world view. "Around the turn of the century," observes Böschenstein, "the sensual form of literary influence—a mode not bound to a particular theme, but based solely on the adaptation of individual words, images, sounds, rhythms, and syntactic figurations—came to supplant an older manner of appropriation, that which could not borrow motifs without accepting their contents as well."[31] For the first time, a poetics can be detached from the total aesthetics from which it had resulted, and be put to other uses. Specifically, Böschenstein claims that Rimbaud's greatest effect on Trakl rested not so much on the mediation of his own radical and iconoclastic world view as on the fact that he brought Trakl into contact with what Böschenstein calls the "heterogeneous poem," which can bring into relationship on the same level elements that originally belong in very different realms of existence.[32] I have often alluded to this phenomenon in Trakl's poetry, and we have encountered it mostly under the form of the oxymoron as structural principle, especially in the course of our discussion of the Baroque poetry of the Passion. But while in Rimbaud this procedure results in a jarring and unfinished form intended to break traditional molds, Trakl can bring the most disparate elements of reality together—*Unrat und Staub der Sterne*[33]—and produce an overarching sublimity of style that truly reconciles and does not merely shock. As I have said before, and as we shall amply see again, such a procedure in Trakl may ultimately be traced back to the christological form of his poetry, particularly under the aspect of the Passion.

Trakl had learned from the Symbolists to create a language that "is resonant in itself and expresses something different from that which language had been accustomed to embody."[34] He had learned from the art of Rimbaud, Baudelaire, and Verlaine that, in the words of Ricoeur, "manifestation and signification are strictly contemporary and reciprocal."[35] This is why we may say of his christology what von Balthasar says of Hölderlin's, namely, that it "is not to be found where one seeks it by 'squeezing' the texts. It will be recognized only as a watermark which has been dissolved into the total expression of the meaning of existence."[36]

Everything I have thus far said about the two fundamentally different kinds of Symbolism has been leading to this theological insight, for in the matter of christology the manner of its poetic representation reaches its confluence with our theological concerns. If it is of paramount importance to stress the Symbolist-Expressionist nature of Trakl's poetics, it is because the form of his christology offers the essential test as to the authenticity of Trakl's transformation—both existentially and aesthetically—in the light of the Christ-form. Form brings together into dynamic unity all the properties of both letter and spirit. We recall what was said in the introductory chapter concerning the nature of a truly Christian art: that it should be Christian in form rather than in content. Only now, however, after surveying the meaning of Symbolism in poetry, are we in a position to grasp the aesthetic presuppositions for the realization of the Christ-form in literature. Thomas Mann, himself largely sharing in the Expressionist aesthetics with its roots in Symbolist technique, has adequately defined these presuppositions in a manner that applies directly to Trakl: "Breakthrough, recovery, reconstruction of the expression and of the highest and deepest appeal to feeling, all of this at the level of a spirituality and a strictness of form that had to be reached in order that the poem might become event."[37]

The thorough absorption by Trakl of the Symbolist poetics—which fundamentally means the ability to create an autonomous image—enables him to produce an art in which the "poem becomes event," in the words of Thomas Mann. Once this has been established, however, we must proceed to determine the identity of such an event. My claim is that the basic contours of this event constitute a realization (in the incarnational sense of "bringing into reality") of the Christ-form of revelation. If this is so, I must attempt to explain in what manner the Christ-form may be realized in this fashion without the literary medium's becoming a kind of poetized dogmatics or dogmatized poetry. This requires an examination of the relationship between the Christ-form and the Symbolist poetics that is to realize it.

Incarnation and the Symbol

We have already seen that the dogma of the Trinity is a necessary presupposition for the Symbolist doctrine of the autonomy of art. We shall now explore the Symbolist understanding of the poetic image from the perspective of another inherently Christian dogma, that of the Incarnation as man of the second Person of the Trinity. Although the history of ideas may show that Symbolist aesthetics has the Christian doctrines of Trinity and, as we shall see presently, of Incarnation, as necessary presuppositions, it is not at all my intention to suggest that, because this is so, there therefore exists a *perpetual* dependence of Symbolist aesthetics upon religious dogma, so that we come to regard such an aesthetics as being intrinsically Christian. Rather, by penetrating to the metaphysical genesis of Symbolism, I endeavor to show the potential it contains for something like the figural realization of the Christ-form of Scripture. In other words, the theological presuppositions of Symbolist aesthetics prepare the way for Trakl's being able to transform the literary symbol into a *figura* (in Auerbach's understanding of the concept) within the Judeo-Christian tradition.

We must now, then, seek the common ground shared by Symbolist aesthetics and the Christian dogma of God's Incarnation. The fundamental question posed by the Symbolist aesthetics is: How can an image become a symbol by fusing (συμ-βάλλειν—"to join together"—yielding σύμβολον) into a single reality both material-sensual "substance" *(hylē)* and invisible-spiritual "meaning" *(logos),* so that what results is a living form *(Gestalt, morphē)?* Now, this question is closely analogous to the christological question of Incarnation: How can the eternal, invisible, and totally Other become identified with and revealed in the visible, limited, and corruptible form of an individually existing human being? Not only are these questions analogous, but the theological question emerges as much the more crucial of the two, since its possibility contains the archetypical conditions for the aesthetic question. The theological question appears to me to be the more fundamental for reasons of chronology as well, since belief in the Incarnation and in the Trinity both antedates Symbolism and conditions the cultural-intellectual context from which it arises.

Belief in the Incarnation of God necessarily modifies all preexistent conceptions of form, so much so that from this belief there flow the corresponding doctrines of the Resurrection of the Body and of the transformation of the heavens and the earth in the eschaton, dogmas totally foreign to Greek antiquity and perceived only dimly by the Jews in their apocalyptic expectation. A Christian theology of form envisages the ultimate transfiguration of spiritual *and* material substance, so that every creature reborn in Christ, whether human or not, acquires an individual claim to eternal glory never before conceived as possible. No Christian poet has given more resplendent aesthetic expression to this vision than Dante, in whose *Paradiso* the souls of the saints gain in uniqueness and specificity precisely as they are more and more intensely bathed in the divine light. From this perspective, then, it appears that the development of a Symbolist aesthetics would have been impossible without the preexistence in Western consciousness of the theological structure of the Incarnation (which is not necessarily to say belief in the reality of this structure). In other words, the existence of the structure of the Incarnation—the divine and human natures existentially united in one person—in the Western imagination makes it possible to conceive of the total autonomy of the poetic image, since analogically the image is no longer the appearance that remains (Platonically) bound to the transcendent reality its signifies, but, similar to the God-man's existence in time, the image has become a symbol with a life of its own that mysteriously unites immanence and transcendence, appearance and reality, form and content, into a single complex entity that radiates life from within itself.

In this context we may at last fully appreciate the reasons for insisting on the primacy of the *total form* of Trakl's poetry. Most of us exhibit our Platonizing bias by regarding an invisible "meaning" as being interior to a more superficial "form," the hidden reality being in fact the heart of the matter, which, when arrived at, allows us to dispense with the sensual forms that have mediated it. The Christian view of total form, on the other hand, does not dispense with a "content" or a "meaning" for the sake of a crude materialism, but holds that that meaning and content are so wholly and inextricably identified with the sensual-spiritual form encountered as to be one with it. This understanding of form, image, and symbol, lying as it does at the heart of Symbolism, may be regarded as the implementation in the aesthetic domain of a world view proclaimed in the Gospels and elaborated by patristic theology. If Ernst Fuchs called the Gospels a "language event" *(Sprachereignis)* it was because they opened up "a new dimension of man's awareness, a new breakthrough in language and symbolization,"[38] thus creating a new life-world. In specific linguistic terms, the Greek words in the New Testament usually translated as "form," "likeness," and "image" (μορφή, σχῆμα, εἰκών) refer "not to the external appearance but to the total reality of the person or thing in question."[39] In this manner, the language of the New Testament overcomes the dichotomies of Platonism and clearly exhibits the extent to which the structure of the Incarnation came to modify men's consciousness and means of expression.

Following from his dualistic metaphysics, Plato's poetic doctrine had necessarily to be one of imitation *(mimēsis)*. Symbolism most acutely shows its antipathy for Platonism by being founded on a poetic doctrine of creation *(poiēsis)*. Now, unless his activity is to acquire a demonic dimension, the artist may be said to "create" not *ex nihilo,* but by participation in God's own continuous act of creation. Artistic activity, so viewed, has a radically religious dimension. But to the Symbolist, the Platonic doctrine of imitation seems a rather lame compromise seeking to combine the opposing views of creation *ex nihilo* and creation by participation. Plato could indicate the difference between man and the eternal only by removing the perfect and the ideal utterly from the human scene. He sensed some irreconcilable contradiction between the divine and the human, and placed an abyss between them in his philosophy, so that the artist could only "imitate" eternal archetypes. This view is not compatible with the Judeo-Christian doctrine of creation, by which God remains present in what he has made by sustaining it with life, and especially not compatible with the Christian doctrine of the Incarnation of the Logos, by which God becomes manifest as a man. Imitation is a static poetic doctrine proceeding from a conservative mind that wishes to close off the realm of the possible.

Symbolism mirrors the structure of the Incarnation by conceiving the possibility that a new image might come into existence that has not been before, as well as by generating enthusiasm for the uniqueness of each individually existing image, so that "in the liberation from mimetic compulsion is found also the liberation of the image."[40] In this sense, the idea of Symbolism may be regarded as a disruptive and revolutionary one that curtails all reductionism and other attempts at "taming" the freedom of the image.

Incarnation and Style

Plato's zeal for salvaging the primacy and purity of the eternal results in a closed and static universe in which the ideal may be glimpsed at only in the highest flights of reason and intuition, and in which, paradoxically enough, it is man who remains the sole agent. The character of Plato's divine is too abstract for action on its part. The same world view that led Plato to a drastic separation of the human from the divine on the philosophical level resulted, on the aesthetic level, in the classical doctrine of the separation of styles. Sublime and august subjects could be dealt with only in the epic, tragic or lyrical modes, and the characters involved had always to be of noble lineage. Frivolous and "base" subjects, on the other hand, were thought fit only for comedy or satires. In addition to this radical separation of styles, Greek literature is governed by what Auerbach terms *Vordergründigkeit*, that is, an impulse to exteriority whereby the phenomena are represented "in a fully externalized form, visible and palpable in all their parts, and completely fixed in their spatial and temporal relations."[41] Corroborating in great detail Ernst Fuchs's terming the Gospels a *Sprachereignis*, Auerbach explains the revolution wrought upon classical aesthetics by faith in the Incarnation. Incarnation was

> totally incompatible with the principle of the separation of styles. Christ had not come as a hero or king but as a human being of the lowest social stature. . . . Nevertheless, all that he did and said was of the highest and deepest dignity, more significant than anything else in the world. The style in which it was presented possessed little if any

rhetorical culture in the antique sense; it was *sermo piscatorius* and yet it was extremely moving and much more impressive than the most sublime rhetorico-tragical literary work. . . . The story of Christ's Passion no sooner comes to dominate the consciousness of the people than it completely destroys the aesthetics of the separation of styles; it engenders a new elevated style, which does not scorn everyday life and which is ready to absorb the sensuously realistic, even the ugly, the undignified, the physically base.[42]

Here it is important to stress the fact that the Christian concept of style does not simply eliminate the sublime for the sake of the deformed and the ordinary, but rather that all subjects are now potentially sublime. But, "if we have here to do with the sublime," writes Auerbach elsewhere, "it is a sublimity of a different kind than that of antiquity, a sublimity which contains and comprehends the lovely and the *biotikon*."[43]

Hans-Eckehard Bahr elaborates the point which regard to the "worldliness" and "temporality" of the Christian vision by reference to the Christian view of the ugly. Referring to contemporary Christian writers such as Georges Bernanos and Flannery O'Connor, Bahr says that by never abandoning the present scene of this world as the stage where their novels take place, these writers are but following the structural logic of the Incarnation. The universality of redemption achieved by Christ's identity as God and the nature of his saving deed likewise effect a revolution in the judgment of the beautiful and the ugly.[44] No longer is an existing individual or thing subject to preconceived aesthetic canons of sublimity or objectionableness; rather, what is ugly and what beautiful is now determined according to the norm of God's self-revelation in Christ. (We recall how Tertullian stressed the humiliated form of Christ's appearance in the world.) Bahr finally establishes the necessary dependence of the aesthetic upon the ethicoreligious, so that the love that Christ manifested by taking on human nature becomes the ruthless judge of every worldly aesthetics. "The repulsively ugly is the real test for the durability of beauty. . . . To take the ugly to oneself in its state of non-transfigured, unregenerate ugliness is possible only for the person who loves. . . . Ever since God descended in this world to the depths of disgrace and allowed himself to be hung on the Cross, every sickly, misshapen, and ugly aspect of creation has by that very fact been permanently delivered from disgrace."[45]

In time we shall come to see how Trakl's poetry may be regarded as an extreme and—due to his Symbolist poetics—particularly thoroughgoing manifestation of that mixed style which, according to Auerbach, is the fundamental and irreversible effect that Christian faith in the Incarnation had on the development of Western literature. Trakl not only "mixes styles"; the uniquely unified style he creates defeats all expectations by winning sublimity out of the repulsive itself, in a manner that can ultimately be understood only as the aesthetic repercussion of the greatest oxymoron of all: the mystery of the incarnate God-Man.

While the disruption of existing aesthetic canons is to be attributed specifically to the coincidence of majesty and humiliation in the Christ-form of Scripture,[46] the Christian conception of the dynamics of time rests directly upon the Old Testament. Sharply contrasting with Greek *Vordergründigkeit,* the Hebraic style is characterized by the "externalization of only so much of the phenomena as is necessary for the purpose of the narrative, all else is left in obscurity. . . . Time and place are undefined and call for interpretation; thoughts and feelings remain unexpressed, are only suggested by the silence and the fragmentary speeches; the whole, permeated with the most unrelieved suspense and directed toward a single goal (and to that extent far more of a unity than the Homeric style), remains mysterious and 'fraught with background' *(hintergründig)*."[47] Every part of this description applies *a fortiori* to Trakl's style, which in this sense could be considered an extreme case of Hebraic narration, achieving the total presence of mystery. We have only to read the first few lines of *Traum und Umnachtung,* for instance, to verify the exactness with which Auerbach's description of the Hebraic style applies to Trakl. This is perhaps an important reason why he has to many seemed akin to Kafka, directly steeped as this writer was in the world of Torah:

> Am Abend ward zum Greis der Vater; in dunklen Zimmern versteinerte das Antlitz der Mutter und auf dem Knaben lastete der Fluch des entarteten Geschlechts. Manchmal erinnerte er sich seiner Kindheit, erfüllt von Krankheit, Schrecken und Finsternis, verschwiegener Spiele im Sternengarten, oder dass er die Ratten fütterte im dämmernden Hof. Aus blauem Spiegel trat die schmale Gestalt der Schwester und er stürzte wie tot ins Dunkel.[48]

Obscurity is achieved at once through the *Verfremdungseffekte;* yet it is a darkness that, far from repulsing, rather attracts and envelops. Highlights of narration are concatenated syntactically as if following one another logically, whereas in fact no cause-and-effect dynamics can possibly apply. Time and place are completely fractured, so that events that normally require decades are contracted to a single moment *(ward zum Greis der Vater, versteinerte das Antlitz der Mutter).* Memories are fused haphazardly, yet they are all unified by their import as moral symbols of degeneracy. Paradoxically, we may note a pervading sense of unreality conveyed by the straightforward realist manner in which quasi-miraculous events are portrayed. In this there is a close affinity to the "miracles" of Scripture, which likewise do not demand exclusive attention for themselves as marvels, but always act as manifestations of religious imperatives. We note, too, that the *tone* of the passage is elevated, sublime, even hieratic, as only an initiation rite can be, in the resonance of its periods and the solemnity of its emphases. And this sublimity is not destroyed, but rather bizarrely intensified, by the action of "feeding rats in the dusk of the courtyard." Each event, although its meaning is far from self-evident, makes an absolute claim to importance. The silences, the fragmentariness, the unrelieved suspense, the singleness of goal, the mysteriousness and *Hintergründigkeit,* are all too obvious in even the few lines quoted to require further elaboration.

The intimate connection that exists between the characteristics of the Hebraic style and the Symbolist use of images is striking. Despite all its obscurity and silences, Scripture does not make us search for a "hidden essence" behind the words. The words themselves convey the experience of a presence, and bear witness to the perennially young and energetic character of that experience and presence. Without lapsing into word-fetishism, we may say that Scripture contains in an inimitable manner the record of a people's experience of the reality of God's action among them. We may therefore approximate the language of Scripture and that of Symbolism because of their shared method of not indicating something beyond the words and yet conveying an experience not equatable with the words. Von Balthasar says that, with regard to the language of Scripture, "every attempt to grasp at the 'body' itself behind the figures and images is in vain. . . . The form of Scripture is purposely loose and perspectivistic, in order that we may not hold on to it tightly and confuse the garment with the actual body."[49] Ambiguity and perspectivism of form are seen to derive ultimately from the Jewish abhorrence of idolatry, since the beauty of the written word can never replace the burning reality of the living God. And yet, the indispensable character of Scripture derives from the role of its symbols to stake out the contours of the experience of God. So, too, poetry. Although it is no end in itself except for the most extreme Symbolists, nevertheless, if poetry is banished from our "republic" as Plato would have it in his, neither shall we have the experience of the depths of Being that poetry of a certain calibre mediates to us.

The Christological Structure of Trakl's Symbolism: **Verwandlung des Bösen**

The preceding sections of this chapter have been an extensive but necessary preamble that provides us with the context in which we may see Trakl's poetry come to life as in its native habitat. We now arrive at the point where something like an intensive examination of Trakl's poetry is in order, an analysis that will enable us, at last, to experience the organic interaction of the different voices of Trakl's poetry, voices that until now we have been straining to single out from the unity of their unhalting polyphony. On the one hand, I have dealt rather extensively with Symbolism, following an intuition that the character of Trakl's poetic praxis is founded upon the Symbolist doctrine of the autonomous or self-sufficient image. On the other hand, I have sought to approximate Trakl's poetry to the Judeo-Christian style of narration, and some reference has been made to the sympathies that exist between this style and Symbolism itself. My present task will consist of demonstrating, on the example of a mature and comprehensive poem, how the traditions of Symbolism and Judeo-Christian stylistics converge in Trakl, resulting in the unique character of his poetry. In other words, I shall seek to penetrate the identity of Trakl's poetry by seeing in what ways the lapidary symbol defined for us in the nineteenth century now receives a figural application, so that Trakl's particular use of the symbol entails a figural realization of the Christ-form of Scripture. We shall see, specifically, that only such a symbolist realization can vouch for the authenticity of that transformation according to the form of Christ demanded by St. Paul (cf. 2 Cor. 3 : 18), since it is only the poetics of Symbolism that is in a position of incarnating the form of the Christ-event. In other words, we may say that we have before us the highest form of religious poetry only when that poetry contains more than a series of references to extrapoetical convictions of piety. Either the poetry contains the whole mystery of the religious event or it is only a poetry about religious feelings.

It goes without saying that positing this extreme conjunction and near-identification of aesthetic means and theological meanings as an ideal makes tremendous demands upon a poet. Trakl withstands the test, however, simply because the paradigm I propose has not been arrived at ideally as a theoretical construction, but has been deduced on the basis of what I have been able to observe as actually occurring in his poetry. It appears that Trakl achieves an extreme approximation of Ricoeur's categories of primary and secondary symbolization, the levels of unreflected *avowal* and of explanatory *myth,* so that we are hardly able to distinguish between the existing symbol and its significance. And this, in passing, may be said to be the very essence of symbol: its fusion of existence and meaning into a single entity. Hans Konrad Neidhart can thus say of Trakl that, "insofar as Trakl's images really *are* what they express, insofar as their form and meaning, their images and meanings merge into one, to that extent do they in actual fact constitute 'symbols' which permit a 'hieroglyphic' view of things."[50]

The very nature of Trakl's poetics forbids us to approach his art prejudiced by what Dorothee Sölle has called an "objectified fixation of the theological concern." The theological critic must seek to make manifest, in a given Trakl poem, the symbolic realization of those events which for theology remain a subject of speculation.[51] This procedure is not exacted merely by a ceremonious show of respect for the inviolability of the aesthetic form, but is enjoined by the most fundamental theological reasons.[52] The essence of Christianity touches upon something that is *substantial* in the technical sense of the philosopher; it implies an existential transformation and not merely a "change of opinion." In other words, Christianity is not an ideology but a new creation. Elisabeth Langgässer can, therefore, see the task of Christian art in the twentieth century as being "the restitution of art from the realm of the ethical-psychological to the realm of pure substance and to the new creation which, because of divine grace, is at work within the realm of substance."[53] The distinction between a religion of ethics and one of substantial change coincides precisely with our previous distinction between meaning and image. Although the ethical can and must become an attribute of substance, it can nowhere subsist autonomously apart from substance. In the same manner, meaning is an attribute of symbol, but cannot exist without it; and this hierarchy of being may never be violated even when the profoundest significance of a symbol has been revealed. Meaning can exist only because of the antecedent existence of a substance that may predicate it. Reality is the foundation for understanding.

All of these aspects of a theological meditation on the essence of symbol must now be demonstrated with reference to a specific poem. The object of this analysis will be to show the adequacy of approximating the Christian view of reality to Trakl's view as it is expressed in particular symbols. What I undertake, then, is a comparison of the Christian and the Traklian grammar of being, with the hope of finally substantiating my claim that, in making a Symbolist application of figural language, Trakl did indeed fulfill Peter Damian's understanding of existence as summarized in his aphorism: "Mea grammatica Christus est."

It would be easy to choose a poem of Trakl's that contains some readily identifiable religious symbolism on which to pin this interpretation, such as *Passion, De Profundis, Crucifixus,* or *Sebastian im Traum.* However, in order to avoid the danger of "begging the question," and also for the sake of having before us a poem of primary status because of its high degree of stylistic maturity and the exhaustiveness of its mythological range, I choose *Verwandlung des Bösen,* a poem written in prose form:

Verwandlung des Bösen

(I)   Herbst: schwarzes Schreiten am Waldsaum; Minute stummer Zer-
           störung; auflauscht die Stirne des Aussätzigen unter dem kahlen

Baum. Langvergangener Abend, der nun über die Stufen von Moos
5   sinkt; November. Eine Glocke läutet und der Hirt führt eine Herde
von schwarzen und roten Pferden ins Dorf. Unter dem Haselgebüsch
weidet der grüne Jäger ein Wild aus. Seine Hände rauchen von Blut
und der Schatten des Tiers seufzt im Laub über den Augen des
Mannes, braun und schweigsam; der Wald. Krähen, die sich zer-
10 streuen; drei. Ihr Flug gleicht einer Sonate, voll verblichener
Akkorde und männlicher Schwermut; leise löst sich eine goldene
Wolke auf. Bei der Mühle zünden Knaben ein Feuer an. Flamme ist
des Bleichsten Bruder und jener lacht vergraben in sein purpurnes
Haar; oder es ist ein Ort des Mordes, an dem ein steiniger Weg
15 vorbeiführt. Die Berberitzen sind verschwunden, jahrlang träumt
es in bleierner Luft unter den Föhren; Angst, grünes Dunkel, das
Gurgeln eines Ertrinkenden: aus dem Sternenweiher zieht der
Fischer einen grossen, schwarzen Fisch, Antlitz voll Grausamkeit
und Irrsinn. Die Stimmen des Rohrs, hadernder Männer im Rücken
20 schaukelt jener auf rotem Kahn über frierende Herbstwasser, lebend
in dunklen Sagen seines Geschlechts und die Augen steinern über
Nächte und jungfräuliche Schrecken aufgetan. Böse.
(II)   Was zwingt dich still zu stehen auf der verfallenen Stiege,
im Haus deiner Väter? Bleierne Schwärze. Was hebst du mit sil-
25 berner Hand an die Augen; und die Lider sinken wie trunken von
Mohn? Aber durch die Mauer von Stein siehst du den Sternenhimmel,
dis Milchstrasse, den Saturn; rot. Rasend an die Mauer von Stein
klopft der kahle Baum. Du auf verfallenen Stufen: Baum, Stern,
Stein! Du, ein blaues Tier, das leise zittert; du, der bleiche
30 Priester, der es hinschlachtet am schwarzen Altar. O dein Lächeln
im Dunkel, traurig und böse, dass ein Kind im Schlaf erbleicht.
Eine rote Flamme sprang aus deiner Hand und ein Nachtfalter
verbrannte daran. O die Flöte des Lichts; o die Flöte des Tods.
Was zwang dich still zu stehen auf verfallener Stiege, im Haus
35 deiner Väter? Drunten ans Tor klopft ein Engel mit kristallnem
Finger.
(III)   O die Hölle des Schlafs; dunkle Gasse, braunes Gärtchen.
Leise läutet im blauen Abend der Toten Gestalt. Grüne Blümchen
umgaukeln sie und ihr Antlitz hat sie verlassen. Oder es neigt
40 sich verblichen über die kalte Stirne des Mörders im Dunkel des
Hausflurs; Anbetung, purpurne Flamme der Wollust; hinsterbend
stürzte über schwarze Stufen der Schläfer ins Dunkel.
(IV)   Jemand verliess dich am Kreuzweg und du schaust lange zurück.
Silberner Schritt im Schatten verkrüppelter Apfelbäumchen. Purpurn
45 leuchtet die Frucht im schwarzen Geäst und im Gras häutet sich
die Schlange. O! das Dunkel; der Schweiss, der auf die eisige
Stirne tritt und die traurigen Träume im Wein, in der Dorfschenke
unter schwarzverrauchtem Gebälk. Du, noch Wildnis, die rosige
Inseln zaubert aus dem braunen Tabaksgewölk und aus dem Innern
50 den wilden Schrei eines Greifen holt, wenn er um schwarze
Klippen jagt in Meer, Sturm und Eis. Du, ein grünes Metall
und innen ein feuriges Gesicht, das hingehen will und singen
vom Beinerhügel finstere Zeiten und den flammenden Sturz des
Engels. O! Verzweiflung, die mit stummem Schrei ins Knie bricht.
55   Ein Toter besucht dich. Aus dem Herzen rinnt das selbst-
(V) vergossene Blut und in schwarzer Braue nistet unsäglicher

> Augenblick; dunkle Begegnung. Du—ein purpurner Mond, da jener
> im grünen Schatten des Ölbaums erscheint. Dem folgt unvergäng-
> liche Nacht.[54]

The text of this second and final version of *Verwandlung des Bösen* dates
from September–October 1913,[55] the period when Trakl had arrived at
the expansive, nonrhymed, psalmlike manner of expression most
characteristic of his mature style. In this genre he is unlike any other
poet. That the present text appears at first sight to be cast in the manner
of a conventional prose narration all the more intensifies its bewildering
effect upon the reader. The tone of each of the five paragraphs of
uneven length greatly contrasts that of the others, and yet there is
present a subtle unity and development in the events of the poem.

The poem may be viewed as portraying a process of transformation, in
keeping with the expectations aroused by the title. The subject of the
transformation is Evil. The most general and fundamental question we
can ask of the poem is, therefore: In what does the promised transformation of Evil consist? We may divide the poem into three main parts,
corresponding to three stages of the transformation, namely: (1) the
statement of the initial situation (I); (2) the conflicts and actions that
eventually effect the process of transformation (II–IV); and (3) the
situation resulting from the transformation (V). The drastically changing
tone, syntax, and rhythm of the initial sentence of each paragraph show
a turning (strophe = στροφή!) which is far more significant than a mere
conventional "change of subject." The change of tone and emphasis, in
fact, signals each time the turning to a new phase of the transformation.

In paragraph I we encounter a broken and fragmentary style that
largely dispenses with connectives, often even with verbs, and relies
heavily on the mute semicolon. The result is a deliberately disjointed
description of obscure and perplexing events that show no apparent
connection among themselves. This paragraph may be qualified as an
extreme example of that *akausale Hintergründigkeit* which Erich Auerbach
has so well defined for us as belonging to the essence of the Judeo-
Christian style. The world is not presented as a psychologically closed
chamber where cause and effect succeed one another relentlessly. The
world here, rather, is broken, which is to say that it is not only fragmentary but also open to the action of providential, acausal, self-motivated
forces that remain in the background.[56] This is why the passage is
"fraught with background," which is to say that its only unity is provided
by the unremitting presence of mystery and silence. Because the words
we read describe events that are not reducible to language, "the objectified form" that we have before us, consisting of such and such symbols,
"can materially be only a selection from the historical events."[57] The

events contained in paragraph I may be summarized in the words *Zerstörung, Auflösung,* and *Böse,* found at its beginning, middle, and end. No transformation has even been initiated.

The opening sentence of paragraph II changes the tone of disjointedness and desolation abruptly. Not only do we pass from fragmentary description to a syntactically complete sentence, but that sentence is a question to a "thou," so that suddenly some mode of communication, dialogue, and community has been established. We may recognize the beginning of transformation at this turning from a disjointed world lying in ruins to a "thou" who will be ineradicably present throughout the rest of the poem. Senselessness has yielded to presence.

The initial interjection of paragraph III continues a form of expression begun in II, and which will persist through IV. These repeated *O!*s express an intense form of reaction, admiration, or recoiling from the events being expressed. They therefore structurally support my localizing the actual event of transformation in the three central paragraphs of the poem. Syntactically, paragraph V returns to a descriptive mode. But, unlike the disjointed and fragmentary character of the description in I, the declarative tone of V is fraught with affirmation and silence—the paragraph is only four lines long—in the face of what may be only obliquely described: *unsäglicher Augenblick, unvergängliche Nacht.* To experience a full sense of what has occured in the course of the poem, we have only to juxtapose its opening and closing phrases: *Herbst: schwarzes Schreiten am Waldsaum; Minute stummer Zerstörung . . .,* the initial phrase, instantly conveys the situation of helplessness and despair. The poem concludes with the image of a green olive tree and the anonymous presence of one whose apparition signals the beginning of incorruptible night: *Dem folgt unvergängliche Nacht.*

If the preceding reflections have provided us with the general structure of the poem, we must now investigate the nature of the transformation I claim has taken place. We must not lose sight of the context of the present discussion, however. I initiated it in view of the nature of Trakl's poetics, particularly in view of his symbolist technique. This means that the discussion of *Verwandlung des Bösen* has the task of demonstrating the central thesis of my inquiry, namely, that Trakl's poetry realizes the Christ-form of Scripture not by reference to it, but in the very form of the poetry. Now, the fundamental structure of the Christ-form is determined by the elements of Incarnation, redemptive Death, and Resurrection. It is therefore my present task to show in what ways Incarnation, redemptive Death, and Resurrection are unmistakably present in Trakl's poetry not as themes comprising a referential content, but as forms determing the shape and structure of the poetry. In other words, we are presently investigating the noetic consequences in poetry of the ontological Christ-event. At this point we must attribute the strangeness of Trakl's language, its fascinating and alienating effect on the reader, to the fact that its extreme stylization is not imitating the empirico-logical order of things, but rather realizing the christological structure of the paradoxical mystery of God's Incarnation and Death as man. Trakl creates a constellation of symbols whose meta-symbolism realizes the *figura* of the mysterious Christ-event. For this reason, the poet appears to be totally absent from his work, since self-expression is not his goal at this point, but rather the manifestation of a particular order of reality. Having foremost in mind, then, the demonstration of the coincidence in Trakl's poetry of aesthetic structure with dogmatic structure, we now return to *Verwandlung des Bösen* in order to establish the structural identity of the events already schematized.

The opening section has no unity of its own. Its sheer assemblage of instances of destruction provides us, however, with the elements that will undergo transformation later in the poem. Thus the initial motif of "black wandering" (2) is brought to a halt in the "standing on the rotten stairway" of II (23), from which the sleeper, dying, "falls into the darkness" in III (42). There is also a second halting point in the for-sakenness at the crossroads at the beginning of IV (43), which finally resolves itself into the triumphant flight of the griffin, which is followed in V by "incorruptible night." In my view, the negative hopelessness of *schwarzes Schreiten* (2) has finally been transformed into the positive darkness of *unvergängliche Nacht* (58–59), comparable to the rich night of Novalis's *Hymnen an die Nacht* and to the jubilant exodus of the Roman liturgy's *O vere beata Nox!*

Another key motif provided by paragraph I is that of the green hunter who disembowels a deer. The deer's utter helplessness, expressed in the sighing of its shade (8), is carried forward in paragraph II by the image of the blue animal, with the difference that here animal and hunter have merged into one and been thus transformed. The liturgical image of priest and victim belongs squarely in the New Testament view of Christ's unique sacrifice, in which alone priest and victim are identical (cf. Heb. 9 : 11–14). In paragraph III the self-slaughtered animal-priest has been hieratically contracted to a dead countenance adorned with flowers. There is here, perhaps, a hint of cultic transformation, the passage from a historical event to its existence in the life of faith. Paragraph IV marks the transformation most emphatically. The dead figure of III is now made dynamic by the image of the snake shedding its skin—a sign of renewal and rebirth—which image finally makes possible the tri-umphant cry of the griffin in flight, a cry that sings of "dark times and the flaming fall of the Angel" (52–54). A catastrophic event becomes transformed into the theme of song, and this indicates the passing over into victory and indirectly speaks of Trakl's view of the transforming power of poetry.

The motif of cruel slaughter from I (7–8), which in II had acquired a meaning by being raised to the level of liturgical sacrifice, and in IV resulted in the griffin's victory cry, appears finally in V resumed in the image of the self-inflicted wound from which the heart's blood pours out. And yet this paragraph has been introduced by the phrase "Ein Toter besucht dich," which creates an unreal field of reference and prevents our taking "Aus dem Herzen rinnt das selbstvergossene Blut" in any naturalistic sense; thus the repulsion is absent that was produced in I by the realistic phrase "Unter dem Haselgebüsch weidet der grüne Jäger ein Wild aus." But, although V lacks the realism of I, we have not here to do with unreal events, but rather with the quasi-liturgical and cultic expression of the meaning of the death involved. That it was self-inflicted must be paramount to the meaning of the poem, given the linguistic oddity of the word *selbstvergossen,* which would not otherwise be employed. There is, further, an intrinsic connection between this image and that of the apparition of *jener* under the olive tree, an event followed by "incorruptible night."

Let us attempt to penetrate more deeply into the identity of this person whose contours are gradually becoming clearer, to whom the poem refers under the images of suffering animal, priest, dead man, and griffin, and under the wholly anonymous pronouns *jener* and *du.* It is my suggestion that there exists a tight simultaneous identity and continuity among the symbolic personae of the poem, and that the differences among the images are intended to manifest aspects of the same reality. If this were not so, the poem would indeed remain totally incomprehensible. As it is, however, the christoformity of its protagonist provides a basis for comparison that readily yields the unity of the poem.

The anonymous presence in paragraph I (at the stage of fragmentation) of the *jener* (13, 20), who, in my view, becomes the *du* of the rest of the poem, witnesses to the incarnational mode of presence of one who effects the transformation in the poem. The victim-priest, who eventually rises in the unified mythological form of the griffin, has been present in the midst of disjointedness and fragmentation even before he could emerge onto a level of awareness where he could be addressed as a "thou." Thus he is not present as one conjured up and introduced by a movement of an external will, but as an unknown, anonymous person who persists in being present despite the obscurity of his identity. There is no *deus ex machina* in the poem, just as there had been none in our initial poem, *Menschheit.* For this reason, the very real transformation of Evil that occurs remains fraught with paradox. The transformations occur from within the poem, in an incarnational manner, and consequently the victory of IV and V nowhere dispenses with the condition of evil fragmentation that has been overcome. The one slaughtered perpetually retains the wounds of the victory. Even after victory he continues to be a dead man (55), because he has not come *back* from the dead, but has gone *beyond* death and in this sense carries his death always with him. Concerning this mystery, Kierkegaard observes that "whoever, being dead, awakens to life in a new sphere, was and is and remains truly dead."[58]

Essential to the identity of the protagonist is his unidirectional intent to carry out his deed. This intent inserts itself implacably between the description of fragmentation in I and the opening question of II: "What compels you to stand quietly on the rotten stairway, in the house of your fathers?" The question is only seemingly rhetorical, for it receives an answer not in any words of the perenially silent "thou," but in his actions that follow. The question must be central to the meaning of the poem, since it is repeated in the past tense again in II (34–35). The difference in tenses indicates that the decisive event must have occurred between lines 23 and 34.

There is a formal similarity between this question, asked in its context of sacrificial death, and the kind of lyrical lament common to the Greek liturgy for Passiontide, in which the Church as a bride repeatedly asks of her bridegroom what it is that makes him persist in his saving deed despite the personal ruination it brings to him. The first of the Lamentations of Great Friday Evening exclaims:

Ἡ Ζωή πῶς θνήσκεις; πῶς καί τάφῳ οἰκεῖς;[59]

And a few verses down we read:

Ἰησοῦ Χριστέ μου, Βασιλεῦ τοῦ παντός,
τί ζητῶν τοῖς ἐν τῷ Ἅδῃ ἐλήλυθας;
ἤ τό γένος ἀπολύσαι τῶν βροτῶν.[60]

The protagonist who is so addressed is said to have lived until now in "dark legends of his race" (20–21), a phrase that reinforces the incarnational presence *ab initio* that I have stressed before. And if the legends have been dark and confused, in the manner of Old Testament prophecies, the passing from legend to actual presence is all the more dazzling in that it is not to be reduced to rational deduction. Hence the use of the question-form that opens paragraph II, which indicates that the reality of the presence is not doubtful, but puzzling. The rhetorical question implies that, if nothing is evidently forcing the protagonist to persist on the rotten stairway, then he is doing it because he wants to do so. The Eastern Fathers, in this connection, use the word ἑκουσίως to refer to the totally free character of Christ's condescension in becoming man and in dying on the Cross. The first of the Resurrection Hymns for Sundays contains the verse:

> Τόν σαρκί ἑκουσίως σταυροθέντα δι' ἡμᾶς,
> παθόντα καί ταφέντα καί ἀναστάντα ἐκ νεκρῶν,
> ὑμνήσωμεν.[61]

The word ἑκουσίως (i.e., "out of one's free will"), therefore, suggests itself as the answer to the question twice repeated in paragraph II, given not only the analogous form of lyrical address in Trakl's poem and in the Byzantine hymns I have cited, but, in the last analysis, on account of the great similarity of context between them. Both Christ's deeds as celebrated by the liturgical assembly and the deeds of Trakl's protagonist have in common the structure of transformation and revitalization of what was fallen and fragmentary. And in both cases this transformation occurs through the incarnational presence and redemptive death of either protagonist.

In paragraph II none of the elements of fragmentation inventoried in I disappears magically, merely by the presence of the "thou." In fact, we may regard the entire desolation and dissociation of I as present in II in the phrase *Haus deiner Väter*. This biblically tinged expression stylizes the blackness and state of destruction initially described by reducing it to a graspable unit. It is precisely here that the "thou" chooses to stand, in the midst of rottenness and superannuation. At the conclusion of I, the "thou" has already been subtly introduced as sole participant in a rite of passage *(schaukelt jener über frierende Herbstwasser)* that brings him to the threshold of evil and despair. We observe him in the contemplation of horrors that will give way to the action of sacrifice. His action is qualified by the adjective *steinern* ("stony," "rocklike"), Trakl's word to connote both pain and dogged persistence.

This curious qualifier *steinern*, describing the immutable attitude of the protagonist's eyes and in close proximity to the *Antlitz* of line 18, is poignantly reminiscent of Isaiah 50:7b: "Darum habe ich mein *Angesicht* dargeboten wie einen *Kieselstein*" ("Therefore have I offered up my face like flint-stone"). In fact, it is extraordinary to note how many lexical items from our poem are found in a similar constellation in this short fiftieth chapter of Isaiah and the beginning of chapter 51. To give only the identical words found in both poem and scriptural text, and not any of the close synonyms also present: *Hand, sehen, Meer, Wasser, hinsterben, Fisch, Dunkel, Zeit, Rücken, Stein, hadern, Stimme, finster, Licht, Feuer, anzünden, Flamme, hingehen, schauen, Vater, Garten, Insel, Augen, Himmel, heben, Rauch, vergehen, Herz.* It would here prove needlessly complex to enter into a detailed textual analysis comparing the poem and the biblical passage. Suffice it to say that Isaiah 50 is one of the essential texts dealing with the key prophetic theme of the messianic "suffering servant" through whom redemption comes. And this is the precise identity and role I discover in the protagonist of *Verwandlung des Bösen*.

The leaden darkness from paragraph I (16) continues to be present in II (24), but is immediately modified by the restrictive *aber* introducing the phrase that achieves the initial breakthrough to transformation: "*But through the stone wall you see the starry heavens, the Milky Way, and Saturn; red.*" The bare tree, which in paragraph I had been the helpless witness to a leper's plight (3–4), is now active, madly knocking against the stone wall through which the heavens have been spotted. Both the persistent contemplation of the "thou" and the knocking of the bare tree unite in their intention to destroy this wall of separation altogether. The presence of the "thou" at the same time activates the elements that had previously lain in ruin, so that now they come into relationship with each other and are named serially as if for the first time: "Du auf verfallenen Stufen: Baum, Stern, Stein!" This fresh giving of names, a kind of new creation, is the direct result of the "thou"'s presence, and the intimate connection between name-giver and thing named is indicated by the mute but suggestive binding function of the colon.

We now arrive at line 29, which is both the numerical and the significant center of the poem: "Du, ein blaues Tier, das leise zittert; du, der bleiche Priester, der es hinschlachtet am schwarzen Altar." The phrase resumes the elements of innocent suffering and inflicted cruelty from paragraph I, but, as noted previously, both are transformed by being raised to a sacral level and especially by being united in the same person: the self-sacrificing "thou." This duality of function within the unity of person is finally emphasized once again in V, where the phrase "aus dem Herzen rinnt das selbstvergossene Blut" recalls the gesture of the Sacred Heart of Jesus, a favorite Baroque theme. The identity of priest and victim is a uniquely christological motif, flowing from the structure of the Incarnation. Only Christ, being God, can offer perfect atonement to the Father. The classical text is from the Letter to the Hebrews: "When Christ appeared as high priest of the good things to come, he entered once for all through the greater and more perfect tabernacle of the heavens [cf. the gazing through the stone wall at the heavens], not made by hands, nor again by virtue of the blood of goats and calves, but by virtue of his own blood [cf. "das selbstvergossene Blut"] into the Holy of Holies, having obtained eternal redemption. . . . The blood of Christ, who by his eternal spirit offered himself unblemished unto God (9:11–14). The identity between priest and victim is resumed by the Fathers in the word αὐτεξουσίως ("through his own power"), which adds another dimension to the ἑκουσίως we have already seen. Christ was the only adequate redeemer because in him alone the willingness to love to the death was identical with his ability as God to raise fallen man. Therefore, αὐτεξουσίως expresses an essential element of the redemption, which exhibits the contrary aspects of light and death (33), corresponding to Christ's divine and human natures.

Paragraph II concludes with the promise of the griffin's flight, since now the luminous angel knocking with a crystal finger at the door of the tomblike "house of the fathers," acting as the metamorphosis of the forlorn tree knocking on the stone wall, awakens (as Angel of the Resurrection) from the sleep of death him whose actual rising will occur by virtue of his own power. Heaven, which could previously be discerned only far off through a stone wall, has now come down to earth in the form of a crystal angel.

But Trakl's poem is christological to the extent that even the Harrowing of Hell must take place before the Resurrection can occur. Paragraph III, consequently, portrays the moment of total extinction of the protagonist, a moment that coincides with his exorcising Descent into Hell. His sleep is characterized as the hellish *somnium mortis* in which an extremity of apparent inaction coincides with an extremity of spiritual effectiveness. The use of the "thou" is temporarily suspended; but the dead man, in the iconic rigidity of his portrayal, encounters the murderer in the house of the fathers (40). This violent encounter of evil and voluntary self-sacrifice may be identified as the actual Harrowing, which makes the reconciling and unifying encounter of V (57) possible. The sleeper is characterized as dying by falling from the very steps where he had been standing (41–42). The deliberate stand taken at the opening of II is here shown to have led to his freely chosen ruination.

The transition from III to IV is not univocally one from death to resurrection. There is a revivification of the "thou," who had slipped away in III to the condition of a dead figure; but darkness and suffering continue to be present (46–47). Paragraph IV, however, is characterized by a steadily mounting luminosity that first strikes one at the transformation of the initial *schwarzes Schreiten* (2) into *silberner Schritt* (44). The bare tree of I and II has first budded flowers in III and now its fruit "shines" among the black branches (44–45). Out of the suffocation of brown tobacco smoke, rosy islands are conjured forth (48–49). To the "thou" is finally attributed a resonant and fiery countenance (51–52). This manner of transformation bears the stamp of authenticity precisely because it is a transformation from within, a transformation in which the elements of decay previously portrayed are not rejected in favor of some facile utopia, but which exhibits at every step a stubborn fidelity to the very corruptibility of I through III. Twice a word for "inner" or "interior" is used in IV (49 and 51) to denote this authentic quality of the transformation portrayed. The oxymoronic nature of the events occurring is nowhere lifted, and the exclamation from II: "O die Flöte des Lichts; o die Flöte des Tods" (33) is echoed in IV in the juxtaposition of *rosige Inseln* and *braunes Tabaksgewölk* (48–49).

There is present also an intermixture of Passion and Resurrection motifs, whose very simultaneity indicates that no chronological narration is here intended, but that, rather, the happenings portrayed are occurring within the mystical time of the prophets. Thus, the *Ort des Mordes* and its *steiniger Weg* from I (14) here reappear as the deserted *Kreuzweg* (43), in which the play of words with *Kreuz* is not only obvious but textually supported by the *Beinerhügel* ("Hill of Bones") of 44, a name that may be regarded as a free translation of Golgotha, "Place of the Skull." In strict counterpoint with these images of the Passion, which themselves are already transformed versions of the raw brutality of paragraph I, are the images of Resurrection: the fruition of the bare tree (45), the shedding of the snake's dead skin (45–46), the alchemical production of rosy islands out of tobacco smoke (48–49), and, most important of all, the cry and flight of the griffin, who with his fiery nature triumphantly sings of dark times from the Hill of Bones. The flaming plunge of the Angel, which he also celebrates, is an unmistakable iconographic portrayal of the fall of Lucifer, and this triumph over "darker times" is in diametrical opposition to the temporary ascendancy of evil at the conclusion of I. The fall of the Angel of Light likewise counterbalances the arrival of the crystal Angel of the Resurrection (35–36). The griffin's fiery countenance finally and permanently supplants the "dead figure, whose countenance had abandoned him" in III. While there the sleeper, "dying, plunged into the darkness" (41–42), here the griffin "dashes in sea, storm, and ice . . . , a fiery countenance that wants to go forth and sing." The obedient helplessness and sinking into death in III here result in permanent triumph over the forces of chaos, represented by the pristine raging of sea, storm, and ice. The sleeper's plunging into darkness in III *(stürzte ins Dunkel)* effects in IV the plunging of the Angel of Evil *(den flammenden Sturz des Engels)*.

The use by Trakl of the mythological-symbolic figure of the Griffin is startling, since this poet almost categorically avoids importing material into his art, in keeping with his Symbolist technique. The wild and sovereign cry of the Griffin is here effective enough as it stands, and the fact that the cry is drawn forth from within reinforces the autonomy of the "thou"'s stance, already summarized in the word αὐτεξουσίως. But the Griffin has a long iconographic and literary history, in which he is a symbol of power and of the sun, an apotropaic being who guards the tombs and gates and thus wards off evil from both the living and the dead.[62] The Griffin's double nature as eagle and as lion has, in particular, made him a symbol of Christ in his twin identity as God and as man, as in the famous passage from *Purgatorio* 29, where Dante portrays Christ as a griffin drawing the chariot of the Church:

> Lo spazio dentro a lor quattro contenne
> un carro, in sù due rote, trïunfale,
> ch'al collo d'un grifon tirato venne.
>
> Esso tendeva in sù l'una e l'altra ale
> tra la mezzana e le tre e tre liste,
> sì ch'a nulla, fendendo, facea male.
>
> Tanto salivan che non eran viste;
> le membra d'oro avea quant'era uccello,
> e bianche l'altre, di vermiglio miste.
>
> Non che Roma di carro così bello
> rallegrasse Affricano, o vero Augusto,
> ma quel del Sol saria pover con ello.[63]

Isidore of Seville compares Christ to the lion "pro regno et fortitudine" and to the eagle "propter quod post resurrectionem ad astra remeavit."[64] All of these features show the adequacy of Trakl's use of the griffin in his poem, since the symbol synthesizes in a particularly rich manner precisely those transformative events which, independently of this symbol, have just been identified as providing the structure of the poem.

The concluding phrase of IV: "O! Verzweiflung, die mit stummem Schrei ins Knie bricht," contradicts the transformation we have noted in IV only superficially. The *mute* cry of despair presents, in fact, a precise complement to the griffin's wild cry of victory, so that there is here not contradiction but reciprocity. This cry may be given the name of *recours absolu*, the term of Gabriel Marcel's to which I referred at the end of the previous chapter. The self-powered nature of the griffin's salvific act requires the total availability of him who is to be snatched up, horse and all, and transported to the mountaintops of India.[65] Despair in this context shows its function as gateway to faith. "Only the sin of absolute despair can paradoxically deliver from despair," writes Michel Estève, commenting on one of Bernanos's characters.[66] That despair here sinks to its knees in humble submission and that it is not the last word—the "unutterable moment" and the "imperishable night" of V follow—demonstrate that this kind of despair plays the transitive role of handing over the self that it might participate in the dark encounter under the green shade of the olive tree (58). Thus this despair plays the same positive role as the *noche oscura* of John of the Cross, which serves as medium for the mystical union. The wholly transformative character of the "night" that concludes the poem may be best realized when we recall two other descriptions of the night in Trakl that enhance and clarify its role in our poem. In *Passion,* the protagonist ardently longs for the coming of a night that he equates with Christ by making this name the night's grammatical apposition:

> O, dass frömmer die Nacht käme,
> Kristus.[67]

And in *Abendland* Trakl defines the night as the "dwelling place of him who loves":

> Denn es ist die Nacht
> Die Wohnung des Liebenden.[68]

Obviously a good deal more could be said about this seemingly inexhaustible poem than has already been said. This very inexhaustibility corroborates my claim as to the Symbolist nature of Trakl's poetics. We have before us not a self-contained narration of events that have occurred elsewhere at another time, but the actual occurrence of these events, under symbolic form. The constellation of symbols Trakl has arranged on the page relate to each other in such a way that the intervening spaces remain perpetually dark and silent. This openness warrants the sovereign freedom of Trakl's poetry, which never attaches itself to externals but exists solely as poetic event.

Nevertheless, a poem such as *Verwandlung des Bösen* ultimately owes its freedom to the fact that it does not set out to create its own world view, but allows itself to exist in the world that crystallizes around the Christ-form of Scripture. References to lepers, shepherds, Calvary, and olive trees are but incidental hints that accompany the presence of the christological mystery. In Western civilization, all of the symbols that populate the Gospel narrative have acquired a sacramental character that evokes a world of associations at the mere mention of a word such as *shepherd* or *leper.* But in Trakl these references serve to frame the actual transformation of the poetic elements themselves, which in their symbolic nature realize postfigurally the actual meaning of the Gospel narrative. The very anonymity of Christ in our poem, and elsewhere in Trakl, reveals the abstractionism of Trakl's Symbolist technique, far more concerned with essence than with nomenclature. The dialogue with the silent but active "thou" realizes the contemporaneity with Christ that was intended by the evangelical *kerygma,* a proclamation concerned with the possibility of coexisting with God and in God rather than with the ability of discoursing about God.

Verwandlung des Bösen, in my interpretation, is an unmistakably christological sequence, which may be summarized in the following five moments, corresponding respectively to its paragraphs:

    I. Dissolution: triumph of evil
   II. Sacrifice: identity of priest and victim
  III. Descent into Hell
  IV. Harrowing and Resurrection
   V. Transformation: triumph over evil.

If we are able to draw up such a scheme, it is only by comparison of the poem with the nature of Christ's redemption as portrayed in Scripture and the liturgico-theological tradition. For, in itself, the poem constitutes such an extreme realization of the Christ-form that it threatens at every instant to lapse into total silence, admittedly the vibrant silence of a total presence that would be tantamount to pure act, but a silence not available to critical scrutiny. In other words, the poem would remain incomprehensible without the independent existence of the Christ-form of which it is the *Abbild* or image. But, granted the existence of this Christ-form, we can recognize that the poem orders itself according to christological structures, which have been so absorbed as to become constitutive and, therefore, anonymous. The extremest communion of subject and object that the poem potrays forbids the naming of exterior differences. The kind of witnessing to the reality of the Christ-event that this poem represents "is not an asseveration that things are so . . . , but rather an open interior space that shows forth the reality of the thing itself [das Seiende selbst]."[69] Symbolist technique, which does not refer but *shows,* allows Trakl to achieve in the aesthetic medium this transition from a *fides qua,* a faith that is still referential and concerned with its objects as objects, to a *fides quae,* the living faith of contemplation, which shows forth spontaneously, and even in spite of itself, the evidence of God's action.

4

The Poem as a Work of Atonement

Klag, Herren frygter ikke, han kan vel
forsvare sig; men hvorledes skulde han
kunne forsvare sig, naar Ingen vover at
klage, som det sømmer sig et Menneske.
Tael, opløft Din Røst, tael høit, Gud kan vel
tale høiere, han har jo Tordenen—men og-
saa den er et Svar, en Forklaring, paalidelig,
trofast, oprindelig, et Svar fra Gud selv,
der, hvis den end knuste et Menneske, er
herligere end Bysnak og Rygter om
Styrelsens Retfaerdighed, opfundne af
menneskelig Viisdom, udspredte af
Kjellinger og Halvmaend.

S. Kierkegaard[1]

Poetry and Guilt

We have thus far examined Trakl's poetry from two perspectives. The
second chapter attempted to establish a context in the history of spirituality that might throw light on Trakl's literary and mystical identity.
The method there was, of necessity, comparative. The last chapter then
approached the poetry as such, asking of it questions that might lead to a
clearer understanding of its aesthetic character. We saw that Trakl's
originality lay in his particular use of Symbolist-Expressionist poetics.
This aesthetic, combined with Trakl's apocalyptic and Passional heritage,
resulted in the use of the symbol for purposes of the post-figural realization of the Christ-form. This process came to light as the conclusion of
our analysis of *Verwandlung des Bösen*.

The historical and aesthetic perspectives, however, call for completion
in a third movement. After having asked of the poetry questions concerning its spiritual filiation and the nature of its language, we must now
ask of it the paramount question: What is the ultimate function of a

poetic process engaged at an apocalyptic level and understanding itself in terms of figural realization? What is the sense of writing such poetry and how is that sense reflected in the nature of the events occurring within a given poem?

At the same time, we may ask the same question of the Christ-form of Scripture, which has been our constant term of reference in this inquiry. If the great events in the structural identity of the Christ-form are Incarnation, Death, and Resurrection, we may then ask the purpose or end of these events. Although event and meaning are existentially one, since the latter should be read solely as the epiphany of the former, nevertheless ontology and teleology are theoretically separable for the sake of understanding. In his Letter to the Ephesians, St. Paul interprets Christ's figural fulfillment of Old Testament prophecies by commenting as follows on Psalm 68:18: "Therefore it is said, 'When he ascended on high he led captivity captive, and he gave gifts to men.' In saying, 'He ascended,' what does it mean but that he also descended into the lower parts of the earth? He who descended is the same as he who also ascended far above all the heavens, that he might fill all things" (4:8–10). The process here described by St. Paul is summarized by Christian tradition in the one word *redemption*, which conveys the grand sweep of the salvific act in which the highest and the lowest are brought together in the indivisible identity of the God-Man: ὁ καταβάς αὐτός ἐστιν καί ὁ ἀναβάς. The term *redemption*, (literally "a buying back") is based on a commercial analogy and is useful for religious language at its mythological level. This term could foreseeably lead to a rather bizarre idea of a retributive God who demands satisfaction in the death of his Son, which "buys back" fallen humanity. Illtyd Trethowan, for one, finds the alternate term, *atonement*, more accurate for the purpose of theological discussion at a dogmatic level. Although the literal aspect of redemption is not absent from scriptural texts and patristic speculation on the meaning of salvation, the "buying back" remains a partial component of the total process of atonement.

If atonement, then, is the "greatest of subjects" of Christian theology, as Trethowan says, since its content is nothing less than the "definitive union of man with God,"[2] we are inevitably led to ask whether this process at the heart of the Christ-form likewise serves as model for the ultimate meaning of Trakl's poetry. In other words, to what extent might we say that Trakl's conception of the act of writing poetry understands itself in the light of Christ's work of atonement? This is the deepest question that my thesis may ask of Trakl's poetry. In order for us to affirm that the form of Trakl's poetry is in-formed (or with G. M. Hopkins, *in-scaped*) by the Christ-form of Scripture, we must first establish a fundamental similarity between the end of Christ's salvific action and the end of Trakl's poetic activity. If we are not able to establish a formal correspondence between them at this ethico-religious level, then everything I have done until now must necessarily remain inconclusive, since the ultimate meaning of every religious phenomenon is found in its eschatology.

If the final sense of the Christ-form is "atonement"—the cancellation of captivity by taking up far above the heavens what had lain forsaken in the lower parts of the earth, the healing of the rift between man and God—then to what extent may we say that the final sense of Trakl's poetry is likewise the reconciliation of man's guilt, which is the cause of man's estrangement from God? The answer to this question provides the final test for the figural nature of Trakl's language, since the very purpose of the appropriation of the Christ-form must be the realization at a subjective level of that atonement effected by Christ. In keeping with my general thesis, moreover, we are to locate atonement not in a passing reference or two that might be contained in Trakl's work, but in the form itself of the poetry. In this final chapter, therefore, we are searching for structures of atonement in the form of Trakl's poetry. The positive verification of their existence will finally establish the integrity and thoroughness of this poetry's "christoformity."

As a convenient way of approaching the subject, I will here again recall Trakl's aphorism that we have already seen in chapter 1. It is the succinct but revelatory statement that he handed Ludwig von Ficker in July 1914, when departing for Galicia and the Russian front, and that may be regarded as a kind of spiritual testament: "Gefühl in den Augenblicken totenähnlichen Seins: alle Menschen sind der Liebe wert. Erwachend fühlst du die Bitternis der Welt; darin ist alle deine ungelöste Schuld; dein Gedicht eine unvollkommene Sühne."[3] Trakl's referring to poetry, or more particularly to each individual poem, as an "imperfect atonement" provides an essential clue to his general understanding of himself as poet. Poetry as atonement sets him off radically, on the one hand, from the aestheticism of the Symbolists, who considered art an end in itself, and on the other hand from the activism of the Expressionists, who considered art a means toward social and political change. Poetry as atonement even distinguishes itself from more traditional Christian conceptions of art, which have as their goal the moral and spiritual improvement of potential readers. Trakl's conception of his identity as poet plainly situates him at a religious and metaphysical *locus coram Deo,* far from aestheticist, activist, and didactic programmes. For him poetry approximates the condition of prayer. A reader of Trakl's poetry is jolted out of any kind of artistic lethargy and political or religious utopianism. The only thing this poetry has to offer is the experience of the poetry itself, and any "enlightenment" derived from it takes the form of rapid metaphysical movement to a new level of awareness, to the consciousness of the guilt and precariousness of the human being in the world. The spirit is left gaping with the need for existence in another sphere.

In his review of Herbert Lindenberger's book *Georg Trakl,* his former student Theodore Fiedler says, concerning the aphorism just quoted, that Trakl's statement "does schematize the moral and religious conception of self, poetry, and the world that stands behind at least the poetry of his last years (1912–14), if not his earlier work. But in terms of the needs of practical criticism to build a critical vocabulary or vocabularies suited to the complexities and peculiar problems of Trakl's poetry as a whole and individual poems in particular, the aphorism is quickly exhausted."[4] One must marvel at the ease with which Fiedler dismisses the moral and religious structure of Trakl's poetry for the sake of developing a vocabulary for "practical criticism." Does, then, practical criticism have nothing to do with the moral and religious concerns that are the very substance of Trakl's work? I suggest that it is precisely such attempts to sever "religious" from "practical" aspects that lie at the root of Trakl's being treated as a genial but incomprehensible poet even by many Germanists. It is my present intention to show that Trakl's aphorism, far from being quickly exhausted, provides *the* basic insight into the structure of his work.

Before beginning our examination of the structures of atonement in Trakl's poetry, we must first consider the reality that makes atonement necessary in the first place, the issue of guilt. We have seen that the fallen state of man in the world is the decisive experience of the apocalypticists; and the dialectical theologians of our century in particular, by establishing the radical difference between man and God, also emphasized the infinite distance separating man from God. Søren Kierkegaard, in the nineteenth century, had largely prepared the way for such assertions by focusing on the *existentialia,* those facts of human existence which, in being peculiar to man, thereby define his relation and disrelation to God. "Sin," writes Kierkegaard, "is not a dogma or a doctrine for thinkers . . ., it is an existence-determinant, and precisely one which cannot be thought. . . / To come into being is to become a sinner."[5] Trakl faithfully echoes Kierkegaard a number of times with a theme that in his poetry is a perpetual refrain or *Grundton.* For Trakl, as for Kierkegaard, *to be* is a synonym for *to-be-in-guilt;* thus we have absolute statements such as:

Gross ist die Schuld des Geborenen. Weh, ihr goldenen Schauer
Des Todes,
Da die Seele kühlere Blüten träumt.[6]

The categorical statement of the universal guilt of all that is born is characteristically followed by the longing for another form of existence (*kühlere Blüten*). In this, too, Trakl mirrors Kierkegaard's understanding of the dialectical sense of guilt-consciousness: "The totality of guilt comes into being for the individual when he puts his guilt together with the relation to an eternal happiness. . . . The consciousness of guilt is the decisive expression for the relationship to an eternal happiness. He who has no relation to this never gets to the point of conceiving himself as totally or essentially guilty."[7] Trakl writes a passage in *Traum und Umnachtung* that appears in this context to be a lyrical dramatization of Kierkegaard's statement:

> Bitter ist der Tod, die Kost der Schuldbeladenen; in dem braunen Geäst des Stamms zerfielen grinsend die irdenen Gesichter. Aber leise sang jener im grünen Schatten des Hollunders, da er aus bösen Träumen erwachte; süsser Gespiele nahte ihm ein rosiger Engel, dass er, ein sanftes Wild, zur Nacht hinschlummerte; und er sah das Sternenantlitz der Reinheit.[8]

As in Kierkegaard, it is the experience of the "burden of guilt" that makes it possible to awaken to a new sphere and to see the "starry face of purity," which here could be taken as a metaphor for Kierkegaard's "eternal happiness."

The essential character of guilt-consciousness within the total process of atonement is emphasized by Tillich when he writes: "The sentimental interpretation of the divine love is responsible for the assertion that Paul's interpretation of the Cross of Christ and his doctrine of atonement contradict the simple prayer for forgiveness in the Lord's Prayer. . . . The consciousness of guilt cannot be overcome by the simple assurance that man is forgiven. Man can believe in forgiveness only if justice is maintained and guilt is confirmed."[9] One can be sentimental in religion only when one feels basically justified and good, incapable of any evildoing. Nothing is farther from Trakl's view, which is in this sense thoroughly Pauline:

> O der Schauer, da jegliches seine Schuld weiss, dornige Pfade geht.[10]

From another standpoint, Paul Ricoeur stresses the structural role played by the recognition of evil in the epiphany of the sacred: "Evil is the critical experience of the sacred *par excellence*. For this reason, the threat that the bond to what man considers sacred may dissolve makes all the more intensely palpable man's dependence on the forces of the sacred."[11] I propose that, in keeping with this statement, the emphasis given by Trakl in his poetry to the reality of evil and the experience of guilt reflects the great degree of intensity that conditions his relationship to the sacred. For this reason I must disagree with Johannes Klein when he states that Trakl's "relationship to Christ shatters the norms of salvation-history and gives preponderance to guilt."[12] Guilt-consciousness need not necessarily be interpreted as a morbid deviation from normal behavior, and may be seen as the negative aspect of an authentic relationship to the sacred. Did not Christ's salvific deed itself disrupt every "expectation *(Vorstellung)* of salvation-history," in the sense that God redeemed Israel not as a triumphant king, but as an utter failure? God's saving love became expressed in Christ as extreme abjection and weakness. What is more, he who was guiltless became sin for our sake (2 Cor. 5:21). The earthly expression for the power of divine love is God's self-surrender to the destructive forces of evil. In this sense, too, Trakl's poetry is an *imitatio Christi.* The guilt of man knows atonement when it sees itself in association with the suffering of him who knew no guilt:

> Weh, des Geborenen, dass er stürbe,
> Eh er die glühende Frucht,
> Die bittere der Schuld genossen.[13]

The objective affirmation of the *fact of guilt* in human existence calls for a subjective appropriation of that fact, a decision with regard to the need for the atonement of guilt. The motor force behind the impulse to atone has already been located in the positive relationship to an eternal happiness, of which guilt-consciousness is the negative expression. But guilt-consciousness provokes an engagement with reality at a very worldly level, precisely because it refuses to turn away to more facile modes of redemption. Trakl's sense of personal and collective guilt, founded on the reality of original sin, contrasts sharply with Gnostic and other heterodox conceptions of salvation, all of which consist in an evasion of history, either through negation of the reality of the world or through (re-)discovery of basic eternal "laws" below all the confusion wrought by men. For Trakl, redemption lies not in enlightenment of any kind, but in atonement. Guilt and its atonement are, essentially, historical and existential concepts, while enlightenment and "confusion" are ahistorical and intellectualistic constructions that make little of existence in time. Here, too, the incarnational character of Trakl's world view reveals itself. "In sin-consciousness," observes Kierkegaard, "the individual becomes conscious of his difference from the humane in general, which becomes by itself conscious of what it is to exist *qua* man. For since the relation to the historical fact of the Deity in time is the condition for sin-consciousness, sin-consciousness could not have been during all the time when the historical fact had not been."[14]

Rudolf Schier presents us with a very faulty and, I think, eccentric interpretation of Trakl's aphorism on atonement when he tells us that the poet's feeling of guilt derives from having broken the "all-embracing and loving unity of the world" through language, and from having rejected traditional religious views, which saw in nature a limpid mirror of the divine presence.[15] Schier seems to overlook the fundamental point about guilt. Trakl's guilt-experience is not the result of breaking the spell of a loving unity with nature, much less of a rejection of traditional norms. It is the guilt derived from original sin, man's essential state of rebellion against God before being redeemed. Trakl's feeling of unity, moreover, is not with nature, but with all men, all of whom are worthy of love, not ideally, but actually in the present moment. Nor is the feeling of the love-worthiness of all men a sentimental adornment of piety, but the sober insight in a moment of "deathlike existence," the experience of St. Paul's "You have died and your life is hidden with Christ in God" (Col. 3:3–4).

The consciousness of guilt provides a solid example of the fact that a Christian perspective rather makes more difficult than facilitates the task of the artist.[16] A certain faithfulness to ugliness and unfinishedness is demanded, for these are the very stuff and matter for transformation. The beauty of poetic creation is not to be gained outside the realm of reality, but within it. As Berdyaev said of Dostoievski, so too we can say of Trakl: that beauty of the kind that saves the world is not a cultural value, but an aspect of Being itself.[17] And if we can speak at all of "beauty saving the world," of beauty transforming chaos into cosmos, it is because the beauty in question is none other than the form of Christ himself, which implants itself gradually as a result of the collaboration of God's grace and man's response to it in action, "until Christ will have taken form in you" (Gal. 4:19). This is the true sense of Trakl's use of figural language, and not the imposition of an arbitrary impersonalism, "that God may speak directly through the poetic means,"[18] as Schier would have it.

The manner in which Trakl's poetry exists in the world, then, exhibits various levels of religious concerns. The love-worthiness of all men is the fundamental insight gained by sharing the divine point of view after a preliminary death to the self as solipsistic entity. The poem mediates between this restitution of love, on the one hand, and the reality of personal and collective guilt diffused in the world, on the other. Poetry as atonement occupies a position that corresponds directly to man's condition as pilgrim in the world. Ahead lies fullness of love; behind lies guilt; in the present, the activity of atonement. The poem is termed an "imperfect atonement" precisely because poetry is conceivable as atonement only figurally, that is, as dependent on the dynamics of the Christ-form and as participating in Christ's work of atonement; in a word, as responsive (ἀνταναπληρῶ) to the divine deed of salvation. Poetry can exist as atonement only as the second movement of an action initiated by God and concluded by God's acceptance of the human act:

> Rechten Lebens Brot und Wein,
> Gott in deine milden Hände
> Legt der Mensch das dunkle Ende,
> Alle Schuld und rote Pein.[19]

The most significant aspect of Trakl's consciousness of guilt and decay is that, with it, comes a consciousness of the possibility of transformation. There is in Trakl's vision a constant simultaneity of the awareness of guilt and the awareness of the presence of grace, so that we may say that there is a promise of grace in his very consciousness of guilt and decay:

> Im grünen Tümpel, glüht Verwesung.
> Die Fische stehen still. Gotts Odem
> Weckt sacht ein Saitenspiel im Brodem.
> Aussätzigen wirkt die Flut Genesung.[20]

The deep darkness evoked by the *ü*'s of the first line is in sharp contrast to the lightness and dancing quality of the vowels and meter of the third line. The indirect reference in the fourth line to the pool of Bethsaida is typical of Trakl's figural procedure. The unity of this vision of healing out of decay, however, can be derived only from a dynamics of love and not merely from a dialectical logic of opposites. If the realization of guilt does not simply lead to despair, it is because hidden within guilt is detected the presence of God's love:

> Ein Lächeln zittert im Sonnenschein,
> Indes ich langsam weiterschreite;
> Unendliche Liebe gibt das Geleite.
> Leise ergrünt das harte Gestein.[21]

That even a stone can cover itself softly with greenness shows a modulation of hardness by love. Elsewhere we read:

> Stille wohnst du im Schatten der herbstlichen Esche,
> Versunken in des Hügels gerechtes Mass;
>
> Immer gehst du den grünen Fluss hinab,
> Wenn es Abend geworden,
> Tönende Liebe.[22]

The juxtaposition here of "just proportion" and "resounding love" offers one more clue into the nature of Trakl's poetic procedure and his understanding of atonement through poetry. There is no discontinuity in Trakl's aphorism between the feeling of the love-worthiness of all men and the truth of guilt-consciousness. It is out of love that Trakl seeks a subordination of the poetic activity to objective justice. This, as we shall shortly see, is the motivation behind his search for impersonal imagery.

The fact of man's guilt-consciousness and the promise of transformation that this fact contains lead us to inquire into the actual process of atonement in Trakl's poetry. In order to identify the different phases of atonement in Trakl's understanding of the event, let us consider the poem *Grodek,* Trakl's last, whose title is the name of a town in Poland and which was written shortly before the poet's death:

Grodek

Am Abend tönen die herbstlichen Wälder
Von tödlichen Waffen, die goldnen Ebenen
Und blauen Seen, darüber die Sonne
5   Düstrer hinrollt; umfängt die Nacht
Sterbende Krieger, die wilde Klage
Ihrer zerbrochenen Münder.
Doch stille sammelt im Weidengrund
Rotes Gewölk, darin ein zürnender Gott wohnt
10   Das vergossne Blut sich, mondne Kühle;
Alle Strassen münden in schwarze Verwesung.
Unter goldnem Gezweig der Nacht und Sternen
Es schwankt der Schwester Schatten durch den schweigenden Hain,
Zu grüssen die Geister der Helden, die blutenden Häupter;
15   Und leise tönen im Rohr die dunkeln Flöten des Herbstes.
O stolzere Trauer! ihr ehernen Altäre
Die heisse Flamme des Geistes nährt heute ein gewaltiger Schmerz,
Die ungebornen Enkel.[23]

The poem may be divided into three sections, each of which represents a distinct event. Section I (2–7)) unfolds a panorama of destruction unleashed by man. But even at this initial stage of the recognition of man's guilt there is present the enfolding receptiveness of the night, which can always be broader and more constant than even human evil-doing. *Tönen tödliche Waffen* is reciprocated exactly by *umfängt die Nacht.*

Section II (8–11), the middle portion of the poem, focuses on a particular event within the horizon of the night: the wrathful God, dwelling within red clouds, is gathering the spilt blood to himself. The unmistakable act of judgment passed upon man's guilt ("rotes *Gewölk,*" "zürnender *Gott*") is delivered of an initial harshness by modifying elements that reveal the meaning of the judgment. The section is introduced by "doch," which marks a deliberate turning away from the destruction occurring in I. God's act of collecting the spilt blood specifies further the night's action of receptively surrounding the dying warriors. The universal and all-encompassing extent of God's action of gathering what is fallen and broken to himself is formally expressed in the syntax of the sentence: The period beginning with "doch stille sammelt" stretches out quite unusually, even for German syntax, by interposing the clause "darin ein zürnender Gott wohnt" between verb and subject, on the one hand, and the object and reflexive pronoun, on the other, which are needed to complete the sense of the sentence. The structure creates considerable suspense and at the same time conveys a feeling of the way in which God's action rounds off and gives shape to chaos. The "lunar coolness" within the red cloud finally reveals mercy, and not wrath, as being the essence of this judgment. What is described externally as fiery and wrathful is experienced interiorly as receptive and healing. We may further corroborate the positive role of purification that Trakl assigns to wrath when we remember his description of Karl Kraus in another poem:

> Kristallne Stimme, in der Gottes eisiger Odem wohnt,
> Zürnender Magier.[24]

We may, then, describe this second movement as the expiation of that guilt whose brutality had been recognized in I. The dispersing action of man in I, experienced sensually in the report of the weapons of death, is reciprocated in II by the gathering action of the wrathful God. In this middle movement mercy is still experienced as judgment, so that guilt determines a relation to God by disrelation or *disjunctio mystica,* as Johannes Klein ingeniously calls it.[25] For this reason, there takes place no resolution at the end of II, and line 11 intensifies the darkness of I even as it imposes an absolute silence: "Alle Strassen münden in schwarze Verwesung."

The very totality of this bleakness, however, announces a ripeness for change, a sudden reversal *ad statum contrarium.* The verb "münden," which has accelerated the tempo of the poem, does not stop at the convergence of all roads in "black decay." A mere lifting of the eyes sees the decay overshadowed by the "golden branches" of the first line of III (12–18). The scene is suddenly transformed from the hecatomb of I into a landscape illuminated from within by stars and golden branches, and in which the sister's greeting, the silence of the grove, and the sound of dark flutes have replaced the explosion of weapons and the wild lament of warriors with crushed mouths. One thinks naturally of the conclusion of Alban Berg's Violin Concerto, in which the desperate struggle for the expression of grief that occupies most of the piece finally comes to rest in the last tranquil and prolonged note. The motif of spilt blood is repeated in "the bleeding heads," but this, too, is transformed by the sacrificial significance ("you brazen altars") given to the destruction of I and the expiation of II. The chaos reigning initially in the poem is ordered in III by the beneficent presence of the sister, whom I regard as the feminine hypostasis of the wrathful God of II, a descendant of Dante's Beatrice who here exhibits exteriorly as well as interiorly the healing receptiveness of divinity. There is no opposition between the figure of the sister who greets the spirits of the heroes and that of the wrathful God who gathers the spilt blood into his cool silence. These two images are continuous with that of the enfolding night of I, and indicate different stages of the atonement of guilt, phases that prepare for one another as judgment conditions reconciliation. They will only be seen as conflicting if the overall unity of the poem's form is neglected.[26]

The last two lines of the poem complete the movement of reconciliation, which I identify as the conclusion of the process of atonement. Here the amorphous pain of the dying warriors is named "a mighty pain." The positive and active role of this pain is emphasized not only by the adjective *gewaltig*, which recalls the αὐτεξουσίως character of Christ's suffering, but by its nourishing function. Suffering is here seen as the wax that sustains the life *(Flamme)* of the spirit. The final phrase—*die ungebornen Enkel*—difficult to integrate into the syntax of the closing sentence, most likely stands in apposition to *ein gewaltiger Schmerz*. This means that the transformative pain experienced by the poet vicariously and symbolically is not merely an existential fact, but one possessing the transitive function of initiating in the present a new kind of humanity. The appositive relationship of "a mighty pain" and "the unborn grandchildren" amounts to a fusion of the two. Suffering for the sake of unborn generations is the very life-blood of the spirit's flame. In this manner, the naked lament of I has become unifying atonement, although the elegiac tone persists to the end. The life of the spirit is not seen as a private abstraction, but concretely as a dimension shared with the whole of humanity. Recalling the context of *Verwandlung des Bösen*, we may say that "the unborn grandchildren" are the new dwellers Trakl envisions for the ravaged "house of the fathers." Between the first condition of the house as desolate and its transformed inhabited state there lies "a mighty suffering" as mediator. The restored innocence of the heirs yet to be born has been hard won from the dilapidation of their fathers' house by the suffering of the poet who, as an *alter Christus,* has made his vision become event in his poem.

Trakl had once written:

Über nächtlich dunkle Fluten
Sing' ich meine traurigen Lieder,
Lieder, die wie Wunden bluten.[27]

The conclusion of *Grodek* takes up the theme again. But the increased stylization and maturity of its form reflect a corresponding deepening in the poet's view of suffering. His song is now more than a wound that bleeds lyrically. The suffering has found a life-giving function: the reconciliation of human violence, hatred, and destructiveness. The harmony and peace that lie at the other side of guilt and suffering, and there only, however, show that they are not the result of a spurious and fabricated eudemonism. Just as the guilt recognized in I had been the result of collective evil-doing, so too the conclusion exhibits a communitarian vision. Although suffering is a particularly individual experience, not to be abstracted or in any way reduced or universalized, the ultimate sense of this suffering is altruistic, motivated in its objectives by the total community of man: "Alle Menschen sind der Liebe wert." The ecclesial character of Trakl's Christianity delivers him from private mythologizing in the manner of a Rilke or Yeats. The peace of the individual depends on the peace of his community; and so the meaning of individual suffering can be found only as the individual relates himself to the welfare of even those yet to exist.

This analysis of *Grodek* enables us to summarize Trakl's understanding of the structures of atonement in the following three movements:

1. The Recognition of Guilt: Guilt is identified as the reality of evil in the self, and this recognition initiates a process of the exorcism of evil. Essential to this exorcism are the aesthetic means at the poet's disposal, for the evil must be *named well* in order for its transformation to begin.

2. The Expiation of Guilt: Essential to the reconciliation of guilt is the suffering experienced as the judgment of a wrathful God. This judgment, however, is ultimately seen to be the necessary exterior, and therefore negative, manifestation of a fundamental mercy that gathers the fragments of existence to itself so as to heal them.

3. The Reconciliation with God: This third movement constitutes the atonement proper, which is the coming to rest of man in God through a transformation of his destructive energies. As God gathered together the pieces of his existence to heal it, so too the individual now gathers together the fragmentation of his community. This is a properly religious work which, for the poet, takes the form of writing poetry.

We note that, while the first aspect of atonement emphasizes the aesthetic means as the mirror of recognition, the second aspect rests upon the negative, ethical imperative of suffering. The third and concluding movement, the coming to rest, has as content the union with God that determines the properly mystical quality of this sphere. We note, too, that this order of movements is valid only descriptively and eschatologically. Reconciliation is the conclusion of atonement both logically and in the reality of the last apocalypse. However, the intervening existence in the *regio dissimilitudinis* is characterized by a constant dialectical alternation of the three movements, so that in Trakl's poetry we find them highlighted in various sequences, according to the interior time of his spiritual rhythms.

In the aphorism I have quoted, Trakl's word for atonement is *Sühne*. This word exhibits a double aspect that is important for our future analyses. A first meaning of *Sühne* connotes "satisfaction, expiation, restoring the damage one has caused." In this sense, the word *Busse* is its synonym. We may associate this meaning of *Sühne* with the second of our schematized movements. More fundamentally, however, *Sühne* derives from the Germanic stem *swon-*, which roughly connotes "appeasement" and "reconciliation." In this sense we have the derived word *Versühnung* or *Versöhnung,* which implies " a reconciling action that restores peace." It is also very tempting, although the etymology probably does not warrant it, to see in *Versöhnung* an expression of the boldest form reconciliation with God can take: the Johannine and Pauline doctrine of "making sons *(Söhne)* by adoption." This second meaning may be regarded as the outcome of expiation, and I have identified it as the third movement of atonement. "Atonement," rather than "expiation" or "penance," seems appropriate in English as the overarching term to resume the entire process of reunification or "at-one-ment," while "expiation" is confined to one phase of atonement.[28]

The remainder of this chapter will be organized according to the three phases of atonement that I have identified in the analysis of *Grodek*. Consequently, let us first examine in greater detail the initial phase of atonement, that of the recognition of guilt.

The Mirror of Recognition

> Unheil als Unheil erwirkt das Heile.
> Heidegger[29]

Guilt may be recognized as guilt only as the result of the activity of grace. Guilt and grace stand in an inescapable dialectical relationship to each other. The two concepts make up the religious reality of man, just as convex and concave, cosmos and nothingness together complete a total *Gestalt.* For this reason, the recognition of guilt is usually portrayed in Trakl as an event or occurrence, a change in the field of consciousness, a *prise de conscience* resulting from the incursion of an initiative from outside of self-awareness.

Often this event takes the form of a confrontation with personal decay by seeing one's image reflected in an actual mirror or pond:

> Mit Schnee und Aussatz füllt sich die kranke Seele,
> Da sie am Abend ihr Bild im rosigen Weiher beschaut.
> Verfallene Lider öffnen sich weinend im Haselgebüsch.[30]

The whole sense of the recognition is that it reveals metaphysical decay; the poetic means of portrayal, therefore, abandon all naturalism in order that the invisible may be perceived. Trakl's symbolism may ultimately be traced to his moral and metaphysical stance, and not to any artistic vogue:

> O des Menschen verweste Gestalt: gefügt aus kalten Metallen,
> Nacht und Schrecken versunkener Wälder
> Und der sengenden Wildnis des Tiers;
> Windestille der Seele.[31]

"Wind lull of the soul": the phrase describes succinctly the locus of Trakl's poetry, the metaphysical point of observation that makes possible the minutest recording of the total condition of man's existence, as spirit and matter interpenetrate and express one another. The mournful recognition continues:

> O die Geburt des Menschen. Nächtlich rauscht
> Blaues Wasser im Felsengrund;
> Seufzend erblickt sein Bild der gefallene Engel.[32]

At other times the eventful quality of the recognition derives from the symbolic role of a cross that signals a time of change, as in *Abendland:*

> In kindlicher Stille,
> Im Korn, wo sprachlos ein Kreuz ragt,
> Erscheint dem Schauenden
> Seufzend sein Schatten und Hingang.[33]

Or as in *Im Dunkel:*

> O das grünende Kreuz. In dunklem Gespräch
> Erkannten sich Mann und Weib.
> An kahler Mauer
> Wandelt mit seinen Gestirnen der Einsame.[34]

These passages begin to define for us Trakl's constant attitude as a witness to man's condition. Words such as *schauen, beschauen, erblicken,* often raised to absolute attributes of identity *(der Schauende),* and other words such as *lauschen* and *hören,* constitute Trakl's vocabulary of recognition. The truth may be perceived because the perceiver has adopted a favorable attitude. Like a seismograph, Trakl's consciousness records the most gentle stirrings in his soul.

I have already said, however, that the importance of Trakl's witness rests upon the fact that he nowhere conceives of himself as a religiously isolated individual. The experience of his painful existential isolation only corroborates for him the reality of metaphysical community with mankind. In this way, we can understand the following passage from a letter to von Ficker as an authentic confession of guilt that Trakl utters in his own behalf and as a representative of his entire generation:

> Zu wenig Liebe, zu wenig Gerechtigkeit und Erbarmen, und immer zu wenig Liebe; allzuviel Härte, Hochmut und allerlei Verbrechertum— das bin ich. Ich bin gewiss, dass ich das Böse nur aus Schwäche und Feigheit unterlasse und damit meine Bosheit noch schände. Ich sehne den Tag herbei, an dem die Seele in diesem unseligen von Schwermut verpesteten Körper nicht mehr wird wohnen wollen und können, an dem sie diese Spottgestalt aus Kot und Fäulnis verlassen wird, die ein nur allzugetreues Spiegelbild eines gottlosen, verfluchten Jahrhunderts ist.– Gott, nur einen kleinen Funken reiner Freude—und man wäre gerettet; Liebe—und man wäre erlöst.[35]

These words convey to us in a descriptive, confessional style what Trakl's poetry embodies as symbolic event. The utter honesty of such a penitent has its reward in the clarity of his vision. There is an energy at work here that enables Trakl to transmute the fact of guilt and depravity into images of strange beauty and fascination. If we are to believe Berdyaev's statement that authentic beauty possesses ontological density and is not limited to a manifestation of cultural values, then we may readily locate the origin of the beauty of Trakl's poetry in the event of his confrontation with the moral truth of his generation, of which he considers himself a demonically faithful reflection.

But this confession of guilt is framed by an even more fundamental striving for love, which in Trakl's letter we encounter as first and last word. The impulse toward love, not love that is received but love that is generated, may indeed be regarded as the motor force behind Trakl's poetic activity. For if Trakl's goal as a poet is to give to truth what belongs to it, and if this truth is partly the accurate portrayal of the absence of love, then the poem as imperfect atonement can be nothing but a work of love. While in his letters Trakl often confesses his guilt and attributes to it the miserable spiritual state in which he finds himself, in his poetry he actively attempts to realize a work of atonement. Therefore the poetry achieves the ontological density as event that is its very identity. The poem must be event, for it conceives of itself as religious act.

Confession here takes the form and specificity of a body inhabiting space.

As we now seek to determine more concretely the ways in which poetry discharges its function as aesthetic means for the recognition of guilt, the following formulation by Ferdinand Ebner will serve as an aid to define the relationship between love and language:

> The real I exists because and insofar as it moves towards a "thou." The real I does not exist in the thought that generates itself only in order to be absorbed once more into the isolation of the I, the thought in which the I thinks itself. The real I exists subjectively in love, and objectively only in the word, but not in the word as it thinks itself, but in the word as it expresses itself. Love and the word are the true vehicles of the I's relationship and movement toward the "thou". . . . In the word, man's spiritual life in its subjectivity has become objective, objective subjectivity, so to speak.[36]

I reproduce this passage at length because it so adequately defines the framework that makes Trakl's poetry possible. Subjectively, Ebner locates in love the event of the true I's coming into existence, and objectively in the concrete self-expression of the I in the word. Both forms of expression necessitate a "thou," who is addressed and who is the object of love. This dynamic conception of existence specifies further Trakl's confession of guilt. The first phase of the exorcism of evil in the self is its expression to a "thou," a movement that subjectively rests on love. Exterior and interior motions coincide in their impulse away from the guilty self, which is left behind as an empty shell. "The essential consciousness of guilt," writes Kierkegaard, "is the first deep plunge into existence."[37]

The expression of guilt in the poetic word constitutes its objectification and, therefore, its exteriorization and inchoate exorcism. When Trakl writes,

> Über die Diele
> Tanzt mondesweiss
> Des Bösen gewaltiger Schatten,[38]

he has accomplished a specification of Evil that initiates a process of expiation. This symbolization of evil occupies a hazardous interim between the possibility of its rising triumphant and destroying him who has confined it in space and time, and the competing possibility that evil may be banished through reconciliation. Ricoeur observes in this vein that "symbolism is the place where progression and regression become identical. To gain a hold on that place would be to gain access to concrete reflection itself."[39] The phrase *concrete reflection* closely describes the kind of movement begun by the objectification of guilt.

The short poem *An die Verstummten* will enable us at this point to witness the way in which Trakl's method of concrete reflection through symbolization objectifies guilt by specifying it in images that make this poem something like an absolute metaphor of guilt:

An die Verstummten

O, der Wahnsinn der grossen Stadt, da am Abend
An schwarzer Mauer verkrüppelte Bäume starren,
Aus silberner Maske der Geist des Bösen schaut;
Licht mit magnetischer Geissel die steinerne Nacht verdrängt.
O, das versunkene Läuten der Abendglocken.

Hure, die in eisigen Schauern ein totes Kindlein gebärt.
Rasend peitscht Gottes Zorn die Stirne des Besessenen,
Purpurne Seuche, Hunger, der grüne Augen zerbricht.
O, das grässliche Lachen des Golds.

Aber stille blutet in dunkler Höhle stummere Menschheit,
Fügt aus harten Metallen das erlösende Haupt.[40]

The title of the poem seems to indicate that the poet intends to become a mouthpiece for the guilt and grief of those too submerged in them to objectify their condition in symbolic lament. The first strophe realizes a condensation of the Spirit of Evil in concrete images: the crippled trees ossifying at the black wall, the silver mask of greed, the magnetic whip of light that violates the integrity of the night. The wrath of God answers the madness of the diabolical city in the second strophe by castigating it with epidemics and hunger, intended to exorcise the Spirit of Evil from the possessed. The raging of God's wrath *(rasend peitscht)* reciprocates, on its own terms, the violence of evil *(Licht mit magnetischer Geissel)*. The whore's still-born child acts, in the middle of the poem, as a silent victim whose ambiguity as symbol both of evil and of innocence anticipates the atonement of the last two verses. The characteristic disjunctive *aber,* like the *doch* of *Grodek,* signals the turning to a reality which, being conclusive in the poem, outdoes in hope the raving despair that precedes. The activity of secret suffering, attributed to a "more silent humanity," supplants the shrill pandemonium of the electric city. The poet, in lending symbolic form to a purposeful suffering, effects the neutralization of the evil that he has first named. I know no better description of the kind of triumph over evil that such a poem as this accomplishes than the one given by Johannes Klein when he refers to Trakl's architectural sense in constructing a poem: "Often, when the content of a poem witnesses to defeats, the form can reveal an actual victory."[41] Form as a means of overcoming chaos: the ontological reality of evil may be countered only by the ontological reality of the terrible image.

The poem's concluding couplet presents us with the explicitly christological mystery of the hiddenness of the work of atonement. The activity of silent, atoning bleeding, which gradually fashions the redeeming Head, takes place "in a dark cave." The two other adjectives qualifying the scene—"quiet" and "more silent"—complete the sense of utter concealment and anonymity: the place is a cave, the color is dark, all sounds are muffled. This process of total blacking out concentrates our attention on the metaphysical sense of the scene. Von Balthasar elucidates the relationship between christological hiddenness and the objectification of guilt, which in our poem gains intense relief by the juxtaposition of the overt and garish vulgarity of evil with the taciturn gesture that follows the *aber:*

> It is man's guilt that forces the Son to manifest himself to the world in the mode of hiddenness. The guilt is, therefore, not excused by the hiddenness, but rather condemned by it. The hiddenness is the objective proof that the guilty have not wanted to see. But because the figure of hiddenness is at the same time a figure of suffering, guilt turns away from this its mirror deliberately, because there is here nothing gratifying and edifying to delight in, but only something worthy of contempt (cf. Isa. 53: 2–3). The last thing that guilt could acknowledge is that precisely this image is its perfect objectification, a self-portrait whose similarity and even identity necessarily unsettle the unprejudiced observer, and increasingly so the longer he contemplates it.[42]

So great is the dependence of guilt on grace that guilt could never become conscious of itself *qua* guilt if left to its own resources. Guilt-consciousness is thus the opposite of despair, since the very sense of guilt is a promise of liberation. It is therefore the objectification of God's mercy in the form of Christ's humiliation that makes possible the objectification of guilt in the form of the images of evil that Trakl dramatizes in lines 2–10 of the poem. Far from being a sort of "pious Christian addition" to a hopeless panorama, as is also often argued, for instance, with regard to the epilogue of Dostoievski's *Crime and Punishment,* the concluding lines 11 and 12, with their explicitly Passional event, are the very condition that makes the rest of the poem possible in retrospect. The mute darkness of the cave is the locus from which the poet speaks; and we recall that the *cave* had been the favorite Baroque metaphor for the wounds of the Crucified in their role as place of refuge and "smithy" where the redemption is wrought.

Ferdinand Ebner insists on the fundamental difference between ordinary self-awareness and guilt-consciousness:

> Self-recognition is recognition of the discrepancy in the self between idea and reality, but it is not yet by far a recognition of sin. . . . In self-

recognition man measures himself according to a human standard, since idea is something human. In the recognition of sin, man sees the reality of his existence and his life *over against* that of Jesus Christ and, therefore, measured by a divine standard, so that his own reality is, ethically, reduced to nothing.[43]

The fact that in the recognition of guilt man experiences himself as judged by a divine rather than a human standard leads Trakl to strive for an ever greater impersonality in his poetry. I recall again the passage from the letter to Buschbeck in which he makes impersonal objectivity the goal of his poetic procedure:

Es fällt mir nicht leicht und wird niemals leicht fallen, mich be-dingungslos dem Darzustellenden unterzuordnen und ich werde mich immer und immer wieder berichtigen müssen, um der Wahrheit zu geben, was der Wahrheit ist.[44]

Impersonalism is adopted by Trakl as his peculiar form of poetic ascesis, "for the sake of the truth." This aesthetic discipline, however, is an extension or application of his personal attitude to reality. In his letters we witness an increasing process of decentralization of the ego. In 1910 he writes to Buschbeck:

Meine Angelegenheiten interessieren mich nicht mehr. . . . Ich möchte mich gerne ganz einhüllen und anderswohin unsichtbar werden.[45]

Two years earlier he had written from Vienna:

Als ich hier ankam, war es mir, als sähe ich zum ersten Male das Leben so klar wie es ist, ohne alle persönliche Deutung, nackt, vor-aussetzungslos, als vernähme ich alle jene Stimmen, die die Wirk-lichkeit spricht, die grausamen, peinlich vernehmbar. Und einen Au-genblick spürte ich etwas von dem Druck, der auf den Menschen für gewöhnlich lastet.[46]

We note here the characteristic turning to the spiritual state of all mankind, the contemplation of which constituted Trakl's most constant medium for poetic creation. In 1911 he had written to Buschbeck in the first of the letters here quoted, referring to the revised version of a poem:

Es ist umso viel besser als das ursprüngliche als es nun unpersönlich ist. . . . Ich bin überzeugt, dass es Dir in dieser universellen Form und Art mehr sagen und bedeuten wird, denn in der begrenzt persön-lichen des ersten Entwurfes.[47]

The result of this rigorous subordination to what Trakl considers an extrapersonal truth is that he is invaded by a throng of destructive demons that ordinarily remain unperceived by the majority of self-deceiving mankind:

> Ich bin derzeit von allzu viel (was für ein infernalisches Chaos von Rythmen und Bildern) bedrängt, als dass ich für anderes Zeit hätte, als dies zum geringsten Teil zu gestalten.[48]

In the same way that the hiddenness and silence at the conclusion of *An die Verstummten* made possible the objectification of evil, so, too, the poet's deliberate search for impersonality in his art leads to the partial containment and taming of chaos through an imposition of form. Amorphousness is the aesthetic manifestation of the ascendancy of evil; the imposition of form is, at the level of recognition, the particular implementation of atonement. Impersonality emerges as the condition *sine qua non* for the exorcism of evil, since the poet encounters the forces of evil not with self-expression, but primarily with the recognition of their reality. The reality of evil is the first and negative aspect of the truth; as long as there is a need for the work of atonement, this aspect remains predominant in Trakl's work of poetry. "The revelation of the world's redemption," writes von Balthasar, "cannot occur as a spectacular theophany that dazzles misery with splendor. It can occur only in the mystery of a love that, by its suffering, survives all the burden of scorn that is heaped upon it."[49] These words, commenting on the modality of Christ's redemptive act, show the extent to which Trakl molded his existence in the image of the Christ-form. The same Trakl who had written: "Zu wenig Liebe, zu wenig Gerechtigkeit und Erbarmen, und immer zu wenig Liebe," shows by the nature of his impersonal aesthetic attitude and practice that it was precisely such love that he sought to realize by moving beyond the confines of the guilty self. Impersonality for him becomes the direct means of objectifying the image of man as he is judged and loved, not by himself, but by God. Impersonality in poetry incarnates theocentricity.

> **Auch, dass wir verdorrt sind, weil wir die Maske leichtfertig abgelegt und nichts weiter als unsere eng begrenzte, kümmerliche kleine Person in den Weltraum gehalten haben; in die schwarzen, geheimnisvoll zehrenden Winde. . . . So wäre also**

> wahrhaftig, mein Felix, die Abstraktion
> unsre heilige Maske, mit der wir Freien
> dem unfreien Satan heute entgegentre-
> ten?[50]

The poet objectifies himself in his words in a manner analogous to God's self-objectification in Christ. The confining of the self in space and in time constitutes a movement away from the ego as center of the universe, and defines the particular modality of Incarnation. Trakl's impersonalism, undertaken for the sake of objectifying guilt in his words, emerges as direct result of the imitation of the God-Man's self-objectification. In order to atone for guilt, Christ becomes identified with the form of guilt, and this action is the expression of the Father's love for man. Writes Ebner:

> Man is delivered out of the ego-isolation of his existence by the word and by love. The love of God, which created man by means of the Word that contained life, became objective in "the Word," which here clearly means that it became historical fact: objectified in God's becoming man and in the God of the Gospel.[51]

The process of symbolic abstraction is the particular manner in which Trakl achieves a purification of the poetic image. Such purification coincides with the extinction of the poet's private ego and thus makes possible the objectification of evil. The poem *Jahr* offers an excellent illustration of this procedure:

Jahr

Dunkle Stille der Kindheit. Unter grünenden Eschen
Weidet die Sanftmut bläulichen Blickes; goldene Ruh.
Ein Dunkles entzückt der Duft der Veilchen; schwankende Ähren
Im Abend, Samen und die goldenen Schatten der Schwermut.
Balken behaut der Zimmermann; im dämmernden Grund
Mahlt die Mühle; im Hasellaub wölbt sich ein purpurner Mund,
Männliches rot über schweigende Wasser geneigt.
Leise ist der Herbst, der Geist des Waldes; goldene Wolke
Folgt dem Einsamen, der schwarze Schatten des Enkels.
Neige in steinernem Zimmer; unter alten Zypressen
Sind der Tränen nächtige Bilder zum Quell versammelt;
Goldenes Auge des Anbeginns, dunkle Geduld des Endes.[52]

The poem strikes us at once by a certain quality of indefinite suspense that abolishes all one's usual points of reference. In particular, we are disoriented by the great number of abstract words that are used as if they were concrete entities: *Stille der Kindheit, weidet die Sanftmut, goldene Ruh, goldene Schatten der Schwermut, der Geist des Waldes, Neige in steinernem Zimmer, der Tränen nächtige Bilder, dunkle Geduld des Endes.* In addition to these abstracta, which become grammatical subjects, we note a specifically Traklian mannerism borrowed from Hölderlin—the conversion of adjectives into neuter nouns: *ein Dunkles, Männliches.* This practice contributes to an even intenser feeling of abstractness and mystery. Syntactically, the poem adopts as a constant structural feature the omission of the definite article, which raises even concrete nouns such as *Eschen, Ähren, Balken, Wasser, Wolke, Zypresse,* and *Auge* to something like types outside a particular place and time.

And yet, at the same time, we grow aware of the fact that this degree of formal abstraction is of such a nature that it does not dissipate reality by falling into the banalities of bad allegory. If Trakl's language alienates the reader because it is so far removed from everyday speech and even from elevated discourse of a conventional kind, it is because the proper object of Trakl's poem belongs to a realm beyond empirical existence. By grounding his poem in a metaphysical domain, Trakl reveals his desire to achieve in his poetry a rapid descent to the foundations of existence, to the realm of spiritual essences. The bits of natural detail that remain— the carpenter hewing his planks and the millstone grinding in the valley—act as the necessary point of entry from the visible world into the world of spirit.

Far from dissipating the concrete, Trakl's procedure of abstraction rather condenses the unseen and makes the visible world a vehicle for its operations. What results is a world of sensual abstraction. Matter stands at the service of spirit. The real agent in Trakl's world is not the individual as he illusorily conceives of himself as lord of his microcosm. The moving forces here are those chaotic or benevolent states that are directly responsible for transformation or decay in the life of the spirit: solitude and peace, the innocence of childhood and the patience of suffering, dejection and meekness, darkness and light. The hypostatic "incarnation" of these spiritual realities makes the world dynamic rather than robbing it of density and vitality. The world is shown in its authentic identity, which results from the interpenetration of matter and spirit. Johannes Klein has accurately remarked that Trakl's abstractionism derives from his attempt to express the absolute without mediation: "In all its struggle with form, his expression strives to become immediate, to *say* something absolute, and in this attempt it exhibits a paradoxical compulsion itself to become absolute. Trakl's statement of life is often worlds removed from everyday life because it seeks out a transformation of the everyday into the spiritual—a lost dimension."[53]

In this sense, Trakl's procedure is comparable to that of Byzantine art, whose stylization is not derived from artistic immaturity any more than

Trakl's deliberate exclusion of the dimensions of empirical space and time. In either case, abstractionism may be traced to the attempt of making visible the triumph of eternity. For this, the rarefaction of human reality is necessary. The particular must yield to the laws of the spirit in order to show itself as being judged by them. "An unfulfillable longing is here expressed to lend body to the sacral and to bring it into a constant epiphany," says Bahr of Byzantine icons. And his conclusion nearly entitles us to speak of Trakl's "Byzantinism": "The basic colors are gold and blue."[54] Byzantine icon and Traklian poem are united in their religious impulse to employ matter as a vehicle of spirit; and therefore the aesthetic reality of each is impersonal as it seeks to liberate the perceiver from the illusion of a sham autonomy and engage him in a process of purification and *ekstasis:* exit from the self.

We should not neglect to see in the conclusion of *Jahr* the biblical basis that becomes transparent as a condition for Trakl's abstracting procedure. The lines

> . . . unter alten Zypressen
> Sind der Tränen nächtige Bilder zum Quell versammelt,

are an indirect allusion to the words of the Psalmist:

> Sammle meine Tränen in deinen Krug; ohne Zweifel, du zählst sie.
> (Ps. 56:9)

The image of tears that are gathered by God into his jug conveys a sense of the transformative power of sorrows, none of which is useless or lost from God's count. For the poet, the Psalmist's tears are specified as *nächtige Bilder,* namely, those images of decline and death he has just enumerated in the poem. These images, abstracted as they are from their quotidian use, become the distillation that acts as a fountain or source *(Quell):* the nourishing well of patience. Abstraction in Trakl, then, assumes the role of transforming the corruptible by distilling it into the imperishable liquor gathered into God's presence.

Trakl's alternative to the quotidian is not the general, which is to say the banal. It is the archetypical, which is to say the foundation of reality. The procedure of the decomposition of man (by his division into states of soul) and the denaturalization of nature (by its becoming an analogue of spiritual entities) manifests Trakl's objective of achieving total interiority. The divine lies neither in nature nor in man, but in the movement beyond them both. The search for the divine necessarily entails the decomposition (a possible rendering of Trakl's ubiquitous *Verwesung!*) of both man and nature in order that they may be reconstituted at another level of reality, beyond the control of accidents that compete with the perception of the absolute.

The confrontation with the absolute produces the inevitable paradox that, while the artist must shun his narrow individuality for the sake of making spiritual events visible, this act engages him in the essence of his personhood. "The creative Self of the artist," observes Maritain, "is his person as person, in the act of spiritual communication, not his person as material individual or as self-centered ego. . . . Poetry's I is the substantial depth of living and loving subjectivity. It is the creative Self, a subject as *act*."[55] This is to say that the act of poetic creation effects the realization of the self at a greater degree of authenticity, where the self abandons its counterfeit subjectivity to enter the domain of "infinite subjectivity," which is Kierkegaard's definition of God. Existence in relation to God's absoluteness brings about a monumental reorganization of the order of spiritual values: "In his condition as spirit," observes Ebner, "which is to say in his origin in God, man was not 'first' but 'second person'; God was and is the first person. And this 'first' and 'second' here literally express the actual spiritual order of things, in contrast to the usual grammatical conventions."[56] The violent reversal whereby the "thou" becomes first person and the "I" takes its proper position as permanent addressee accounts for the destruction in Trakl's poetry of the natural order of things so that the true spiritual hierarchy may shine through. Thus we have this illumination of death:

> Sanfte Harmonien, da wir in kristallnen Wogen
> Fahren durch die stille Nacht
> Ein rosiger Engel aus den Gräbern der Liebenden tritt,[57]

which sharply contrasts with the following view of evil:

> Schlafwandler treten vor ein Kerzenlicht,
> In eine Spinne fährt des Bösen Geist.[58]

In each case we experience a recognition: in the first instance that of the manner in which love immortalizes, in the second an incarnation of the Spirit of Evil. The first dramatizes life out of death; the second, death in life. Likewise, the following verses communicate events that are as mysterious as their portrayal is bold:

> Hirten begruben die Sonne im kahlen Wald.
> Ein Fischer zog
> In härenem Netz den Mond aus frierendem Weiher.[59]

The compression of the cosmic and the commonplace in this case bears witness to the sovereign freedom with which Trakl moves in the realm of spirit. These verses are an excellent illustration of the "sublime humility" of Auerbach's *sermo piscatorius,* and here in a quite literal sense! We are not to fabricate an allegorical explanation for every symbolic event we encounter in this poetry. Much more essential is the nature of the process itself which, in effecting the commutation of language into a means for spiritual regeneration, stakes out an uncharted sphere of Being.

T. J. Casey fittingly describes the unity of Trakl's poetry when he says that "in materializing what is spiritual, it spiritualizes the material world."[60] This observation points unawares to the christological form of Trakl's poetry. We may say that the interpenetration of the spiritual and the sensual in this poetry accomplishes a breakthrough that overcomes the natural human tendency, especially endemic to the modern era, to sever spirit and matter as one would empty abstraction and corporal inertia. Let us note well that when speaking of Trakl's "abstractionism" I have been referring to an aesthetic technique, and not to his conception of man, world, or God. The fact that his world view rests upon a sense of the vitality of the spiritual is too obvious to require demonstration. The temptation of man is to seek escape from reality by fleeing into an abstract spiritualism or a spiritless sensualism, or both simultaneously.[61] Trakl overcomes by an ethicoreligious act—the writing of poetry—the temptation to flee from the God of creation, the desperate attempt that at bottom propels the feat of splitting the spirit and the senses radically. The living God may be encountered only by whole persons, indeed as God himself encounters us in Christ as a true human being. The inner depth and luminosity of the Traklian symbol is at the same time the result (as being made possible by) and an imitation (through conscious participation) of the Christ-event of Incarnation: "The senses are an externalization of the soul, and Christ is the externalization *(das Ent-äusserte)* of God, of the God who, as creator, has already externalized himself in *erōs.* In the Incarnation God definitively confirms this, in such a way that the destitution of Being and its sensuality can at a deeper level manifest the only treasure it contains, namely, love."[62] At this point we witness the convergence of Trakl's ethico-aesthetic procedure with the structure of the Christ-event. The depersonalization of the lyrical voice in his poetry takes the form of images that abstract the quotidian and condense the spiritual. This aesthetic process may be considered the exact realization of the Christ-form which, being a perceptible aesthetic reality, "raises" the sphere of humanity by "lowering" that of divinity (cf. the kenotic hymn of Phil. 2), so that, as von Balthasar says, the activity of love may be revealed as the "blending of horizons" in the theandric fact.

> **Finsternis ist nicht finster bei dir,**
> **Und die Nacht leuchtet wie der Tag.**
> **Finsternis ist wie das Licht.**
>
> **Ps. 139:12**

Why, then, we may ask, does Trakl's Christianity—his existence as one
transformed by the action of Christ—take such a problematic, evasive
form in his poetry? The answer is that his poetry, as a participation in
and realization of Christ's salvific act in the subjective sphere, achieves
such an extreme contemporaneity and mystical identity with the Christ-
event that it demonstrates in the present tense the process itself of
atonement and does not refer to it as an accomplished fact. By reaching
such a level of subjectivity, Trakl is unable to consider the atoning
Passion of Christ anything but an event simultaneous with his own
existence. This total contemporaneity is the extreme of the figural realization of the Christ-form. No longer can eternity and the absolute be
regarded objectively as a realm separate from earthly decay. "The new
era which Christ inaugurates cannot be a *figura* in the same sense as the
old era had been. It still has form, even provisional form; but Christ's
hypostatic unity embraces both the corruptibility of the earthly form and
the imperishability of the heavenly form."[63] Trakl's continual insistence
upon the predominance of decay in this earthly life is not a sign of
despair. The *form* in which he presents decay witnesses to a transforming
presence. The decline of the earthly, in fact, precisely signals the rise of
imperishable realities, just as the destruction of Christ's body in the
Passion was the condition for Resurrection.

This mystery must not be understood mechanically as a necessary
sequence of events (that is, that after death there can only come rebirth).
Rather, Resurrection is an event that occurs simultaneously with the
Passion, because in them both is revealed the triumph of love:

> Einsam dunkelt der Himmel,
> Sinkt gewaltig das weisse Haupt am Waldsaum hin.
> Steigt aus finsteren Schluchten die Nacht.[64]

The deliberate and powerful falling (ἑκουσίως καί αὐτεξουσίως) releases
the emergence of the night of transformation. The strict interdependence of the two antipodal events is expressed in the syntactic parallelism of the two verses: *sinkt gewaltig . . . // steigt aus finsteren . . . ,* in
which the postposition of the subjects and the strong asyndeton strive to
say both things at once, if that were possible. In a similar way, Christ's
humiliated but powerful lament, full of groans and tears (μετά κραυγῆς
ἰσχυρᾶς καί δακρύων), is shown to be essential to his glorified position as

model of patience and as mediator (ἔμαθεν ἀφ᾽ ὧν ἔπαθεν τήν ὑπακοήν—Heb. 5:7–8). Only a historical narration presents the Christ-event chronologically. A poetic realization, being the event's subjective appropriation, communicates it all at once. Trakl's lyrical language does not impart information; in its form it adjusts subjective reality to the archetype of the Christ-form. Trakl's poetry recognizes the reality of Christ as it did the reality of guilt: by objectifying its operations. Trakl does not name Christ. Trakl repeats Christ. And therefore the poetry shows anonymously what it refuses to name explicitly, thus fulfilling on the aesthetic plane a properly evangelical principle: "The tree is known by its fruit" (Matt. 12:33), or, even more poignantly, "Not every one who says to me, 'Lord, Lord,' shall enter the kingdom of heaven, but he who does the will of my Father who is in heaven" (Matt. 7:21). In either case there is a trenchant distinction made between the ontological reality of what a thing is, as manifested in its silent actions, and what it might pretend to be by camouflaging itself with language.

Stressing this decisiveness of existential reality, von Balthasar calls our attention to the dramatic character of the Christian faith, that is, that

> if God re-presents himself in the world, this event implies an emi-
> nently free deed which is of the greatest consequence for human
> action. God's entrance as the Lord of the world and its history cannot
> avoid triggering the most colossal of dramas. . . . Passive reception
> and a detached recording of facts are no longer possible. Whoever is
> deeply struck by what his faith shows him must climb up on the stage
> and participate in the action. . . . God's Christian *epiphaneia* has
> nothing further in common with Plato's Sun of the Good, which
> merely bestows its light. This epiphany is a deed of the freest coming-
> into-presence which boldly lays at stake the uttermost depths of both
> divine and human love.[65]

Trakl's poetry conforms with the fact that God's love has, in Christ, become manifest as a free person who can choose to lay down his life. Christ is not primarily a teacher, but the one who fulfills the atonement. He not so much "enlightens," in a Gnostic sense, as transforms by his action. Christ would be no less the Redeemer had he never spoken a word. In fact, it is possible that he never uttered any of the words the Gospels attribute to him in the particular manner they have recorded them. The silence of Christ, especially in the Passion, most perfectly reveals the depths of his reconciling activity. F. X. Durrwell says that the expiation of Christ "was not so much a debt to pay as a gulf to bridge."[66] Christ not so much concluded a pending transaction as he became the *pontifex* between humanity and God, who carries on his metaphysical labor in utter obscurity. The work of atonement as poem must present an exterior anonymity in order that it may become pure form, for form is the symbolic equivalent of action. The actual events of a poem occur in its form or not at all. Whoever participates in the work of atonement must enter the stage as an actor. We cannot be innocent bystanders; for, as Paul wrote to the Corinthians: "I think that God has exhibited (ἀπέδειξεν) us apostles as the last of all, like men sentenced to death; for we have become a spectacle (θέατρον!) to the world, to angels, and to men" (1 Cor. 4:9). For the poet *to say is to do,* and for this reason the degree of abstractionism in Trakl's poetry corresponds to the degree at which he participates in the Christ-form that his poetry realizes. For Trakl, remembering Christ's deed of atonement and making it present by dramatizing it (i.e., putting it into action) are one and the same spiritual movement: "Recall (ἀναμιμνήσκεσθε) the former days when, after you were enlightened, you endured a hard struggle with sufferings, sometimes being publicly exposed (θεατριζόμενοι) to abuse and affliction, and sometimes being partners with those so treated" (Heb. 10:32).

The fact of Christ's anonymity in Trakl's poetry and its decisive importance for the authenticity of Trakl's Christianity may be realized most acutely if we compare an early poem that is explicitly christological with a late poem that is so "only" in form. The first of these was written in 1909:

Crucifixus

Er ist der Gott, vor dem die Armen knien,
Er ihrer Erdenqualen Schicksalsspiegel,
Ein bleicher Gott, geschändet, angespien,
Verendet auf der Mörderschande Hügel.

Sie knien vor seines Fleisches Folternot,
Dass ihre Demut sich mit ihm vermähle,
Und seines letzten Blickes Nacht und Tod
Ihr Herz im Eis der Todessehnsucht stähle—

Dass öffne—irdenen Gebrests Symbol—
Die Pforte zu der Armut Paradiesen
Sein todesnächtiges Dornenkapitol,
Das bleiche Engel und Verlorene grüssen.[67]

The poem's conventional form and Latin title, something of a mannerism for a twentieth-century Lutheran, reflect its turgid religiosity, a fervor that views Christ in Nietzschean manner as the projection of the world's misery, the God of the death-seekers. Trakl self-consciously announces that the crucified Christ is a symbol of earthly frailty, and thereby indicates the distance that still separates him from the interior reality of his subject. The poem is reminiscent of bad passages in Rilke's *Stundenbuch,* where easy rhymes proliferate and actually adapt the religious subject matter to the exigencies of sound and meter! We note, however, that the essential is already here: the problematic of Passion and transformation, and the dynamism that involves the observer in the drama of the Crucified.

For contrast, let us consider the following short poem, written in mid-1914, at the apex of Trakl's artistic maturity:

Gesang einer gefangenen Amsel
Für Ludwig von Ficker

Dunkler Odem im grünen Gezweig.
Blaue Blümchen umschweben das Antlitz
Des Einsamen, den goldnen Schritt
Ersterbend unter dem Ölbaum.
Aufflattert mit trunknem Flügel die Nacht.
So leise blutet Demut,
Tau, der langsam tropft vom blühenden Dorn.
Strahlender Arme Erbarmen
Umfängt ein brechendes Herz.[68]

After the awkward circumlocutions of *Crucifixus*, this poem strikes one by the extremity of its simplification and, above all, its silences. The Passion has been transformed from theme to essence. The mystical identification of Trakl with the suffering Savior is so complete that a new and limpid symbol is sought to incarnate uttermost solitude, meekness, and mercy: the captured ouzel. The physical reality of the symbol comes from such a different realm than that of the scriptural figure of Jesus that, precisely for that reason, it is capable of abstracting and fusing into unity the metaphysical features of the Christ-event. The Passion has become pure song because all of its external accidents are omitted. We are thrust willy-nilly into the process of the spiritual events themselves. We fall with *ersterbend* and rise with *aufflattert*. We are blinded by the night only to be dazzled with mercy. And at the center of it all, the bleeding of Meekness makes even the thorn blossom. Surrounding the immensity of this solitude are the resplendent arms of Mercy that enfold the breaking heart, much as the brief form of the poem dams in a sea of sorrow. The thematic content of *Crucifixus*, what could there indeed appear to be a literary motif, has been wholly absorbed by the very texture and structure and gestures of the language, so that the "theme" may no longer be described explicitly. Presence forbids reference and enjoins silence. "True religiosity," says Kierkegaard, "is the religiosity of the secret inwardness. . . . Just as the criterion of God's omnipresence consists in his being invisible, so the criterion of true religiosity is its invisibility, i.e. there is nothing outwardly to be seen. The god that can be pointed out is an idol."[69]

Trakl's process of stylization and abstraction evokes the presence of the invisible without violating its sacrality. Such poetry relates to God as

God. The initial *anagnōrisis* of guilt has led to the *anamnēsis* of Christ's salvific act, in which God's judgment of the world's guilt coincides with the love that reconciles it.

The Night of Expiation

> **Mais la souffrance nous reste, qui est notre part commune avec vous, le signe de notre élection, héritée de nos pères, plus active que le feu chaste, incorruptible.**[70]

Between the recognition of guilt and its definitive abolition, there lies a painful night of expiation. In this night the individual experiences the total solitude of being remote from both Egypt and Jerusalem. The darkness of this phase of atonement, its inarticulateness in particular, conceals the deep and crucial activity taking place: the work of suffering. Trakl avows the necessity of entering the awesomeness of this night:

> O Nacht, du stummes Tor vor meinem Leid . . .
> O Nacht, ich bin bereit!
>
> O Nacht, du Garten der Vergessenheit
> Um meiner Armut weltverschlossnen Glanz,
> Das Weinlaub welkt, es welkt der Dornenkranz.
> O komm, du hohe Zeit![71]

These verses are the figural realization of the words of Jesus on the eve of the Passion: "Jetzt ist meine Seele betrübt. Und was soll ich sagen? Vater, hilf mir aus dieser Stunde? Nein, darum bin ich in diese Stunde gekommen" (John 12:27). The hour of suffering that has arrived, moreover, corresponds to the moment of his glorification: "Die Zeit ist gekommen, dass des Menschen Sohn verherrlicht werde" (John 12:23). Both the Jesus of John and Trakl's persona in this poem show the same awareness of the arrival of the *kairos* of suffering, and they both embrace it.

The extraordinary frequency of the theme of suffering in Trakl makes it one of the basic characteristics of his view of existence. Kierkegaard repeatedly stresses the fact that suffering is the very life-blood, as it were, of the religious personality. "The religious individual has suffering constantly with him. He requires suffering in the same sense that the immediate individual (i.e., the person who lives for the moment) requires fortune, and he requires and has suffering even in the absence of external misfortune."[72] "Viewed religiously, it is necessary . . . to comprehend the suffering and to remain in it, so that reflection is directed *upon* the suffering and not *away* from it."[73] Trakl echoes Kierkegaard's insistence on the seemingly absolute necessity of suffering when he writes to von Ficker in 1913:

> Heimgesucht von unsäglichen Erschütterungen, von denen ich nicht weiss ob sie mich zerstören oder vollenden wollen, zweifelnd an allem meinem Beginnen und im Angesicht einer lächerlich ungewissen Zukunft. . . .[74]

The ambiguousness of this state—whether the faceless trials are intended to destroy or to perfect him—determines the very structure of expiation.

For Kierkegaard, however, suffering's necessity does not rest upon its irrational absurdity or upon a Dionysian conception of man that would seek the joyful destruction of the individual. Suffering is the *modus essendi* of the person pilgrimaging to reconciliation with God. The death involved is a salutary one: "The significance of the religious suffering is that it is a dying away from immediacy; its reality consists in its essential persistence; but it belongs to the inwardness of a man, and must not express itself outwardly, as in the monastic movement."[75] This affirmation of Kierkegaard's is verified in Trakl even to explicit rejection of the cloister. Hans Limbach reports a conversation in which, to the question as to why he did not enter a monastery and thus forsake the corrupt world, Trakl answers: "Ich bin Pro-tes-tant. . . . Ich habe kein Recht, mich der Hölle zu entziehen."[76] This conversation is important, in addition, because it contains Trakl's explicit statements concerning his Christianity. Suffering, both for Kierkegaard and for Trakl, is not an amorphous and senseless state of misery; it is "the highest action in inwardness," the quotidian reality of essential existence.[77]

Thus, for Trakl, pain attains to the status of a mode of knowledge:

> O Schmerz, du flammendes Anschaun
> Der grossen Seele![78]

Pain is the mode of apprehending truth:

> Der Wahrheit nachsinnen—
> Viel Schmerz!
> Endlich Begeisterung
> Bis zum Tod.[79]

Trakl also portrays suffering as a transforming force in which the religious individual persists:

Leise kommt die weisse Nacht gezogen,

Verwandelt in purpurne Träume Schmerz und Plage
Des steinigen Lebens,
Dass nimmer der dornige Stachel ablasse vom verwesenden Leib.[80]

The ultimate sense of embracing the religious suffering, however, is that this mode of cognition makes way for the realization of love:

O Liebe, es rührt
Ein blauer Dornenbusch
Die kalte Schläfe,
Mit fallenden Sternen
Schneeige Nacht.[81]

Trakl's poetry may, then, be considered a "religious address" in Kierkegaard's sense of an utterance that has essentially the task of uplifting through suffering. "The religious man believes that it is precisely in suffering that life is to be found."[82] We recall in this connection Trakl's short aphorism: "Nur dem, der das Glück verachtet, wird Erkenntnis."[83]

For Trakl, suffering is not primarily the measure of the fallen creature's distance from the Creator. The logic of Trakl's immersion in suffering is to be found in his fidelity to the Christ-form's structure of atonement. Von Balthasar observes that "the aesthetics of faith is inextricably attached to the mystery of suffering. This is the bridal mystery between Christ and the Church, a mystery exacted by the incessant contemplation of the 'head full of blood and wounds' *(das Haupt voll Blut und Wunden)*, which is the act of existential unification of the bride with Christ."[84] The mystery of suffering as an aesthetic principle: Should we not seek a verification of the Bride's commiseration with the Bridegroom and her participation in his suffering (participation as con-formation) in the repeated instances Trakl's poetry presents the gesture of attendance upon the dead Bridegroom? Occasionally, the commiserating figure is explicitly called "bride":

Es hat mit Sternen sich die Braut geziert,
Die reine Myrthe
Die sich über des Toten anbetendes Antlitz neigt.[85]

Or love is personified in this same role:

Seine Wunden voller Gnaden
Pflegt der Liebe sanfte Kraft.[86]

Or we contemplate the hieratically enshrined face of the dead Savior:

> Blaue Blümchen umschweben das Antlitz
> Des Einsamen.[87]

Often these same poems contain the ecclesiological motif called *Bräutlichkeit* by von Balthasar, under the form of the Bride's enfolding receptiveness for the suffering Bridegroom:

> Blühender Schauer voll
> Umfängt dich endlich der blaue Mantel der Herrin.[88]
>
> Strahlender Arme Erbarmen
> Umfängt ein brechendes Herz.[89]
>
> Dein blauer Mantel umfing den Sinkenden;
> Dein roter Mund besiegelte des Freundes Umnachtung.[90]

In *Klagelied* the bridal kiss, full of ecclesiological significance, is borrowed explicitly from the Canticle of Canticles. The union of Bride and Bridegroom in this poem occurs within the medium of the latter's suffering:

> Goldener Mund, der meine Lippen rührt,
> Und sie erklingen wie die Sterne
> Über dem Bache Kidron . . .
> O! meine Freundin deine Lippen
> Granatapfellippen
> Reifen an meinem kristallenen Muschelmund.[91]

In an amazingly concise way Trakl effects in these lines nothing less than the union of Old and New Testaments, the marriage of Christ and Israel.

Perseverance in the religious suffering has its sense only as the imitation of Christ's deed of atonement, repeated by Trakl in the images of his poetry. To this mystery may be traced the feminine aspects of his art: the silences and the patience, the attitude of listening as *Grundton,* and the sensitivity to the most tenuous spiritual tremor.

> **Ich schütte meine Klage vor ihm aus
> und zeige an vor ihm meine Not.
> Wenn mein Geist in Ängsten ist,
> so nimmst du dich meiner an.
> Ps. 142:3–4**

Trakl's poetry of suffering, says Klein, breaks through the wall that has long separated us from the world of spirit.[92] His concentration on suffering has an interior religious sense; its objective is to move us from one metaphysical location to another: from the state of moral stagnation to the sphere of pure and free relation. For Trakl, suffering is the bridge that unites the individual with God; therefore his lyrical lament conceals, as its last secret, a song of praise.

The reasons usually given for throwing Trakl's identity as a Christian in doubt often coincide with the mob's taunt to the crucified Jesus: "Now the passers-by were jeering at him, shaking their heads, and saying: 'If you are the Son of God, come down from the cross! . . . He trusted in God; let him deliver him now, if he wants him'" (Matt. 27:39–43). Johannes Klein, for instance, judges that "to be a Christian actually means to believe in the redemption and to have knowledge of grace. Trakl, too, evokes the image of the redeemer on Golgotha, but the redemption itself, the condition of being redeemed, is missing."[93] This definition of being a Christian is wholly intellectualistic and dogmatic—a belief and a knowing in the Gnostic style—rather than existential and ontological. It borders on the concept of Christianity as an ideology, which Rahner discards. Trakl is judged to offer an "incomplete" picture of Christianity. But, on the other hand, Christians who are too emphatic and univocal in their affirmation of the reality of redemption are accused by the same type of humanistic critic of displaying an arrogant triumphalism that ignores the existential anguish of modern man in his experience of godforsakenness. The solution to this impasse would seem to lie in a closer examination of the structure of the Christ-form of revelation itself.

Jesus nowhere offers salvation to those who would conceptually affirm faith in and knowledge of his saving deed. Rather, he invites those who would follow him simply to drink of the cup the Father has given him. And St. Paul speaks of the necessity of dying with Christ, a death that is permanent in this world: "You have died and your life is hidden with Christ in God." It is a serious misunderstanding to think of Passion and Resurrection as episodes that must automatically follow one another in succession. The Father's glorification of the Son occurs simultaneously with the latter's death on the cross, and does not take place "magically" as some sort of miraculous overcoming of death, but as the result of the divine and human identity of the one who died and of the inner logic of his death, which is obedience, out of love, to the will of the Father.[94] The Resurrection is real, but apparent only to the eyes of faith; it is not to be (ab)used as a self-evident, quasi-empirical truth. This is why no one recognized Jesus spontaneously when he first encountered his friends after he had risen from the dead.

We cannot expect Trakl, or anyone else for that matter, to achieve the kind of perfect fullness of form that we see in the scriptural presentation of the Passion and Resurrection narrative. Precisely for this reason we say that Scripture is "inspired," which I here interpret as meaning "unsubstitutable": only it has achieved a perfect balance between the elements of destruction and those of regeneration. But Trakl, in his limited way, understood well the sense of Christ's lament as he expired: "Eli, Eli, lama sabachthani?" (Matt. 27:46), and he structured the whole of his poetry around this critical experience of God's abandonment, the intensity and awesomeness of which powerfully convey the creature's awareness of its need for deliverance. We can therefore say of Trakl what von Balthasar says of Claudel: that his work expresses primarily the "basic experience of creatureliness: existence as the experience of not-being-God, as the vibration of relationship; the experience of 'being-with' through that of 'being-exposed'; the knowledge of the First Cause through the experience of the boundaries."[95]

In this connection, we can understand the christological import of Trakl's definition of man as essential lament:

> Wer sind wir? Blaue Klage
> Eines moosigen Waldquells,
> Wo die Veilchen
> Heimlich im Frühling duften.[96]

The secret wafting of the violets in the spring adds to the blue lament of the forest-spring a dimension that is analogous to the inner identity of Trakl's lament as being praise:

> O des Knaben Gestalt
> Geformt aus kristallenen Tränen,
> Nächtigen Schatten.[97]

The form and proportion assumed by the youth's crystal tears completes our impression that Trakl's lament is not merely a desperate shout in the void. In his epitaph for Novalis, Trakl reveals the nature of his lament as being the drawing of the boundary between man and God:

> Es nahm von sanftem Munde ihm die Klage der Gott,
> Da er in seiner Blüte hinsank.[98]

Not only is there receptiveness, but God is also presented as taking the lament from the poet's mouth, an action that finally shows God as himself the initiator of elegiac song.

Trakl's lyrical lament not only bemoans the decayed state of man in the world; in its positive aspect it is a measure of the distance between man and God and an affirmation of the fact that to live without idols means to wait for the event of redemption. "The paradox of Christian eschatology," says von Balthasar, "makes it clear enough that an existence totally lived in a faith oriented toward Christ must wait out the Christ-event in the 'vestibule of Hell' *(Vor-Hölle),* until it can achieve its own inner fulfillment."[99]

But to speak of "distance" between God and man has only a metaphysical sense, since God's "absence" is a spatial term that can only mean the emphatic difference between God and man. For this reason, critics obscure Trakl's real theological acumen when they say that God's silence in the poetry proves the extent to which Trakl can relate to God only negatively.[100] Trakl inserts himself in the apophatic tradition of a work such as *The Cloud of Unknowing,* in which the intensest sense of God's "absence" is paradoxically the warrant for the intimate presence of the living God. The deep silence surrounding this awareness testifies to the fact that this is the real God and no idol. Trakl can, therefore, give God's silence a nourishing function, which is structurally one with the sweat of the Passion flowing from Elis's brow:

> Gottes Schweigen
> Trank ich aus dem Brunnen des Hains.[101]
>
> Blaue Tauben
> Trinken nachts den eisigen Schweiss,
> Der von Elis' kristallener Stirne rinnt.[102]

A crass materialism and a singular lack of theological imagination characterize the opinion of critics who see in God's silence and Trakl's consequent lament evidence of his atheism. I say "materialism" with something specific in mind: these critics expect the poet to give evidence of his faith by a blatantly objectified fixation of the God-image. Karl Rahner counters such demands theologically, by reminding us that God is not a reality among others, but that He is always present as the "transcendental horizon or 'space' within which a determined object is encountered." God, in other words, is not "an 'object' represented by one idea within this horizon."[103] For Trakl's poetry, this means that the silence of God, the refusal to put words into God's mouth, is the very ground that makes possible the apprehension of other realities, such as guilt, evil, and atonement:

> So leise erlöscht ein Unkrautbrand, verstummt
>   der schwarze Weiler im Grund
> Als stiege das Kreuz den blauen Kalvarienhügel herab,
> Würfe die schweigende Erde ihre Toten aus.[104]

Here the extinction of human and natural noises is like the taking of a great breath. The stillness that ensues sets the stage for the descent of the

Cross from Calvary and the earth's violent action of spewing forth her dead. The whole effect rests on the contrast between *schweigend* and *auswerfen*—the auditive void is filled with the praeternatural event. We note that the particular manner of God's action is here a figural representation that superimposes the two *kairoi* of an Austrain hamlet and that of Christ's death on Calvary, which immediately caused the resurrection of a number of the blessed: "Aber Jesus schrie abermals laut und verschied. . . . Und die Erde erbebte, und die Felsen zerrissen, und die Gräber taten sich auf, und standen auf viele Leiber der Heiligen, die da schliefen" (Matt. 27:50,52).

The silence of God assumes sensual form as the lament of man. But for Trakl, this interpenetration of silence and lament comes to rest on the Christ-form that his poetry realizes. Not only is his poetry an absolute statement of the divine/human disparity; not only does his elegiac tone "recognize the precariousness of objects, and thus capture them in their immediacy;"[105] there is much more. Trakl's lament, which populates the silence of God, is to be regarded as the most fitting expression for the atoning function of his poetry as religious act. Trakl's lament directly imitates the silence of the New Testament in the face of the reality of Christ's presence. "The Scriptures, being an eschatological statement and the last word of history," writes van Esbroeck, "proclaim a God whose imminent Word calls out only in silence, since this Word has already depleted itself in the Gospel that is Jesus Christ. As God's definitive Word, Jesus is, until the end of the world, the God who speaks by his silence."[106] In an unexpected manner, we here encounter a confirmation of what I have been saying from the beginning concerning the primacy of form in Trakl's poetry: God does not keep silence in Trakl because he is absent but, as in the New Testament, because he must. "And behold, a Canaanite woman from that region came out and cried, 'Have mercy on me, O Lord, Son of David; my daughter is severely possessed by a demon.' But he did not answer her a word" (Matt. 15:22–23). God's words in the Old Testament had been an imperfect means of communication, because they concealed as much as they revealed, and, therefore, they were a (necessary) obstacle between man and God. With the presence of Christ as perfect Word of God, all other language becomes superfluous. In like manner, the total absorption of statement into form, of abstract discourse into ontological existence, in Trakl's poetry imitates the manner in which God becomes incarnate in human history: as total presence, total act, total existence, the object of which is the reconciliation of man with God through participation in the reality of Christ. Total form, being the symbolic counterpart of pure presence, realizes in the mode of language what Christ's incarnation realizes in the mode of existence.

We can now see in what way an extremity of lament coincides with pure praise. Essential lament is a manifestation of a faith that refuses to transcend the realities that inform it by becoming a secure knowledge of objects. "La foi," says Gabriel Marcel,

> n'est pas l'approximation imparfaite de quelque chose qui pourrait être un savoir; mais elle fait corps avec les réalités auxquelles elle se suspend; on la mutile, c'est trop peu dire: on la nie dans son essence même en prétendant la scinder de ces réalités elles-mêmes.[107]

Faith is the "vibration of relation" (von Balthasar's *Schwingung des Bezuges*), and refuses to collapse into a monistic serenity that offers a sham sort of security:

> Leise verliess am Kreuzweg
> Der Schatten den Fremdling
> Und steinern erblinden
> Dem die schauenden Augen,
> Dass von der Lippe
> Süsser fliesse das Lied.[108]

The forsakenness at the cross-roads and the blinding of the eyes stand in functional relationship to the song, which can therefore flow "more sweetly" from the lips. The vision of the eye, that can still objectify a reality and thus keep it at a distance, yields to the sweeter song of the lips as the result of being forsaken by all images: the confession of a relation that is all the more real as it is totally interiorized. Trakl's lament,

> Frost und Rauch. Ein weisses Sternenhemd verbrennt
> die tragenden Schultern und Gottes Geier zerfleischen
> dein metallenes Herz,[109]

completely merges at this point with the most absolute hymn of praise pronounced by Jesus as a man: "Eli, Eli, lama sabachthani?" (Matt. 27:46). The confession of God's reality becomes all the more precious as it is uttered in total dejection and forsakenness. This is the stillpoint of atonement, as it were, where all images have sunk into overpowering darkness and the believer experiences the terrors of continuing to exist in a relationship he no longer enjoys because there is nothing there to be enjoyed. The delight in images of Evil must be expiated by a denial even of the images of the Good. A new manner of enjoyment and perception must be acquired, or else the very images of the Good will soon be turned to idols. Guilt has been objectified and left behind; union can not yet take place:

> Stunde unendlicher Schwermut,
> Als erlitt' ich den Tod um dich . . .
> Als wohnt' ich ein sanftes Wild

In der kristallenen Woge
Des kühlen Quells
Und es blühten die Veilchen rings.[110]

This, too, is the point where Trakl's poetry achieves its greatest tension by involving the reader in the indeterminateness of salvation that it presents.[111] Salvation can be no ready-make assurance that reduces the suffering of Calvary to an *ad interim* make-believe. Salvation lies beyond Calvary, at the other side of Hell, and this not as a cliché, but as the necessary order of things. Thomas Mann writes of the *Wehklage* of Adrian Leverkühn in a way that describes Trakl's poetry precisely:

Wie, wenn der künstlerischen Paradoxie, dass aus der totalen Konstruktion sich der Ausdruck—der Ausdruck als Klage—gebiert, das religiöse Paradoxon entspräche, dass aus tiefster Heillosigkeit, wenn auch als leiseste Frage nur, die Hoffnung keimte? Es wäre die Hoffnung, jenseits der Hoffnungslosigkeit, die Transzendenz der Verzweiflung,—nicht der Verrat an ihr, sondern das Wunder, das über den Glauben geht.

And then, as if commenting on the conclusion of the Alban Berg Violin Concerto, which I have compared to the typical conclusion of a Trakl poem, Mann goes on:

Hört nur den Schluss, hört ihn mit mir: Eine Instrumentengruppe nach der anderen tritt zurück, und was übrig bleibt, womit das Werk verklingt, ist das hohe g eines Cello, das letzte Wort, der letzte schwenkende Laut, in pianissimo-Fermate langsam vergehend. Dann ist nichts mehr,—Schweigen und Nacht. Aber der nachschwingend im Schweigen hängende Ton, der nicht mehr ist, dem nur die Seele noch nachlauscht, und der Ausklang der Trauer war, ist es nicht mehr, wandelt den Sinn, steht als ein Licht in der Nacht.[112]

This marvelous description applies quite exactly, for instance, to the poem *De Profundis*. After presenting a panorama of desolation and decay, the poem experiences a turn when the persona is nourished by God's silence instead of being crushed by it, as we have seen. Then the conclusion:

Auf meine Stirne tritt kaltes Metall.
Spinnen suchen mein Herz.
Es ist ein Licht, das in meinem Munde erlöscht.

Nachts fand ich mich auf einer Heide,
Starrend von Unrat und Staub der Sterne.
Im Haselgebüsch
Klangen wieder kristallne Engel.[113]

The extinguishing of the light in his mouth immediately leads to the resounding of crystal angels. The sense of sight again yields to total sound; as the private light is swallowed up, a resonant glow emerges. And on that note the poem concludes physically in order to prolong the epiphany into infinity.

The aesthetic and religious paradoxes have coincided, as Thomas Mann conjectured. Just as ordered chaos is no longer chaos, so too an *avowed* extremity of hopelessness is the beginning of hope. For this reason, if we imagine situating Trakl's poetry on the continuum of the liturgical year, we would come to call it a *Karfreitagsdichtung*, a poetry that chooses its stance at the heart of Christ's Passion. Trakl's poetry is literally faithful to the essence of Good Friday, the German word for which *(Karfreitag)* has as root the prefix *Kar-*, deriving from the Old High German *chara*, meaning "mournful lamentation." Good Friday is, then, by definition, the "Day of Lamentation." The word ultimately derives, along with the English *care*, from the Indo-European root *gar-*, connoting "to call or cry out."[114]

Josef Weinheber has remarked that Trakl "in a certain sense begins where Hölderlin concludes. Trakl has the courage to let himself fall, to fall from the outset. He is a pure instrument of God, while Hölderlin still summons up the will to save himself from his fate."[115] By "letting himself fall from the outset," Trakl imitates the Christ of the Passion, for whom to glorify his Father was identical with being forsaken by his Father. For Trakl, utter exposure changes, according to a logic Rilke called the "law of reversals,"[116] into complete security. Utter lament is transformed from within into perfect praise. The creative power of the poet assumes the form of a love that, in imitation of Christ's deed, gives shape and transforms by reconciling apparently incompatible states: death and life, decay and incorruptibility, time and eternity.[117] Trakl's poetry lives from the mystery of Good Friday. Death and Descent into Hell are revealed as the formal conditions required for the accomplishment of the act of love through which Christ and his followers can attain to a definitive victory.[118]

In the image of the Christ of the Passion, the image of man finds a genuine way out of the dead end imposed by decay and death. Death and suffering are not made into illusions, but their confrontation with indestructible love, meeting them as it does on their own terms, raises them to a pitch of reality that at last reveals them in their temporality and limitation:

> Wo an Mauern die Schatten der Ahnen stehn,
> Vordem ein einsamer Baum war, ein blaues Wild im Busch,
> Steigt der weisse Mensch auf goldenen Stiegen,
> Helian ins seufzende Dunkel hinab.[119]

Where there had been only the void of dead ancestors, the isolation of a
forlorn tree, a hidden deer in the woods: *there* takes place the great condescension *(steigt hinab)* of the healing Savior *(Helian = Heiland,* from
heilen: "to make whole") who, descending to the sighing abyss ($\overset{\text{Ω}}{} τῆς$
συγκαταβάσεως![120]), transforms it by the radiance of his presence. The
form that Trakl's poetry imposes on the natural events of death and
decay makes of it a poetry steeped in the Christian mystery, which
reveals newness of life in death. "Only Christianity has converted death
itself into salvation," insists Gerhard van der Leeuw. "All savior-religions
preach life out of death. The Gospel of the Cross proclaims salvation in
death. The uttermost powerlessness here becomes the highest blossoming of power, and the most radical ruination becomes salvation."[121]
Trakl's *Karfreitagsdichtung* realizes, incarnates the structure of this mystery, which says that indestructible life is not a dialectical construction
alternative to death, but a triumph of love from the heart of the forces of
corruption:

> Im Frühling; ein zarter Leichnam
> Erstrahlend in seinem Grab
> Unter den wilden
> Hollunderbüschen der Kindheit.[122]

The identity of Cross and Resurrection, love and glorification, in the
figure of the forsaken God enables us to decipher the self-contradicting
hieroglyph that is man when taken by himself. Trakl writes his poetry
and lives his life from the center of this event where death is transmuted
into life. Only such a location makes it possible for him to place these two
strophes alongside each other:

> Wie scheint doch alles Werdende so krank!
> Ein Fieberhauch um einen Weiler kreist;
> Doch aus Gezweigen wirkt ein sanfter Geist
> Und öffnet das Gemüte weit und bang.
>
> So schmerzlich gut und wahrhaft ist, was lebt;
> Und leise rührt dich an ein alter Stein:
> Wahrlich! Ich werde immer bei euch sein.
> O Mund! der durch die Silberweide bebt.[123]

The vision that can see truth and goodness in the decay of all living
things is founded figurally upon the promise cited in the seventh line,
which is a rephrasing of the last verse of Matthew's Gospel: "Und siehe,
ich bin bei euch alle Tage bis an der Welt Ende" (28:20). This promise,
sealed by Christ's archetypal submission in his person to the forces of
destruction, transfigures decay in a way that reveals its sinking into the
void as a precipitation toward resurrection.

Reconciliation in Silence: **Ein Teppich**

> **Aus schwarzem Verfall**
> **Treten Gottes strahlende Engel.**[124]

The whole sense of the two stages of guilt's recognition and of its expiation lies in their movement toward the reconciliation of the individual with God through crossing the bridge constructed by Christ's act of atonement. This is the ultimate goal of religion: the binding together of what has fallen asunder.

But a Christian understanding of reconciliation cannot rest upon a merely dialectical conception that would make of it the necessary third movement, concluding the clash of guilt and its undoing in expiation. For this reason, the metaphor of the bridge built by Christ's Passion is adequate: one cannot build a bridge and at the same time walk on it; the bridge of salvation must come from the other bank. The individual's participation in the act of atonement occurs always in response to Christ's unique action and as a particular realization of it.

We have seen repeatedly that realization is part of the figural scheme that underlies the Judeo-Christian understanding of salvation-history. In seeking to specify the manner in which the concluding movement of atonement occurs in Trakl's poetry, we must identify an abstract pattern that will show clearly, on the one hand, the coincidence of the process of postfigural realization peculiar to the Christian tradition with, on the other, the most salient structural procedure in Trakl's poetry. I believe that such a pattern is the Kierkegaardian category of *repetition*.

> **Forsoningen, hvilket er**
> **Gjentagelsens dybeste Udtryk.**[125]

Most critics are unanimous in the opinion that repetition is one of the determinant features of Trakl's poetry. Another word for repetition is monotony, the effect caused by the constant return of the same images and phrases. Walter Muschg speaks of the "amazing monotony of his lyricism," which he says is not an artistic mannerism, but the immediate expression of his destiny.[126] Eduard Lachmann compares the unremitting return of the same words and series of words to the rings in the trunk of a tree.[127] Rudolf Schier says that "we can readily affirm that this repetitiousness in sound and rhythm is one of the very essential elements of Trakl's poetry." And he adds: "The varied repetitions which we encounter throughout Trakl's work are all to be understood as an expression of the figural conception of the world, a conception which is founded upon the recognition of repetition."[128] We may further conclude on the religious nature of Trakl's use of repetition as structural principle when we remember Adolf Stöhr's criticism of Ferdinand Ebner's *Das Wort und die geistigen Realitäten,* a work very close in spirit to Trakl's poetry and world view: "It is a considerable torture to have to make one's way through 300 pages with nothing but the eternal repetition of one simple thought, and besides to have the feeling of always turning around the same point."[129] A remark intended as disparaging by Stöhr calls our attention to the solidity of Trakl's and Ebner's work, the fact that they forsook all else in order to dwell on the "one thing necessary" (Luke 10:42). Repetition as poetic principle reminds us too, of course, of at least two other great religious poets of our century, whose company Trakl here joins: the Péguy of a poem such as *Eve* and the Eliot of the *Four Quartets.*

Rilke's penetrating remarks concerning *Helian,* further, which exhibit his intuitive genius, recall the parable of the man who, having found a treasure of great price, went and sold all else in order to buy the whole field (cf. Matt. 13:44):

> Ganz ergreifend ward es mir durch seine inneren Abstände, er ist gleichsam auf seine Pausen gebaut, ein paar Einfriedigungen um das grenzenlos Wortlose: so stehen die Zeilen da. Wie Zäune in einem flachen Land, über die hin das Eingezäunte fortwährend zu einer unbesitzbaren grossen Ebene zusammenschlägt.[130]

The metaphor conveys with Rilke's usual mastery the tension between the reality of the unseen treasure hidden in the field, "which a man found and covered up," and the reality of the poem, which encloses the field like a fence. The poem does not call attention primarily to itself, Rilke tells us, but to the mystery that it seeks to realize. For this reason, the typical Trakl poem looks neither to the past nor to the future, but gyrates around a hidden center. The words of the poem relate to the reality that thus becomes present as does the Baptist to Jesus: "He must increase, but I must decrease" (John 3:30). The monotony of Trakl's poetry may thus be ascribed to its transitive character, that is, to the fact that it nowhere seeks to make an absolute pronouncement but rather makes possible the occurrence of an event that it does not itself manufacture.

The monotony of Trakl's world picture derives from the sublime monotony of the Christian view of salvation-history upon which it is based, the elements of which are sin, grace, and redemption. Elisabeth Langgässer compares the simplicity of the Christian mystery to the monotony (i.e., "one-tone-ness") of a fugue, which is "the monotony of eternity itself and, therefore, the opposite of metaphysical boredom."[131] Repetition is a way of witnessing to the finality of the Christ-event, just as the luminous sameness of God's silence is a necessity enjoined by the fact that God has "talked himself out" in the revelation that is Jesus Christ.[132] Repetition supplants, in the Christian tradition, the key position held by recollection or remembering in Greek philosophy. Kierkegaard says that "repetition and recollection are the same movement, only in opposite directions; for what is recollected has been, is repeated backwards, whereas repetition properly so called recollects forward."[133]

This abstract definition of repetition is shown by Dorothee Sölle in its christological application. For her, the repetition by the individual of the mystery of the Christ-event is, simply, to be equated with the exercise of discipleship. Neutral *Wieder-holung* ("taking up again," i.e. repetition) is specified by her as the likewise spatial but existentially pregnant category of *Nach-folge* ("following after," i.e. discipleship). "Repetition suspends passive remembering and is the only adequate relationship to the Cross."[134] The specifically Christian character of repetition derives from the claim the Gospel makes upon the individual to reform his life in its light, a claim so essentially a part of the Gospel's structure that the Scripture may be considered a perpetually unended story that awaits its conclusion at the end of time. Elisabeth Langgässer says of the characters of the modern Christian novel something that apply perhaps even more directly to the personae of Trakl's poetry: "They are not really plastic and corporeal, individual and non-interchangeable. They are in existence and possess a figure only insofar as they coincide with the archetype on which they have been modelled. . . . The approximation of the type to its archetype brings about the extinction of all traits that are without meaning for the event of the mystical coming into oneness."[135] The abstractionism of Trakl's forms here merges with the repetitive pattern of his periods. They both serve the purpose of making the poem an epiphanic medium that may realize the event of the Christ-form, exclusive center of the poetry.

The mystery of the death and resurrection of Christ is not, according to Durrwell, "prised out of the past in order to be translated into the present": this would be the Greek mode of recollection. Christ's action, "performed once in the past, remains fixed in an everlasting actuality in the Christ of glory."[136] The believer achieves contemporaneity with the Christ-event by appropriating the grammar of its structure, its rhythms, its forms; in other words, by repeating it symbolically and thus realizing it in his own life. Repetition, in this light, is seen as a transcendental category that describes abstractly the specific application of the Redemption. It is the particular form in which the individual exercises his freedom in choosing his metaphysical position with regard to Christ's deed. But the choice to understand one's existence in the light of the Christ-event means the substantial con-formity of the individual with the archetype that is Christ: "Christ suffered for you, leaving you an example [ὑπογραμμόν = "rough draft," "writing-pattern," "model"], that you should follow in his steps" (1 Peter 2:21). The believer's existence, therefore, *repeats* the ever-present reality of the mystery of the Christ-form: "If we have been planted and have grown together (σύμφυτοι) into the likeness of his death, this has been only in order to grow together into the likeness of his resurrection," (Rom. 6:5). The necessity of repetition emphasizes Christ's uniqueness as model for the believer. The believer realizes in his person the claim of the Christ-form by disposing his life in such a way that it is decipherable only in comparison with the Christ-Archetype. Repetition of the Christ-form in the personal sphere revitalizes the figure of Christ in Scripture by removing it from a mythological distance whose static character would make of it something closed both historically and aesthetically. The Christ-form by its very nature calls for realization, that is, for existence within the sphere of the individual's subjectivity. The authentic Christ-form exists for man only under the modality of its repetition. Repetition is the manner in which, as Berdyaev says, "the mystery of Christ is transferred from its material fixation to the inner man: Christ becomes immanent in man and man takes upon himself the whole burden of measureless freedom. Christ ceases to be only one in an objective series, among others."[137]

Kierkegaard describes a moment at which the illusory freedom of the aesthete despairs of itself and is transformed. "In the moment of despair," he says, "there occurs an exchange with repetition, and freedom gives itself a religious expression whereby repetition emerges as atonement, which is repetition *sensu eminentiori*."[138] The crisis of private freedom raises the will to the absolute freedom of choosing to do as Christ did. Genuine religious freedom is seen to lie only in the repetition of Christ's atoning deed. At this point, the aesthetic form of Trakl's poetry becomes the direct expression of its religious dimension. The repetition of this particular form, the Christ-form, "is not merely for contemplation, but is the task of freedom."[139] Repetition is a contemplative work only in the dynamic way of the torso of Apollo in Rilke's famous poem, which brings its beholder to the conclusion: "Du musst dein Leben ändern."[140]

By way of illustrating the actual use Trakl makes of the Kierkegaardian category of repetition, we turn to a late untitled poem:

>   Ein Teppich, darein die leidende Landschaft verblasst
>   Vielleicht Genezareth, im Sturm ein Nachen
> (I)   Aus Wetterwolken stürzen goldene Sachen
>   Der Wahnsinn, der den sanften Menschen fasst.
> 5   Die alten Wasser gurgeln ein blaues Lachen.
>
>   Und manchmal öffnet sich ein dunkler Schacht.
>   Besessene spiegeln sich in kalten Metallen
> (II)   Tropfen Blutes auf glühende Platten fallen
>   Und ein Antlitz zerfällt in schwarzer Nacht.
> 10   Fahnen, die in finstern Gewölben lallen.
>
>   Andres erinnert an der Vögel Flug
> (III)   Über dem Galgen der Krähen mystische Zeichen
>   In spitzen Gräsern versinken kupferne Schleichen
>   In Weihrauchkissen ein Lächeln verhurt und klug.
>
> 15   Charfreitagskinder blind an Zäunen stehen
>   Im Spiegel dunkler Gossen voll Verwesung
> (IV)   Der Sterbenden hinseufzende Genesung
>   Und Engel die durch weisse Augen gehen
>   Von Lidern düstert goldene Erlösung.[141]

The difficulties of the poem derive from the fact that it is a true repetition of salvation-history in the subjective sphere, and not merely a retelling of a story already well-known. The word *Genezareth* in the second line offers the clue to the meaning of the whole poem. But there is no sequential faithfulness here to the actual order of events in the Gospel. The repetition of them shows the kerygmatic meaning of the events in a nonhistorical perpsective.

We move into the poem by the contemplation of a faded tapestry representing something like a boat in a storm. Trakl shows his immersion in the figural imagination by suggesting at once that it is the storm on the Lake of Genezareth that Jesus calmed. By turning to the text of Mark's Gospel describing this episode, we encounter a series of pericopes following the actual story of the storm, fragments of which reappear in Trakl's poem in transformed ways. But our poem presents them in an atemporal interpretation which, in its formal expression, intermingles details from the various events and thus shows them in a subjective contemporaneity with the believer. We are dealing here with a section of the Gospel of Mark that runs from 4:35 to 6:29. While reference to this passage does not resolve every difficulty of the poem, there is nevertheless good reason to believe that this text provided the original stimulus for the poem, which appropriates it subjectively by repeating it. This manner of appropriation itself is what concerns us, rather than any sterile "uncovering of sources."

The appropriation begins at once in Trakl's interpretation of the tapestry he contemplates: he calls it a "suffering landscape," which resumes from the beginning the events of the poem: the fear in the storm (I), the madness of the possessed and the martyrdom of John the Baptist (II), the death on Calvary (III), and the blindness of the lamenting Children of the Passion (IV).

Trakl repeats the scene in such a way that he interprets, and thereby realizes, its meaning. He does not attempt a realistic portrayal of Jesus calming the storm. Rather, he states in the present tense: "From storm-clouds there tumble golden things," which things are specified at the conclusion as being golden redemption (or deliverance). This irruption of light brackets the fear of the disciples, who see themselves swallowed up in the storm: "Was seid ihr so furchtsam? Wie habt ihr denn keinen Glauben?" (4:40). The fear for themselves becomes a wonderment as to Jesus' identity: "Wer ist der? Selbst Wind und Meer sind ihm gehorsam" (4:42). Lines 3 and 4,

> Aus Wetterwolken stürzen goldene Sachen
> Der Wahnsinn, der den sanften Menschen fasst,

may be considered the figural parallel of,

> Und es erhob sich ein grosser Windwirbel . . .
> Und er bedrohte den Wind und sprach zu dem Meer:
> Schweig und verstumme! . . .
> Und sie fürchteten sich sehr.

(37, 39, 41)

The storm is the occasion for Jesus to manifest his identity as savior; and therefore the instrumentality of the storm as epiphany of Jesus' inner identity is evoked by Trakl when he calls the illumination issuing from it "golden things."

The third line of strophe I introduces in reverse form the episode that follows in Mark: the healing of the possessed Gerasene. "The old waters gurgle a blue laugh" is an anticipation of the drowning of the pigs into which the devils have entered: "Und die Herde stürzte den Abhang hinunter ins Meer . . . , und sie ersoffen" (5:13). The juxtaposition by Trakl of the possible drowning of the disciples in the storm and the actual drowning of the possessed pigs reveals the authority of Jesus over the forces of destruction in either case, a correct exegesis of the biblical passages in question. Jesus dispels the fear of the disciples by calming the storm and, in healing the possessed man, shows his power over evil. These specific instances of deliverance provide the events that lead up to the more abstract conclusion of the poem: "Golden redemption."

The episode of the possessed Gerasene is continued in strophe II, where the *Grabhöhlen* of the German Bible (5:3), which were the demoniac's dwelling in Mark, have become a mine-shaft *(ein dunkler Schacht)*.

The particular form of demonic possession portrayed here seems to be all-consuming greed, since the laughing of the drowning demons, in connection with the mine, suggests *das grässliche Lachen des Golds,* which we saw in *An die Verstummten,* and further anticipates the lascivious laughter of line 14. The manner in which the possessed reflect themselves in the mine's "cold metals" (i.e., the imprisoning gold) also anticipates the reflection in strophe IV of the "convalescence of the dying" on the "mirror of dark gutters full of decay." *Dunkle Gossen* closely parallels *dunkler Schacht.* This return to health of the dying, moreover, is a figural dramatization of the healing of Jairus's daughter by Jesus, which immediately follows the healing of the possessed man: "Meine Tochter liegt in den letzten Zügen; du wollest kommen und deine Hände auf sie legen, dass sie gesund werde und lebe" (5 : 23).

The child appears in line 15 in stylized form, as a plural: "the Children of the Passion stand blind at the fences." Their blindness makes it impossible for them to see themselves as the possessed had seen themselves. Only their "sighing in death" can reflect itself transitively as a plea for healing by the anonymous protagonist from whose "eyelids redemption shimmers." Trakl was apparently aware of the fitness of calling "Good Friday's children" those who in their blindness can only sigh. Especially by spelling *Karfreitag* in the archaic manner *Charfreitag,* he is emphasizing the literal root meaning of the Old German word *chara,* which as we have seen means "woeful lament" or "dirge."

The third strophe refers again to the tapestry of the beginning and to other features in it that remind Trakl *(andres erinnert)* of the mystical meaning of the flight of crows over the gallows, which in this context may be considered the gibbet of the Cross. In fact, in an earlier draft of the poem Trakl had here written *Kreuz* before he finally decided on *Galgen.*[142] The words *Vögel* and *Galgen,* in close proximity, make inevitable their association in *Galgenvögel,* "jail-birds." This fusion crystallizes two other lines of the poem, namely,

> Tropfen Blutes auf glühende Platten fallen,

and

> In Weihrauchkissen ein Lächeln verhurt und klug.

The connection of blood upon a platter with the beheading of John the Baptist is reinforced by the fact that the narration of this event follows, in Mark's Gospel, shortly after the healing of Jairus's daughter. We read there how the daughter of Herodias persuaded Herod with her dancing to offer her the Baptist's head on a platter. "Und alsbald schickte der König den Henker hin und hiess sein Haupt herbringen. Der ging hin und enthauptete ihn im Gefängnis" (6:27). John and Jesus shared their identity as prisoners *(Galgenvögel)* of Herod, and therefore the death of the first is associated in the poem to that of the second. The crows' "mystical signs" indicate the concealed meaning of the storm on Genezareth and the death of the gibbet of the Cross, a meaning that the last line of the poem names *goldene Erlösung*. Thus the event that revealed Jesus' power over the forces of destruction is closely associated with the kenotic event of his death, which showed the coincidence of his power with his helplessness. The line

> In Weihrauchkissen ein Lächeln verhurt und klug

conjures up the decadent self-assurance of Herodias against John the Baptist at Herod's banquet. The word *Weihrauchkissen* ("cushions of incense") in particular, which Trakl had originally qualified with the adjective *seiden* ("silken"),[143] has an immediate Oriental effect of rich sensuality and compresses the scriptural verse: "Und es kam ein gelegener Tag, da Herodes an seinem Geburtstag ein Mahl gab seinen Grossen und den Obersten und den Vornehmsten in Galiläa" (6:21). John and Jesus, by their condition as "jail-birds," sharply contrast with the splendor of the mighty portrayed here. And the words *verhurt und klug* succinctly summarize Herodias's concubinage with Herod and her careful insidiousness against the Baptist: "Denn Johannes hatte zu Herodes gesagt: Es ist nicht recht, dass du deines Bruders Frau hast. Herodias aber stellte ihm nach und wollte ihn töten und konnte nicht" (6:18–19).

The poem began as a portrayal of a "suffering landscape." It concludes with the presence of angels that walk through blind eyes and cause redemption to appear. The inner logic of this transition is provided by the intervening repetition of salvation-history in the course of the poem. The highly symbolic, often wholly anonymous nature of the language witnesses to the depths at which the redemption has been appropriated. Trakl's understanding of the inner structure of atonement is further reflected by the manner in which he freely abstracts and stylizes the Gospel story so as to reveal its kerygmatic objectives. Trakl brings the scriptural narration forward, so to speak, making it congruous with his own space and time. In this manner he fulfills Kierkegaard's definition of repetition as a "remembering forward" that models the life-structure of the repeater upon the ineradicable presence of God in human form. Repetition is a movement of immanence that relates to the Incarnation on its own terms: "The Deity's presence in time . . . prevents the individual from relating himself backwards to the eternal, since now he comes forward into being in order to become eternal by relationship to the Deity in time."[144]

Trakl's manner of repeating the events of salvation-history so as to realize them in the subjective sphere defines the area of free creativity with regard to the atonement that is the proper exercise of the Christian life. "God himself," says Berdyaev, "who gave His Only Son to be broken on the tree, atones for the sin of man and He expects that man, having partaken of the mystery of redemption, will accomplish the great deed of creativeness, will realize his human destiny."[145] The genuinely liberating character of the redemption *(Er-Lösung)* is revealed on the aesthetic plane in the freedom with which the artist shows the world of nature as transformed by the power of grace. "Existing within the Christian kerygma," writes van Esbroeck, "every believer is invited to a free and new creation by participating in the definitive exegesis of the one Hermeneut."[146] For Trakl, such a transforming exercise of freedom takes the shape of an extreme stylization and abstraction that attempt to present spiritual events in their essence.

Insofar as the work of God in the redemption is for the sake of man, to that extent we may say that the work of God is incomplete without the cooperation of man. The freedom upon which rests the integrity of man's relationship to God is expressed by Trakl precisely in his fidelity to the work of redemption accomplished by Christ. Trakl has penetrated to the heart of the atonement and seen that the decisive battle for the recovery of holiness is waged between the forces of Good and Evil, between the indestructible power of God's love as manifested in Jesus' utter self-emptying and the destructive power of Satan, who wishes to hide his condition as irredeemably fallen angel by filling the world with illusory images of light.

By taking his position at the heart of the mystery of the Cross, Trakl enters that night of the self in which only obedience to the Father's will provides the air to sustain the failing senses. In Trakl the silences are always powerful, pregnant. It is silence not from emptiness, but from excess of presence. This is why the poems create a sense of mystery and of soundless vibration, rather than of unqualified dejection and despair. Obedience may finally be said to be the very form of Trakl's poetry, the imitation of Christ as he lapsed into a silence filled with love. The concluding movement of atonement in Trakl's poetry achieves the reconciliation at a level beyond the ken of words. The utter abandonment experienced in the night of expiation finally reaches the sphere of elemental peace that can be the result only of Christ's kenotic act. The dejection and lamentation of Good Friday yield to the silence and austere luminosity of Holy Saturday. The *quies sabbatica* that reigns in the tomb of Christ can issue forth only from total self-emptying reciprocated by total acceptance:

> Über das Antlitz des Schläfers neigt sich der greise Vater
> Des Guten bärtiges Antlitz, das ferne gegangen
> Ins Dunkel.[147]

The trinitarian gesture portrayed here—the Father bending down over the dead Son, with an imperturbable Peace between Them—may be regarded as a characteristic movement that continually rounds off Trakl's protrayal of decay and suffering. In the end, all the isolation, dejection, and near-despair are framed and thus transformed by the receptive presence of the Father, who encloses all deformity and fragmentation in the form-giving reality of his Love. Thus the repetitive litany of isolated sorrows in the poem *Psalm*, which ruthlessly extinguishes one by one all human reasons for hope, quietly leads to the certainty of a hope that is given by the illumining presence of the Father:

> Schweigsam über der Schädelstätte öffnen sich
> Gottes goldene Augen.[148]

This last verse of the poem transfigures the earthly disintegration portrayed at length in the earlier portions by subsuming it under Christ's kenotic act on Golgotha, "Place of the Skull." The same gesture, whereby the wilting of the divine into the human effects the blossoming of the human into the divine, surrounds Helian's descent into essential darkness:

> Der stille Gott die blauen Lider über ihn senkt.[149]

This is the limit of Trakl's poetry, the point at which it passes over into silence. Resurrection is apophatically present precisely as an interior light of peace, which outwardly manifests itself by an intensification of darkness. Resurrection is not a triumphal possession of glory, but a state of radical obedience in which the individual can have his reality only in his dependency upon God. For this reason, the concluding verse of the poem we have been analyzing,

> Von Lidern düstert goldene Erlösung,

presents such a paradoxical manner of redemption. The line may be translated: "Golden redemption (or deliverance) shines forth darkly from the eyelids." This oxymoronic expression of redemption, and the eccentric use of the verb *düstern* with a positive connotation and governed by a subject other than the usual impersonal *es* (as a substitute for a verb such as *glänzen*), indicate Trakl's insistence on a wholly interior and supernatural event which, in the eyes of the world, is even more fraught with contradictions than ordinary death and decay. Deliverance comes to the one who has entrusted so much suffering and decomposition over into the hands of an expectant God:

> Gott in deine milden Hände
> Legt der Mensch das dunkle Ende,
> Alle Schuld und rote Pein.[150]

If the silence of Trakl's poetry is so deep and so thorough as to constitute a structural principle, it is because this silence is rooted in the absolute condition of one who has died:

> Sag wie lang wir gestorben sind.[151]

Within the poetry's perspective as the utterance of one dead, there can at last take place the reconciliation that sees in the passing of the temporal the definitive rise of a life beyond decay. But this passing and this rising are not mutually contradictory events. The transformation that takes place raises that which falls and makes it incorruptible. It does not supplant the temporal with something else. The guilt and suffering that have been deposited in God's meek hands are the stuff that, by this eucharistic act of Man and God, is transformed into the nourishment that sustains a burning peace:

> Auch ist dem Guten
> Das Herz versöhnt in grüner Stille
> Und Kühle hoher Bäume.
> Speise teilt er mit sanften Händen aus.
>
> (Thus, too, the good man
> Finds his heart reconciled in green silence
> And in the cool of high trees.
> He gives out food with gentle hands.)[152]

Notes

Introduction: Critical Approaches to Trakl

1. Walter Killy, *Über Georg Trakl*, 3d ed. (Göttingen: Vandenhoeck & Ruprecht, 1967), p. 38.

2. Erich Auerbach, *Mimesis: The Representation of Reality in Western Literature*, trans. Willard R. Trask (Princeton: Princeton University Press, 1953), p. 14.

3. Walter Muschg, *Von Trakl zu Brecht* (Munich: R. Piper, 1961), pp. 101–2.

4. Alfred Focke, *Georg Trakl: Liebe und Tod* (Vienna: Buchreihe "Wissenschaft und Weltbild," 1955).

5. Eduard Lachmann, *Kreuz und Abend* (Salzburg: Otto Müller Verlag, 1954).

6. Walter Muschg, *Die Zerstörung der deutschen Literatur* (Berne: Francke, 1956), p. 106.

7. *Merkur*, no. 61 (1953), pp. 226–58.

8. Elisabeth Langgässer, *Das Christliche der christlichen Dichtung* (Olten: Walter-Verlag, 1961), p. 46.

9. [Dying, the head bows in the darkness of olive trees.] 70 (LG 77).

10. Lachmann, *Kreuz*, p. 81.

11. Walter Falk, *Leid und Verwandlung: Rilke, Kafka, Trakl und der Epochenstil des Impressionismus und Expressionismus* (Salzburg: Otto Müller Verlag, 1961).

12. Muschg, *Von Trakl*, pp. 101–2.

13. Giuseppe Dolei, *L'arte come espiazione imperfetta: Saggio su Trakl* (Stuttgart: Akademischer Verlag Hans-Dieter Heinz, 1978), p. 171.

14. Maire Jaanus Kurrik, *Georg Trakl* (New York: Columbia University Press, 1974), p. 45.

15. Ibid., p. 30.

16. Ibid., p. 34.

17. Ibid., pp. 3–4.

18. Francis M. Sharp, *The Poet's Madness: A Reading of Georg Trakl* (Ithaca: Cornell University Press, 1981), p. 9.

19. Ibid., p. 10.

20. Ibid., p. 162.

21. Michael Hamburger, "Georg Trakl," in *Contraries: Studies in German Literature*, pp. 291–323 (New York: E. P. Dutton, 1970), pp. 295 and 300.

22. Sharp, *Madness*, pp. 194–95.

23. In the preface to Lachmann, *Kreuz*, p. 7.

24. [In the night, the lovely string-music of the soul resounds / full of dark / raptures, at the silver feet of the penitent / in the blue silence / and atonement of the olive tree.] *Passion*, 2d version, 397.

25. *Ion*, 534 and 536; *Phaedrus*, 245.

26. Killy-Szklenar, 1:463.

27. Langgässer, *Das Christliche*, p. 48.

28. Hans-Eckehard Bahr, *Poiesis: Theologische Untersuchung der Kunst* (Stuttgart: Evangelisches Verlagswerk, 1960), p. 193.

29. Ibid., p. 184.

30. Hans Konrad Neidhart, *Georg Trakls Helian* (Schleitheim, 1957); Rudolf D. Schier, " 'Nur dem, der das Glück verachtet, wird Erkenntnis': A Study of Georg Trakl's 'Helian' " (Ph.D. diss., Cornell University, 1965).

Chapter 1. The Poetics of Incarnation

1. Herbert Lindenberger, *Georg Trakl* (New York: Twayne Publishers, 1971), p. 79.
2. Ibid., p. 74.,
3. Henri de Lubac, *Exégèse médiévale*, vol. 1, pt. 1 (Paris: Aubier, 1959), pp. 323–24.
4. Dorothee Sölle, *Realisation* (Darmstadt: Hermann Luchterhand Verlag, 1973), p. 38.
5. Ibid., p. 22.
6. Ibid.
7. Ibid., p. 100.
8. de Lubac, *Exégèse*, p. 306.
9. Sölle, *Realisation*, p. 23.
10. Cf. ibid., p. 27.
11. Walter Killy and Hans Szklenar, eds., *Georg Trakl: Dichtungen und Briefe* (Salzburg: Otto Müller Verlag, 1969), 1:486.
12. Rudolf D. Schier, *Die Sprache Georg Trakls* (Heidelberg: Carl Winter Verlag, 1970), pp. 97–98.
13. de Lubac, *Exégèse*, p. 305.
14. Schier, *Sprache*, p. 44 and *passim*.
15. Sölle, *Realisation*, p. 29.
16. Ibid., p. 101.
17. Ibid., p. 44.
18. "My grammar is Christ." In Jean Leclercq, *L'Amour des lettres et le désir de Dieu* (Paris: Editions du Cerf, 1957), p. 241.
19. de Lubac, *Exégèse*, p. 317.
20. Cf. Hans Urs von Balthasar, *Herrlichkeit: eine theologische Ästhetik* (Einsiedeln: Johannes Verlag, 1961), 1:523.
21. Ibid., p. 526.
22. [When Helian's soul sees itself in a rosy mirror / and snow and leprosy descend from his forehead.] 73 (LG 79).
23. Cf. von Balthasar, *Herrlichkeit*, 1:392–93, on the spiritual senses.
24. Auerbach, *Mimesis*, p. 73.
25. Von Balthasar, *Herrlichkeit*, 1:496.
26. Ibid., pp. 404–5.
27. "The activity of art is founded upon the activity of nature." *Summa theologiae*, I, q. 45, ad. 8.
28. Jacques Maritain, *Art et scolastique*, 4th ed. (Paris: Librairie de l'Art Catholique, 1947), p. 89.
29. "Activity follows (i.e., is determined by) being."
30. Maritain, *Art*, p. 95.
31. Lindenberger, *Trakl*, p. 79.
32. Maritain, *Art*, pp. 97–98.
33. [The pale man / dwells in blue crystal, his cheek leaned upon his stars, / or he bows his head in purple slumber.] *Ruh und Schweigen*, 113 (LG 111).
34. Maritain, *Art*, pp. 37–38.
35. Ibid., p. 43.

36. In the preface to Langgässer, *Das Christliche*, p. 7.

37. Maritain, *Art*, p. 94.

38. [*Mankind:* Mankind aligned at edge of fiery gorge, / a rolling drum, the foreheads of dark warriors, / footsteps through mists of blood; black iron clangs, / despair and night in saddened brains: / Eve's shadow here, the hunt, and the red loot. / Clouds, the light breaks through, the evening meal. / There dwells in bread and wine a gentle silence / and they are now assembled, twelve in number. / At night they scream in sleep under olive branches; / Saint Thomas thrusts his hand into the wound.] 43.

39. "O God, by the *humiliation* of your Son you have *raised up* the fallen world . . ."

40. "The Lord of life, having died, reigns alive."

41. Lachmann, *Kreuz*, p. 12.

42. Schier, *Sprache*, p. 44.

43. [If the world existed in order to instruct man concerning God, surely his divinity would shine forth from all sides in an unquestionable manner. But since the world subsists only by Jesus Christ and for Jesus Christ, and in order to instruct man concerning both his corruption and his redemption, everything in it dazzles with the proofs of these two truths. What we experience in the world conveys neither a total exclusion nor a manifest presence of divinity, but rather the presence of a God who hides. Everything bears this characteristic.] Blaise Pascal, *Oeuvres complètes*, ed. Jacques Chevalier, *Pensée* #602 (Paris: Pléiade, 1954), pp. 1281–82.

44. [Good Friday's children, blind, stand at the fences. / In the mirror of dark gutters full of decay / the sighing of the dying people's convalescence / and angels that walk through white eyes / from eyelids golden redemption shines forth darkly.] 301.

45. [The night has come up over the ravaged forehead / with beautiful stars, / over the countenance petrified with pain. / A wild animal ate the lover's heart. / A fiery angel / drops on a stony field with a broken breast / as a vulture flutters up again. / Woe! In unending lament / fire, earth, and blue mountain-water intermingle.] *Nächtliche Klage*, 2d version, 329.

46. Von Balthasar, *Herrlichkeit*, 1:466–67.

47. [Feeling in moments of deathlike existence: all men are worthy of love. Awakening, you feel the bitterness of the world; in it is all your unresolved (unredeemed) guilt; your poem an imperfect atonement.] 463.

48. [I am convinced that it will say and mean more to you in this universal form than in the narrow personal form of the first draft. You can believe me when I say that I never have and never will easily be able to subordinate myself unconditionally to what is to be represented, and I will over and over again have to correct myself in order to give the truth what belongs to the truth.] 485–86.

49. Von Balthasar, *Herrlichkeit*, 1:527.

50. Ferdinand Ebner, *Schriften: Fragmente, Aufsätze, Aphorismen: Zu einer Phänomenologie des Wortes* (Munich: Kösel Verlag, 1963), 1:317.

51. Ibid., p. 316.

52. Ibid., p. 317.

53. Cf. von Balthasar, *Herrlichkeit*,1:527.

54. [I saw many cities the prey of flames / and the times heaping horror on horror, / and I saw many peoples decay to dust / and all things glide into oblivion.] 216.

55. [Dull heat of fever / makes poisonous flowers bloom from my mouth . . . // From a mirror's deceptive emptiness / there slowly rises—as into the approximate— / a face of dread and darkness: Cain! // Then I am alone with my murderer.] 220.

56. Walter Muschg, *Von Trakl*, p. 32.

57. Von Balthasar, *Herrlichkeit*, 1: 456–57.

58. Schier, *Sprache*, pp. 43–44.

59. [We can make an idol even out of truth itself. Outside of charity, truth is not God; it is his image, an idol which must be neither loved nor worshiped.] Pascal, *Oeuvres*, p. 1277 (*Pensée* #597).

Chapter 2. Trakl and the Apocalyptic Tradition

1. "You say: 'I see water, I see fire, the air, and the earth and all their combinations, how they come to decay and how short they last. . . .' / But your *life* is breathed forth without mediation by the Highest Goodness, and He enamours it so of Himself that it thereafter desires Him continuously." *Paradiso VII*, 124–26 and 142–44.

2. [In the last few days such horrible things have happened to me that I shall never be able to rid myself of their shadow as long as I live. Yes, respected friend, in just a few days my life has been unspeakably crushed and all that remains is a speechless pain to which even bitterness is denied. . . . Perhaps you can write me a couple of words. I no longer know whether I'm going or coming. It is such an indescribable calamity when one's world breaks apart. O my God! What a judgment has irrupted upon me! Tell me that I must still have the strength to live and to do what is true. Tell me that I am not crazy. A stonelike darkness has irrupted upon me. O my friend, how small and unhappy I have become.] 529–30, emphasis mine.

3. [At the window are wilting the warm, red flowers / which someone brought the beautiful child today. / How he raised his hands and laughed quietly . . . / They're praying there. Perhaps someone lies dead.] 369.

4. [Dreamlike the dark spirits / of the mountain convulse the heart, / gloom / that falls over the ravines.] 157 (LG 157).

5. In the preface to Ebner, *Schriften*, 1 : 17.

6. Hans Szklenar, ed., *Erinnerung an Georg Trakl: Zeugnisse und Briefe*, 3d ed. (Salzburg: Otto Müller Verlag, 1966), p. 24.

7. Cf. Søren Kierkegaard, *Concluding Unscientific Postscript*, trans. David F. Swenson and Walter Lowrie (Princeton: Princeton University Press, 1941), p. 405.

8. William M. Johnston, *The Austrian Mind: An Intellectual and Social History 1848–1938* (Berkeley: University of California Press, 1972), p. 165.

9. Otto Basil, *Georg Trakl in Selbstzeugnissen und Bilddokumenten* (Reinbek bei Hamburg: Rowohlt Verlag, 1965), p. 32.

10. [You mighty cities / built up from stone / on the plain! / Just as mute / and with darkened forehead / the homeless man follows the wind, / the naked trees on the hill. / You distant rivers, filling with darkness! / The ghostly sunset / stirs violent fear / in the storm-clouds. / You dying peoples! / Pale wave / breaking on the beach of night, / falling stars.] 140 (LG 141).

11. [Alas! I grieve, O fellow citizens, that you are made so dull concerning the world. / One man runs out to consult his luck, another tells omens from looking at birds. / Still another looks around after the blood of warriors has been spilt, / and the cruel man wishes to hear favorable predictions.] Commodianus, *Carmina*, recensuit Bernhardus Dembart (Vindobonae: Apud C. Geroldi Filium, 1887), pp. 27–28.

12. [The trumpet gives a sign in the sky under the Lion / and suddenly darkness descends with the clamor of the heavens. / The Lord casts down His eyes, that the earth might tremble. / He even shouts into the sphere of the world that all may hear: / "Behold, long have I kept silence, putting up with your ways for so great a time!" / Both those who beat their breasts and those who lament too late wail equally. / There is howling and

weeping, but no chance is given to the wicked. / What shall a mother do for the child she nurses when she herself burns? / In a flame of fire the Lord shall judge the wicked.] Ibid., p. 61.

13. [The stars of heaven fall; the planets are judged along with us. / The dwellers of heaven are troubled as the ruination of the world is accomplished. . / It will profit only those who are known to Christ. / It will be as dew for them, but for the rest a deathly punishment.] Ibid., p. 181.

14. [O the bitter hour of decline, / when we behold a stone face in black waters. / Still, in radiance those who love raise their silver eyelids: / One race. Incense flows from rosy pillows / and the sweet song of the resurrected.] 119 (LG 121).

15. [Everything which we endure in this world is a torment. / To this extent our hope must be sought in the world to come. / God, the Law, the Passion of Christ exhort us / to believe that we shall rise in a new world. / Thus God's law proclaims it: when the Exalted One was made lowly, / hell yielded so that Adam might rise up from his death. / The Lord went down into the tomb out of compassion for his creation. / And thus, in a hidden manner, he depleted the strength of death.] Ibid., p. 135.

16. [If the Lord says that we must eat our bread mingling it with our tears, / what are you now doing, you who wish to live happily? . . . / He who is merry is already alien to the Lord . . . / Therefore, be such as Christ wants you to be: / Meek and joyful in Him, but sad to the world.] Ibid., pp. 81–82.

17. [Always you return, melancholy, / O gentleness of the solitary soul. / A golden day glows to its end. // Humbly the patient one bows to pain, / resounding with harmony and soft frenzy. / Look! Darkness already falls.] 40.

18. Dionysius of Alexandria, in *The Works of Gregory Thaumaturgus, Dionysius of Alexandria, and Archelaus,* trans. S. D. F. Salmond, *Ante-Nicene Christian Library* (Edinburgh: T. & T. Clark, 1871), 20:239–40.

19. [In the evening autumnal forests resound / with deadly weapons; darkly the sun rolls / over golden plains, blue lakes. / Night enfolds / dying warriors, the wild lament / of their broken mouths. / Yet quietly in the meadow / a red cloud, temple of an angry God, / gathers the spilled blood to itself, coolness of moon; / all roads converge in black decay.] 167.

20. Cf. Schier, *Sprache,* pp. 62–63.

21. Cf. Lachmann, *Kreuz,* p. 14, and Schier, *Sprache,* p. 53.

22. Dionysius, *Works,* p. 254.

23. [Fear, you venomous snake, / black one, die among the stones! / As wild rivers of tears / plunge down, mercy of storm, / in threatening thunder / snowy peaks echo all around. / Fire / purges mutilated night.] 157 (LG 159).

24. Von Balthasar, *Herrlichkeit,* 1:485–86.

25. [Alive you were, my God, within the monstrance. / Punctured through by your Father with a needle of fire. / Throbbing like the wretched heart of a frog / that technicians shut up in a glass container.] *Oda al Santísimo Sacramento del Altar. Obras completas,* p. 630.

26. Tertullian, *Latin Christianity: Its Founder, Tertullian. The Ante-Nicene Fathers* (Buffalo: Christian Literature Publishing Co., 1885), 3:530.

27. Ibid., p. 524.

28. [Rosy mirror: an ugly image / that appears on its black backside, / weeps blood out of broken eyes / and plays blasphemously with dead snakes. // Snow runs through the stiffened shirt, / purple over the black countenance / that shatters into heavy fragments / of planets, dead and alien. // Spider appears on the black backside, / lust, your countenance dead and alien. / Blood runs through the stiffened shirt, / snow weeps out of broken eyes.] 302.

29. Methodius of Olympus, in *The Writings of Methodius, Alexander of Lycopolis, Peter of*

Alexandria, and Several Fragments. Ante-Nicene Library (Edinburgh: T. & T. Clark, 1869), 14: 224.

30. Ibid., p. 95.

31. Von Balthasar, *Herrlichkeit*, 1: 442.

32. In Maritain, *Art,* p. 226.

33. Amos N. Wilder, *The Language of the Gospel: Early Christian Rhetoric* (New York: Harper & Row, 1964), p. 226.

34. [What an abomination! The entire world is falling to ruin and, alas, our sins do not crumble within us . . . We live as if we were to die on the next day and we build as if we were forever to live in this world. The walls, the ceilings, the columns' capitals are all aglow with gold, gold, gold, and before our very doors Christ dies naked and hungry in the poor man.] In David S. Wiesen, *St. Jerome as Satirist: A Study in Christian Latin Thought and Letters* (Ithaca: Cornell University Press, 1964), pp. 45–46.

35. [In the dark an old man scurries along like a puppet / and the tinkling of money laughs lustfully. / The halo of sanctity falls on that little girl / waiting meek and white in front of the café . . . // Carriages move in the evening through storms. / Through the dark a corpse tumbles, empty and livid. / A light-colored steamer docks in the canal, / a Moorish girl calls out in the wild green. // Sleepwalkers come before a candle's light, / the Spirit of Evil enters a spider. / A swarm of epidemics circles around drinkers. / A forest of oaks breaks into bare rooms. // In the foreground appears an old opera house. / From alleys there flow forth unsuspected masks / and somewhere a conflagration still blazes with rage. / The bats shriek in the blasts of the wind. // Tenements threaten, full of misery and stench. / The color of violets and musical chords pass by hungry people in cellar-holes. / A sweet child sits dead upon a bench.] 295–96.

36. Eusebius Pamphilus, *The Ecclesiastical History,* trans. C. F. Crusé (London: Bell & Daldy, 1866), p. 372.

37. Ibid., p. 373.

38. Cf. von Balthasar, *Herrlichkeit*, 1: 442.

39. Cf. ibid., pp. 367–68.

40. [Come now as you wish to exact the race's guilt. / The body, that heavy garment, may tear and go to mould, / but this decaying adorns it with new splendor. / I want to accustom it (the body) little by little in advance and with joyful longing to the slumber / in which henceforth no vain dream may oppress it.] In Szklenar, *Erinnerung,* pp. 206–7.

41. "The bitterest verses which a German poet has ever written." Ibid., p. 205.

42. Cf. Gisela Luther, *Barocker Expressionismus? Zur Problematik der Beziehung zwischen der Bildlichkeit expressionistischer und barocker Lyrik* (The Hague: Mouton & Co., 1969), p. 171.

43. [The field-shouts of my youth bring on now mute songs of lament. / The seed and the poison of inherited mortality / is already germinating and fermenting through all my members.] From another strophe of *Bussgedanken,* in J. C. Günther, *Gedichte,* ed. Hanns-ludwig Geiger (Berlin: Erich Schmidt Verlag, 1947), p. 196.

44. [O unheard-of tumult! / Whatever flies and swims today takes leave: / fire, water, air, and earth. / Woe to them here / who have not already turned to God.] *Von dem Jüngsten Gericht,* in Herbert Cysarz, ed., *Barocklyrik: Schwund- und Kirchenbarock,* 2d ed. (Hildesheim: Georg Olms Verlagsbuchhandlung, 1964), 3: 135.

45. [Our body and flesh and blood, full of the vices of these times / and unprepared for existing eternally because of their corruptibility, / become adequate for eternity—incorruptible, new, and young— / most wonderfully through God's power, by means of this transformation.] *Das Jüngste Gericht,* Cysarz, *Hoch- und Spätbarock,* 2: 100.

46. [In the clear mirror of the purified waters / we see the dead times come strangely to life. / And our passions, by bleeding themselves empty, / raise our souls up to far-off

heavens. // We go through the deaths newly formed, / into deeper tortures and deeper ecstasies / wherein the unknown Godhead reigns—/ and eternally new suns perfect us.] *Einklang,* 244.

47. [This is the flame of the dread revenge, which the enkindled wrath has fanned: / Here is the curse of unending punishments, here is the evermore increasing rage: / O Man! Decay now in order not to decay there.] *Von dem Jüngsten Gericht,* Cysarz, 2:191.

48. Gryphius generally delights in such paradoxical statements, which we will ultimately see as deriving from the Christ-form of the Passion. In another poem he says of one who suffers though innocent: "Er lebt in dem er stirbt, er steigt in dem er fällt . . . / Der ist kein rechter Christ, dem für dem Creutze grauet." (*An einen Unschuldigen Leidenden,* Cysarz, 2:186–87.)

49. [That I may fulfill the last torment in myself, / I oppose you not, you dark enemy forces. / You are the road to the great silence, / upon which we walk into the coolest of nights.] 223.

50. [And so, oppressed heart, things have reached an extreme. / Misery has taken the springtime of my age away. / Contempt, poverty, pain, and struggles have still yielded no peace . . . / And wherever my complaint knocks, there the door slams shut.] Cysarz, 3:80.

51. [Now it beats to the rhythm of finished dances, / to the sad melodies of despair, / and all the while the starry garlands of former hopes / wilt on an altar long deprived of its god.] *Ermatten,* 242.

52. [This world with its pleasure / is but filth and refuse / compared to that which is eternal . . . / This world with its pleasures / will perish, dear Christians.] Cysarz, 2:80.

53. [Why do I ask concerning the world! It will stand in flames . . . / Beauty is like snow, this life is death.] *Verläugnung der Welt,* Cysarz, 2:181.

54. [Fear and silence and dark horrors, gloomy chills cover the land . . . / Then, when the day suddenly breaks, whatever has been spoken, done, or thought / will find itself without cover before the judgment of the terrible God.] *Mitternacht,* Cysarz, 2:190.

55. [A field of stubble. A black wind storms. / The violet-colors of sadness blossom. / Train of thought that weathers the brain with gloom . . . / Then the soul keeps silent, dreadfully convulsed, / along rooms, empty and dark-colored.] *Melancholia,* 361.

56. [The towers stand in fire, the church has toppled over. / The townhall lies destroyed, the strong men have been cut down. / The virgins are disgraced, and wherever we may look / there is fire, pestilence, and death that penetrate heart and spirit. / Here, through the trenches and the city, there constantly flows fresh blood. / It is already three times six years that the waters of our streams, / almost clogged up with corpses, can scarcely make advance.] Cysarz, 2:186.

57. [A chorus of rats squeaks enamored on the rubbish. / Women carry entrails in baskets; / in a loathsome procession of rotting filth / they emerge from the twilight. // And suddenly from beneath the slaughterhouse / a canal spews rich blood into the calm river. / Föhn winds color the sparse shrubs brighter / and the red creeps slowly through the stream.] *Vorstadt im Föhn,* 51 (LG 53).

58. [The heap of intestines protrudes through the skin, / which has been bitten through by the maggots. / I see the intestines (Oh, what horror!) / pour out with pus, blood, and water! // The flesh which has not already rotted with time is now eaten up, under the cover of snake-blue mould, by an insatiable swarm of many different worms.] *Gedancken, Über dem Kirch-hof und Ruhe-städte der Verstorbenen,* Cysarz, 2:177.

59. [How sick all living things seem to be! / A feverish haze circles round a hamlet. . . .] *Heiterer Frühling,* 2d version, 49.

60. "Only he receives knowledge who spurns happiness." 463.

61. [Yes! Yes! Double your beatings and your zeal! / Strike yet more sharply and do not restrain yourself! / Although the pain irritates my gout and my spleen / I spit it back into

your face . . . / And if my wish could come true, / each of my wounds would have lips / that I might despise you in the cruel manner you deserve.] Cysarz, 3:77.

62. [Strike now, pain! The wound glows. / I pay no heed to this torment! / Look: out of my wounds there is blossoming mysteriously a star in the night! / Strike now, death! I am perfected.] 261.

63. "To murder the nightingale there came / three thousand men, armed with glittering knives." *Oda al Santísimo Sacramento del Altar. Obras,* p. 632.

64. [You refuge of my anguish, you widely gaping rifts, / wherein I am secure when the wrathful God / rebukes me for my sins . . . // How happy am I then, when delivered I sit / in the bosom that is your cave.] Cysarz, 2:10.

65. [Wake up, my spirit! Rise up! / Wake up! Here are the five death-stabs and wounds of your Lord. / Wake up! Leave world and lust aside. / I want to lock you up in Emmanuel's cave . . . // This place shows us five caves, / which the Father's Word bears on his person . . . // You, too, my spirit: Do not hesitate / in case a strong thunderbolt breaks / the clouds of great grace. / Crawl into the Lord's wounds . . . / There strikes you neither lightning nor wrath.] Cysarz, *Vor- und Frühbarock,* 1:251.

66. [An organ chorale filled him with God's trembling. But he passed his days in a dark cave, lied and stole and hid himself.] *Traum und Umnachtung,* 147 (LG 147).

67. [God's thunderous wrath lashes the forehead of the possessed . . . // But more silent humanity bleeds quietly in a dark cave, / shapes the redeeming Head out of dark metals.] *An die Verstummten,* 124 (LG 125).

68. [Here you find the oil of gladness. / Here shine golden stars. / Here is hidden a jewel of such worth / the like of which has never been seen . . . // I take the Lord's wounds to myself, / the best adornment on earth. / Whoever lacks it can never / be allowed into / the honor of this little lamb's wedding-feast. / Only he who is decorated with this jewel / will be led into this great banquet.] Cysarz, 1:252.

69. [Under the arch of thorns you lay, and the spike / bore its way deep into the crystal flesh / that the soul might wed the night in greater fire. // The bride has decked herself with stars, / the pure myrtle / that bends over the dead man's adoring countenance.] 322.

70. [Up, soul! You have stained yourself and are so ugly. / You have desecrated the likeness of the Most High in yourself. . . . / Go out from vanity's seductive domain / and keep your faith's eye for your Bridegroom. . . . / Look on your Savior from his crown to his feet, / and see: what a wretch, yes, what a worm he is! // His head of finest gold is full of pus and boils. / His dove-eyes are glued shut with spittle . . . / His raven-black hair, from which dew has always flowed, is now all stuck together with clotted blood. . . . / Out of his nose there now runs black clotted blood,— / his nose, which used to smell of apples and nard oil. / His lips, that told of myrrh and roses, are swollen brown and blue, gnarled and full of bruises. . . . / The limbs' ivory, inlaid with turquoises, is a freely flowing spring from which mere blood-foams bubbles. . . . // The hands and feet, with which He hung earth and sea in the air, are now fastened with nails to the Cross. . . . / He who has angels round about Him, and stars at His feet, must now bend back and neck to the burden of His Cross . . . / The Judge who will judge all flesh Himself kneels damned, / and He who gives all clothing is Himself naked as a finger. / He who is truth itself must allow calumny to be heaped upon Himself, / and God, the Father's delight, is saddened unto death. // We who stink with sins are indeed smelling God, / since Jesus now anoints us with the balm of His blood. / In order that our soul might beautify its ugly face, His foul pus must now be for us as the purest ointment.] Cysarz, 2:222–24.

71. [In the cool of a tree and without pain / That Which Is Perfected breathes / and has no need for autumnal stars . . . / Thorns, over which that man falls. / Long afterwards, those who love ponder over / his deplorable fall.] 310.

72. [O you silent mirrors of truth! / The ivory temples of the solitary / reflect a radiance

of fallen angels.] *Nachtlied,* 68 (LG 73).

73. [My Father, does Thou not wish to inquire concerning Thy Child? / I who am Thy very mouth ask Thee, O God of wrath, whether Thou remainest unmoved? . . . / Thy will be fulfilled. . . .] Cysarz, 3:129.

74. [Or when holding his father's hand / he silently climbed the black Hill of Calvary / and in the darkening rock crevices / the blue shape of man moved through his legend, / blood ran crimson from the wound under his heart. / O how softly the Cross rose up in his dark soul.] 89 (LG 91–93).

75. Writes Jacob: "Le culte du Sacré-Coeur, le coup de lance ou cinquième plaie est le culte et la marque physique de l'intelligence profonde. Les grandes pensées viennent du coeur, dit un moraliste. Ce qui signifie qu'on ne pense bien que les idées devenues force de conviction ou sentiment. C'est avec cette intelligence physiologique qu'il faut écrire." *Art poétique* (Paris: Emile Paul Frères, 1922), p. 11.

76. [Humbly the patient one bows to pain, / resounding with harmony and soft madness . . . // Shuddering under autumnal stars / each year the head bows more deeply.] *In ein altes Stammbuch,* 40 (LG 41).

77. [O pain! Life itself dies! O wonder! God must suffer! / He who supports all things falls down, Honor itself is despised. / He who covers all things is naked; / the comforter is scorned. / He who created air and forests must now bid them farewell.] Cysarz, 2:188.

78. [A fiery angel / you now lie with crushed breast on a field of stones.] *Nächtliche Klage,* 328.

79. [Five cellars here appear / which stand all full of wine before you, / a wine that quenches thirst.] Cysarz, 1:250.

80. [At night / blue doves drink the icy sweat / which flows from Elis' crystal brow.] *Elis,* 3d version, 85 (LG 88).

81. [Oh, look at the meadows of his limbs, / how wilted they are! Was not his countenance / a veritable valley of roses? How has this come to pass? / The wild swines of Cocytus have dug up with their snouts / his hazel-brown hair, his unbroken legs.] *Trauer- und Klagegedicht,* Cysarz, 2:87.

82. [But he became a snowy tree / on the Hill of Bones, / a deer peering out from a suppurating wound, / then again a silent stone.] 396.

83. Walter Muschg, *Von Trakl,* p. 113.

84. Cf. Langgässer, *Das Christliche,* pp. 51–52.

85. Paul Tillich, *Theology of Culture* (London: Oxford University Press, 1959), p. 68.

86. Karl Barth, *The Epistle to the Romans,* trans. Edwyn C. Hoskyns (London: Oxford University Press, 1933), p. 42.

87. On this point, and on the whole relationship of theology and Expressionism, see Wolfgang Rothe's pioneer article, "Der Mensch vor Gott: Expressionismus und Theologie," in Rothe, ed., *Expressionismus als Literatur* (Berne: Francke, 1969), p. 49 and *passim.*

88. Ebner, *Schriften,* 1:96.

89. Cf. Hans-Eckehard Bahr, *Poiesis,* pp. 250–51.

90. Kierkegaard, *Postscript,* pp. 492–93.

91. Gabriel Marcel, *Du refus à l'invocation* (Paris: Gallimard, 1940), p. 217.

92. T. J. Casey, *Manshape That Shone: An Interpretation of Trakl* (Oxford: Basil Blackwell, 1964), p. 17.

93. [The blue of my eyes is extinguished in this night, / the red gold of my heart. O how quietly the light burned. / Your blue robe enfolded him as he fell, / your red mouth sealed the friend's passing over into night.] *Nachts,* 96.

94. Karl Hammer, *W. A. Mozart—eine theologische Deutung: Ein Beitrag zur theologischen Anthropologie* (Zurich: EVZ-Verlag, 1964), p. 289.

95. Cf. Tillich, *Culture,* p. 73.

96. In von Balthasar, *Apokalypse der deutschen Seele: Studien zu einer Lehre von letzten Haltungen* (Salzburg: Verlag Anton Pustet, 1939), 3:46.

97. Johannes Klein, *Geschichte der deutschen Lyrik von Luther bis zum Ausgang des zweiten Weltkrieges* (Wiesbaden: Franz Steiner Verlag, 1957), p. 807.

98. Von Balthasar, *Apokalypse,* 3:61.

Chapter 3. The Traklian Grammar of Being

1. "The human drama is of necessity a moral one, engaged at the level of a struggle with passionate vices and crimes. And when this struggle is expressed purely and poetically, it no longer exhibits the former language of agitation, concupiscence, and strife, but possesses a new voice that conveys a knowledge of storms, horrors, and shame, that sees things in a new perspective and with new proportions, and that answers with the chasteness of its images and words to the chasteness which has become implanted in the heart." Benedetto Croce, *Poesia antica e moderna* (Bari: Gius. Lateza e Figli, 1966), p. 401.

2. "Christ is the spirit of the very letter," Johannes Scotus, *In Johannem, Patrologia Latina,* vol. 122 (Paris: Apud Garnier Fratres, 1879), c. 331B.

3. Rothe, *Expressionismus,* p. 387.

4. Paul Tillich, *Systematic Theology* (Chicago: University of Chicago Press, 1951), 1:40.

5. Tillich, *Culture,* p. 70.

6. Cf. Bahr, *Poiesis,* pp. 158–59.

7. Romano Guardini, *Die Sinne und die religiöse Erkenntnis: Zwei Versuche über die christliche Vergewisserung* (Würzburg: Werkbund-Verlag, 1950), p. 18.

8. Maritain, *Art,* pp. 78–79.

9. Maritain, *Creative Intuition in Art and Poetry* (New York: Meridian Books, 1954), p. 50.

10. Susanne K. Langer, *Feeling and Form: A Theory of Art* (New York: Charles Scribner's Sons, 1953), p. 52.

11. Cf. Joseph Chiari, *"Symbolisme" from Poe to Mallarmé: The Growth of a Myth* (London: Rockliff Publishing Corp., 1956), p. 47.

12. Nikolai Berdyaev, *The Meaning of the Creative Act,* trans. Donald A. Lowrie (London: Victor Gollancz Ltd., 1955), p. 245.

13. Chiari, *"Symbolisme,"* p. 46.

14. Walter Muschg, *Von Trakl,* pp. 20–21.

15. In Michael Hamburger, *The Truth of Poetry: Tensions in Modern Poetry from Baudelaire to the 1960s* (London: Weidenfeld and Nicolson, 1969), p. 188.

16. [Crimson curses of hunger / echo in rotting darkness, / black swords of the lie, / as if a bronze gate slammed shut.] *Vorhölle,* 132 (LG 133).

17. Paul Ricoeur, *Finitude et culpabilité, II: La symbolique du mal* (Paris: Editions Montaigne, 1960), p. 16.

18. Ibid., p. 19.

19. Chiari, *"Symbolisme,"* p. 59.

20. G. Ingli James, "The Autonomy of the Work of Art: Modern Criticism and the Christian Tradition," *Sewanee Review* 70 (1962): 299.

21. Ibid., p. 300.

22. Ibid., p. 301.

23. Cf. ibid., p. 316.

24. Ibid., p. 298.

25. Ibid., p. 311.

26. Ibid., p. 312.

27. Ibid., p. 313.

28. Ibid., p. 301. In this connection I offer the following fascinating, if controversial, statement by Henrich Steffens, a religious phenomenologist of the early nineteenth century: "Die europäischen Sprachen sind nur Ton; die Buchstaben, die Sylben, die Worte haben nur Bedeutung für das Ohr, der Klang schliesst sich an das innerste, lebendigste, beweglichste Dasein an, und diejenige Sprache vor allen, die den Ausdruck betont, wo die Töne sich, steigend und fallend, hervorgehoben und zurückgedrängt, an die innere Bedeutung an jede Gemüthsbewegung eng und leicht anschmiegen, kann recht eigentlich eine christliche Sprache genannt werden, und deutet auf den Sieg der Liebe über das Gesetz." *Caricaturen des Heiligsten,* pt. 1 (Leipzig, 1819), p. 350.

29. Cf. Rothe, *Expressionismus,* p. 381.

30. Lindenberger, *Trakl,* p. 89.

31. Bernhard Böschenstein, "Wirkungen des französischen Symbolismus auf die deutsche Literatur der Jahrhundertwende," *Euphorion* 58 (1964): 395.

32. Ibid., p. 389.

33. "Refuse and dust of the stars."

34. Rothe, *Expressionismus,* p. 374.

35. Ricoeur, *Symbolique,* p. 18.

36. Von Balthasar, *Herrlichkeit,* 3/1: 665.

37. Thomas Mann, *Doktor Faustus: Das Leben des deutschen Tonsetzers Adrian Leverkühn, erzählt von einem Freunde* (Stockholm: Bermann-Fischer Verlag, 1947), p. 736.

38. Amos N. Wilder, *Language,* p. 18.

39. Ibid., p. 33.

40. Franz Schupp, *Glaube—Kultur—Symbol: Versuch einer kritischen Theorie sakramentaler Praxis* (Düsseldorf: Patmos Verlag, 1974), p. 254.

41. Auerbach, *Mimesis,* p. 6.

42. Ibid., p. 72.

43. Auerbach, *Neue Dantestudien* (Istanbul: Ibrahim Horoz Basimevi, 1944), p. 3.

44. Bahr, *Poiesis,* p. 248.

45. Ibid., pp. 289–90.

45. Ibid., pp. 289–90.

46. Auerbach observes: "Jésus-Christ devient le modèle à suivre, et c'est en imitant son humilité qu'on peut approcher de sa majesté; c'est par l'humilité qu'il a atteint lui-même le comble de la majesté." *Dantestudien,* p. 7.

47. Auerbach, *Mimesis,* pp. 11–12.

48. [In the evening the father grew old; in dark rooms the mother's face turned to stone, and the curse of a debased race weighed down upon the boy. At times he remembered his childhood, filled with sickness, horror, and darkness, with secret games in the garden of stars; or he was feeding the rats in the dusky courtyard. His sister's slender shape emerged from the blue mirror, and he plunged as if dead into darkness. . . .] 147 (LG 147).

49. Von Balthasar, *Herrlichkeit,* 1:520.

50. Hans Konrad Neidhart, *Helian,* p. 162.

51. Cf. Sölle, *Realisation,* p. 105.

52. Karl Rahner writes concerning the nature of Christianity that, "because man is mediated to the historical event of salvation and this mediation does not take place merely by way of theoretical information—since he experiences this mediation as the *event* of his own transcendental and supernaturally elevated being—he has always gone beyond the basic forms of ideology." *Theological Investigations,* trans. Karl-H. and Boniface Kruger (Baltimore: Helicon Press, 1969), 6:54, emphasis mine.

53. Langgässer, *Das Christliche,* p. 58.

54. [*Transformation of Evil:* Autumn: black footsteps by the forest edge; moment of speechless destruction; foreheads of lepers eavesdrop beneath the bared tree. Long bygone evening now sinking over steps of moss; November. A bell rings out and the shepherd leads a herd of black and red horses into the village. Under the hazelbush the green hunter disembowels a deer. His hands smoke of blood, and in the leaves above the man's eyes the deer's shadow sighs in brown silence; the forest. Three crows scatter, their flight a sonata resonant with faded chords and the sorrow of man; softly a golden cloud dissolves. Boys light a fire by the mill. Flame is the brother of the palest things, and buried in his purple hair he laughs; or it is a place of murder beside a stony path. The barberries are gone, all year long dreams lie in leaden air under pines; fear, green darkness, gurgling sounds of a man drowning. From the starry pond the fisherman draws a great, black fish, face of horror and madness. Voices of reeds, behind quarreling men the man sways in a red boat across icy waters of autumn, living in the dark legends of his race and his eyes open like stone over nights and virgin terrors. Evil.

What compels you to stand quietly on the rotted staircase in the house of your fathers? Leaden blackness. What do you lift with silver hand to your eyes; and your eyelids sink as if drunk with poppy? Yet through the wall of stone you see the starry sky, the Milky Way, and Saturn; red. The bare tree frantically pounds the stone wall. You upon decayed stairs: tree, star, stone! You, a blue deer gently trembling; you, the pale priest who slaughters it on a black altar. O your smile in the darkness, so mournfully evil that a child turns pale in his sleep. A red flame leaped from your hand and a moth burned in it. O flute of light; o flute of death. What made you stand still on the crumbled steps in the house of your fathers? Below, an angel taps the gate with crystal finger.

O you hell of sleep; dark lane, small brown garden. Softly through the blue evening the shape of the dead resounds; about them flutter green flowers and their face has abandoned them; or ashen it bows over the murderer's cold temples in the darkened hallway. Adoration, purple flame of lust; dying, the sleeper plunged over black steps into darkness.

Someone left you at the crossroads and for a long time you gaze back. Silver footstep in the shadows of small and crippled apple-trees. The fruit glows purple in the black branches and the snake sheds its skin in the grass. O the darkness; the sweat shed by the icy brow, and sorrowful dreams from the wine of the village tavern, beneath smoke-blackened beams. You, still a wilderness that conjures rose-tinged islands from the brown tobacco cloud, and draws from his core the wild cry of a griffin as he dashes around black cliffs in sea, storm and ice. You, a face of fire within green metal, wanting to go there and from the Hill of Bones to sing of dark ages and the flaming fall of the angel. O despair, falling on its knees in a soundless scream.

A dead man visits you. Self-spilled blood flows from his heart and in that black brow nests an unspeakable moment; dark encounter. You—a purple moon, as he appears in the olive tree's green shadow. Incorruptible night follows him.] 97–98 (LG 99–103).

55. Killy-Szklenar, 2 : 165.

56. *Cf.* Langgässer, *Das Christliche,* p. 34.

57. Von Balthasar, *Herrlichkeit,* 1 : 472.

58. Kierkegaard, *Postscript,* p. 400.

59. [O Life, how canst Thou die? / How canst Thou dwell in the tomb?] Papadeas, Ἀκολουθίαι, p. 387.

60. [O my Jesus, King of all, why hast Thou come / to seek out them that are dead in Hades? / Or to release the race of mortals?] Ibid., p. 388.

61. [Let us praise him who, out of his own free will, was crucified in the flesh for us, suffered, was buried, and rose from the dead.] Emmanouel G. Mytilenaiou, ed., Ἱερά Σύνοψις τῶν Προσευχῶν (Athens: N. Alikiotes, 1952), p. 328.

62. For the symbolism of the griffin see the following works: Richard Barber and Anne

Riches, *A Dictionary of Fabulous Beasts* (New York: Walker & Co., 1971), pp. 73–75. Catherine B. Avery, ed., *The New Century Classical Handbook* (New York: Appleton-Century-Crofts, Inc., 1962), p. 507. Maria Leach, ed., *Standard Dictionary of Folklore, Mythology, and Legend* (New York: Funk and Wagnalls, 1972), p. 467. *Meyers Enzyklopädisches Lexikon* (Mannheim: Bibliographisches Institut, 1974), 10:734. Engelbert Kirschbaum, ed., *Lexikon der christlichen Ikonographie* (Freiburg: Herder Verlag, 1970), 2:202–3.

63. [The space within the four of them contained a triumphal chariot on two wheels, which came drawn at the neck of a griffin; / and he stretched upwards one wing and the other between the middle and the three and three bands so that he did harm to none by cleaving. / So high they rose that they were lost to sight; he had his members of gold so far as he was bird, and the rest was white mixed with red. / Not only did Rome never gladden an Africanus or an Augustus with a chariot so splendid, but even that of the Sun would be poor to it.] *Purgatorio* 29:106–17. Dante Alighieri, *The Divine Comedy*, trans. Charles S. Singleton. *Purgatorio* (Princeton: Princeton University Press, 1973), pp. 321–23.

64. "For his kingliness and his strength . . . Because after the resurrection he returned to the stars." Isidori Hispaliensis Episcopi, *Etymologiarum sive Originum Libri XX*, ed. W. M. Lindsay (Oxford: E Typographeo Clarendoniano, 1911), 7, ii, 42–44.

65. Cf. Barber and Riches, *Dictionary*, pp. 74–75.

66. Bernanos, *Oeuvres*, p. 1763.

67. [O that the Night might more devoutly come, / Krist.] [sic] 395.

68. [For the night is the dwelling-place of him who loves.] 399.

69. Von Balthasar, *Herrlichkeit*, 1: 593.

Chapter 4. The Poem as a Work of Atonement

1. Søren Kierkegaard, *Samlede Vaerker*, ed. A. B. Drachmann, J. L. Heiberg, and H. O. Lange (Copenhagen: Gyldendalske Boghandel, 1963), 5: 170. "Lament! The Lord is not afraid. He is well able to defend himself. But how should he be able to defend himself if no one dares to lament as it befits human beings to do? Speak, lift up your voice, speak loudly: God can surely speak louder still. He possesses the thunder—but that too is an answer, an explanation, reliable, trustworthy, authentic, an answer from God himself, an answer which even if it crush a man is more glorious than smalltalk and mumblings about the righteousness of providence, rumors invented by human wisdom and spread about by coquettes and half-men."

2. Illtyd Trethowan, *The Absolute and the Atonement* (London: George Allen & Unwin, Ltd., 1971), p. 152.

3. Cf. chap. 1, n. 47.

4. In *Comparative Literature* 26, no. 1 (Winter 1974): 82.

5. Kierkegaard, *Postscript*, p. 518.

6. [Great is the guilt of all that is born. Woe, you golden shudders / of death, / when the soul dreams of cooler blossoms.] *Anif,* 114.

7. Kierkegaard, *Postscript*, p. 471.

8. [Bitter is death, food of the guilt-laden. Grinning in the ancestral tree's brown branches, earthen faces disintegrate. But one sang quietly in the green shadows of the elder-bush as he awoke from evil dreams; a rosy angel, sweet playmate, came near him so that he, a gentle deer, slumbered into night. And he saw the star-filled face of purity.] 150 (LG 151).

9. Tillich, *Systematic Theology*, 1:288.

10. [O the terror when every thing knows its guilt, walks pathways of thorns.] *Traum und Umnachtung,* 149 (LG 151).

11. Ricoeur, *Symbolique*, p. 13.

12. In Rothe, *Expressionismus*, p. 384.

13. [Woe to him who has been born: that he should die / before enjoying the glowing fruit, / the bitter fruit of guilt.] *Passion*, 1st version, 392.

14. Kierkegaard, *Postscript*, p. 517.

15. Schier, *Sprache*, pp. 67 and 80.

16. Cf. Maritain, *Art*, p. 102.

17. Cf. Berdyaev, *Meaning*, pp. 245–46.

18. Schier, *Sprache*, p. 67.

19. [The bread and wine of upright living, / God, into your gentle hands / man lays the dark end, / all guilt and red pain.] *Herbstseele*, 2d version, 107 (LG 109).

20. [Decay glows in the green pool, / the fish are still. God's breath / softly awakens a lyre in the haze. / The waters bring about healing for lepers.] *Kleines Konzert*, 42 (LG 43).

21. [A smile trembles in the sunshine, / while I slowly walk on by. / Unending love provides direction. / The hard stones quietly grow green.] *An Mauern hin*, 309.

22. [You live quietly in the shade of the autumnal ash tree, / submerged into the hill's just proportion. // Always you walk down the green river / when evening has come: / Resounding love.] *Anif*, 114 (LG 113).

23. [*Grodek:* In the evening autumnal forests resound / with deadly weapons; darkly the sun rolls / over golden plains, blue lakes. / Night enfolds / dying warriors, the wild lament / of their broken mouths. / Yet quietly in the willow thicket / a red cloud, temple of an angry God, / gathers spilled blood to itself, coolness of moon; / all roads flow into black decay. / Under golden branches of night and stars / the sister's shadow sways through the silent grove / to greet the spirits of the heroes, the bleeding heads; / and the dark flutes of autumn play softly in the reeds. / O prouder grief! you altars of bronze, / today the hot flame of the spirit is nourished by a mighty pain— / the unborn grandchildren.] 167 (LG 169).

24. [Crystalline voice, wherein dwells God's icy breath. / Angry magician.] *Karl Kraus*, 123 (LG 125).

25. Rothe, *Expressionismus*, p. 387.

26. Such myopia leads the French critic Jean-Michel Palmier to dismiss the issue of Trakl's Christianity with journalistic insouciance, basing himself, among other things, on this instance in *Grodek*. Quoting Heidegger with glee, Palmier asks: "Pourquoi le poète, dans la dernière détresse de son suprême dire, n'invoque-t-il ni Dieu, ni le Christ, s'il est resolument chrétien? Pourquoi nomme-t-il à la place 'l'ombre vacillante de la Soeur' et elle-même comme la 'Salutante'? Pourquoi le chant ne finit-il pas sur la perspective de la confiance en la redemption chrétienne?" *Situation de Georg Trakl* (Paris: Editions Pierre Belfond, 1972), p. 166. Such questions offer a flagrant instance of that objectified fixation of theological concerns deplored by Dorothee Sölle (cf. pp. 18–19), and plainly indicate a disregard of the existential dynamics of theology. Would Palmier then not argue that Dante was not ultimately a Christian poet because of the central role as mediatrix given by him to Beatrice, in this case analogous to Trakl's *Schwester*? Such critics are unwilling to grant any room for play to a Christian poet's creative imagination. Unless they find practically the whole creed and catechism recited over in every poem, they withhold the epithet "Christian"!

27. [Over waters, dark at night, / I sing my mournful songs, / songs that bleed like wounds.] *Nachtlied*, 235.

28. Cf. Gerhard Wahrig, *Deutsches Wörterbuch* (Gütersloh: Bertelsmann Lexikon-Verlag, 1968), cols. 3492 and 3845.

29. "Evil as evil effects the good," or "The fragmented as fragmentation brings about a healing wholeness," or "Damnation as damnation effects salvation," etc. Martin Heidegger,

in the essay on Rilke: "Wozu Dichter in dürftiger Zeit?" *Holzwege* (Frankfurt/Main: Vittorio Klostermann Verlag, 1950), p. 249.

30. [The sick soul fills up with snow and leprosy, / when in the evening it considers its image in the rosy pond. / Decayed eyelids open up, weeping, in the hazel-bush.] 424.

31. [O the decayed form of man; fashioned out of cold metals, / night and terrors of sunken forests / and the animal's scorching wilderness; / wind lull of the soul.] *Siebengesang des Todes*, 126 (LG 129).

32. [O the birth of man. Nocturnal blue water / murmurs in the rocky earth; / sighing, the fallen angel perceives his image.] *Geburt*, 115.

33. [In childlike tranquillity, / in the field of grain, where speechless a cross rises, / there appears to the beholder / his shadow and his demise, sighing.] 408.

34. [O the greening cross. In dark discourse / man and wife recognized each other. / Along the bare wall / the solitary walks with his stars.] 143.

35. [Too little love, too little justice and compassion, and always too little love. Too much harshness, arrogance, and all kinds of criminality: this is what I am. I am certain that I keep from doing evil only out of weakness and cowardice, and in this way I disgrace even my wickedness. I long for the day when my soul will no longer want or be able to dwell in this unholy body of mine, plagued by melancholy as it is. I long for the day when my soul will abandon this laughable figure consisting of filth and putrefaction, a figure which is an all too faithful reflection of a godless and accursed century.— God, only a small spark of pure joy and one would be saved! Love, and one would be redeemed.] 519.

36. *Schriften*, 1: 196.

37. *Postscript*, p. 473.

38. [Across the floor / comes dancing white as the moon / the powerful shadow of evil.] *Der Schlaf*, 1st version, 412.

39. Ricoeur, *De l'interprétation: Essai sur Freud* (Paris: Editions du Seuil, 1965), p. 475.

40. [*To the Silenced:* O the madness of the great city, when at nightfall / crippled trees grow stiff beside the black wall, / the spirit of evil gazes from a silver mask. / The stony night banishes light with magnetic scourge. / O sunken tones of evening bells. // Whore, who in icy tremors gives birth to a dead child. / God's thunderous wrath lashes the foreheads of the possessed, / purple pestilence, hunger crushes the green eyes. / O the horrible laughter of gold. // But a more silent humanity bleeds quietly in a dark cave, / fashions the redeeming Head out of hard metals.] 124 (LG 125).

41. Rothe, *Expressionismus*, p. 390.

42. Von Balthasar, *Herrlichkeit*, 1:502.

43. Ebner, *Schriften*, 1:315.

44. Cf. chap. 1, n. 48.

45. [My own affairs are no longer of interest to me. . . . I would gladly like to conceal myself and become invisible somewhere else.] 477.

46. [When I arrived here I had the impression of seeing life for the first time clearly, as it really is, without any personal interpretation, naked, without any presuppositions, as if I perceived all those voices which reality speaks, fierce voices not to be perceived without pain. And for a moment I felt something of the burden that habitually weighs man down.] 471–72.

47. [It is better than the original to the extent that it is now impersonal. . . . I am convinced that it will say and mean more to you in this universal form than in the narrow personal form of the first draft.] 485.

48. [At present I am greatly oppressed by such a hellish chaos of rhythms and images that I have time for nothing other than giving form at least partially to all of this.] 479.

49. Von Balthasar, *Herrlichkeit*, 1:501.

50. [Then, too, that we are withered up because we have thoughtlessly cast off the mask and have nothing to hold out into space but our own narrow, limited, and pitifully small

person—out into the black and mysteriously consuming winds. . . . In this sense, my dear Felix, would not abstraction truly be our holy mask, with which we could today as free beings come to the encounter of the freedomless Satan?] Elisabeth Langgässer, *Märkische Argonautenfahrt* (Hamburg: Classen Verlag, 1950), pp. 57 and 60.

51. Ebner, *Schriften,* 1 : 197.

52. [*Year:* Dark stillness of childhood. Under greening ash trees / gentleness grazes with a blue gaze; golden repose. / A scent of violets charms the darkness; in the evening / waving corn, grain and the golden shadows of sadness. / A carpenter hews the beams; the mill grinds / in the darkening valley. A purple mouth arches in hazel leaves, / masculine redness bent over silent waters. / Quiet is the autumn, the forest spirit; golden cloud / and the black shadow of the grandchild follow the solitary. / A bending in a stone room; beneath old cypress trees / the tears of night images are gathered at their source; / golden eye of the beginning, dark patience of the end.] 138 (LG 137).

53. Rothe, *Expressionismus,* p. 388.

54. Bahr, *Poiesis,* p. 302.

55. Maritain, *Intuition,* p. 106.

56. Ebner, *Schriften,* 1 : 97.

57. [Gentle harmonies, when in crystalline waves / we pass through the silent night, / a rosy angel steps out of the lovers' graves.] 313.

58. [Sleepwalkers step in front of a candle's light / The Spirit of Evil enters a spider.] *Unterwegs,* 2d version, 296.

59. [Shepherds buried the sun in the barren forest. / In a net of hair / a fisherman drew the moon from the freezing pond.] *Ruh and Schweigen,* 113 (LG 111).

60. Casey, *Manshape,* p. 13.

61. Cf. von Balthasar, *Herrlichkeit,* 1 : 392.

62. Ibid., p. 393.

63. Ibid., p. 603.

64. [Lonely, the sky darkens, / and the white head sinks mightily at the forest's edge. / Out of gloomy ravines the night emerges.] 320.

65. Von Balthasar, *Herrlichkeit,* 2/1 : 10–11.

66. F. X. Durrwell, *The Resurrection* (London: Sheed & Ward, 1961), p. 71.

67. [*Crucifixus:* He is the God to whom the poor ones kneel, / He, their destiny's mirror and their earthly torments', / a livid God, humiliated and spat on, / ending His life in the shame of Murderer's Hill. // They kneel to the tortures of His flesh, / in order that their meekness may wed His, / and that his final glance's night and death / may steal their heart in the ice of death-longing— // so that his death-benighted capitol of thorns / may open— symbol of earthly frailty— / the gate to Poverty's Paradises, / greeted by livid angels and lost men.] 245.

68. [*Song of a Captive Ouzel,* For Ludwig von Ficker: Dark breath in the green bough. / Small blue flowers hover round the face / of the solitary, his golden step / expiring under the olive tree. / Night flutters up on a drunken wing. / So gently Meekness bleeds, / dew that slowly drops from the blossoming thorn. / With radiant arms Compassion / enfolds a breaking heart.] 135.

69. Kierkegaard, *Postscript,* p. 424.

70. [But suffering remains to us, which is the lot we hold in common with you, the sign of our election inherited from our fathers, more active than a chaste fire, imperishable.] Bernanos, *Oeuvres,* p. 307.

71. [O Night, you mute gate before my suffering . . . / O Night, I am ready! / O Night, you garden of forgetfulness / around my poverty's splendor, closed to the world. / The foliage of the vine is withering, the crown of thorns is wilting. / O come, you fullness of time!] *Gesang zur Nacht,* 223.

72. Kierkegaard, *Postscript,* p. 389. Parenthetical expression my addition.

73. Ibid., p. 397.

74. [I am persecuted by unutterable jolts, and I do not know whether these are supposed to destroy me or perfect me. I am in doubt concerning everything I undertake and I face a ridiculously uncertain future.] 504.

75. *Postscript*, p. 446.

76. Szklenar, *Erinnerung*, pp. 122–23. "I am a Pro-tes-tant. . . . I have no right to withdraw from Hell."

77. Cf. Kierkegaard, *Postscript*, p. 388.

78. [O pain, you flaming contemplation / of great souls!] *Das Gewitter*, 157 (LG 159).

79. [To ponder the truth— / much pain! / At last, enthusiasm / until death.] *Nachtergebung*, 1st version, 414.

80. [Quietly the white night approaches, // transforms into dreams the pain and vexation / of stony existence, / that the prickly thorn may never cease to pierce the rotting body.] *Föhn*, 121 (LG 121–23).

81. [O Love! A blue thornbush / touches the [head's] cold temple, / the snowy night / with falling stars.] *Abendland*, 3rd version, 410.

82. Kierkegaard, *Postscript*, p. 390.

83. Killy-Szklenar, 1:463.

84. Von Balthasar, *Herrlichkeit*, 1:504.

85. [The bride has decked herself with stars, / the pure myrtle / that bends over the dead man's adoring countenance.] 322.

86. [The gentle power of Love / nurses his wounds, full of graces.] *Im Winter*, 383.

87. [Small blue flowers hover round the face / of the solitary.] *Gesang einer gefangenen Amsel*, 135.

88. [Full of blossoming tremors / the lady's blue mantle enfolds you at last.] 322.

89. [With radiant arms Compassion / enfolds a breaking heart.] *Gesang einer gefangenen Amsel*, 135.

90. [Your blue robe received him as he fell, / your red mouth sealed the friend's passing over into night.] *Nachts*, 96 (LG 99).

91. [Golden mouth that touches my lips, / and they resound like stars / over the torrent Kedron . . . / O my Beloved! Your lips— / pomegranate lips— / ripen on my mussel-like crystalline mouth.] 280.

92. Rothe, *Expressionismus*, p. 374.

93. Ibid., p. 384.

94. On the whole question of atonement, particularly on the simultaneity of Christ's glorification and humiliation, and on the Son's obedience out of love and the meaning of his abandonment by the Father, see: Norbert Hoffmann, "Atonement and the Ontological Coherence between the Trinity and the Cross," in: *Towards a Civilization of Love* (San Francisco: Ignatius Press, 1985), pp. 213–262. The article is dense but very lucid, and most rewarding for anyone wishing to pursue the matter in depth.

95. Von Balthasar, *Herrlichkeit*, 1:385–86.

96. [Who are we? Blue lament / of a mossy forest spring, / where the violets / secretly waft in the springtime.] *An Johanna*, 330.

97. [O, the boy's figure, / formed of crystalline tears / and nocturnal shadows.] *Abendland*, 3d version, 405.

98. [The God took the lament from his gentle mouth, / as in his full bloom he sank.] *An Novalis*, version 2a, 325.

99. Von Balthasar, *Herrlichkeit*, 1:598.

100. Cf. Rothe, *Expressionismus*, p. 385.

101. [God's silence / I drank from the fountain in the grove.] *De Profundis*, 46 (LG 47).

102. [Blue doves / drink at night the icy sweat / which flows from Elis' crystal brow.] *Elis*, 3d version, 86 (LG 89).

103. Rahner, *Investigations*, 6:237.

104. [So quietly a blaze of weeds dies out, and the black hamlet becomes mute in its foundations, / as if the Cross were descending the blue hill of Calvary, / as if the silent earth were expelling her dead.] *Psalm*, 346.

105. Lindenberger, *Trakl*, p. 47.

106. Michel van Esbroeck, *Herméneutique, structuralisme et exégèse: Essai de logique kérygmatique* (Paris: Desclée, 1968), p. 33.

107. [Faith . . . is not the imperfect approximation of something that could become knowledge. Faith constitutes a 'body' continuous with those realities on which it is dependent. We mutilate faith—no, this is too weak—we deny faith in its very essence by attempting to sever it from the realities themselves which inform it.] Gabriel Marcel, *Du refus*, pp, 193–94.

108. [The shadow quietly abandoned / the stranger at the crossroads; / and his intent eyes / became blind as stones, / that the song might flow more sweetly / from his lips.] *Abendland*, version 1a, 399.

109. [Frost and smoke. A white shirt of stars burns the shoulders that wear it and God's vultures mangle your metallic heart.] *Winternacht*, 128 (LG 129).

110. [Hour of unending sadness, / as if I were undergoing death because of you, . . . / as if I, a gentle deer, / were dwelling in the crystalline waters / of the cool spring / and the violets were blooming all about.] 321.

111. Cf. Langgässer, *Das Christliche*, p. 33.

112. [But take our artistic paradox: grant that expressiveness—expression as lament—is the issue of the whole construction: then may we not parallel to it another, a religious paradox, and say too (though only in the softest whisper) that out of the deepest despairedness hope might germinate? It would be a hope beyond hopelessness, the transcending of despair—not a betrayal of despair, but the miracle which surpasses belief. . . . Listen to the end, listen with me: one group of instruments after another retires, and what remains, as the work fades on the air, is the high G of a cello, the last word, the last fainting sound, slowly dying in a pianissimo-fermata, then nothing more: silence, and night. But that tone which vibrates in the silence, which is no longer there, to which only the spirit hearkens, and which was the last sound of mourning, is so no more. It changes its meaning; it abides as a light in the night.] Mann, *Doctor Faustus*, trans. H. T. Lowe-Porter (New York: Alfred A. Knopf, 1948), p. 491, with slight alterations.

113. [Cold metal treads upon my brow. / Spiders search out my heart. / There is a light that dies in my mouth. // By night I found myself upon a moor, / stiff with rubble and the dust of stars. / In the hazel bush / crystal angels sounded once more.] 46 (LG 49).

114. Wahrig, *Wörterbuch*, col. 1980.

115. In Casey, *Manshape*, p. 108.

116. Cf. ibid.

117. Cf. von Balthasar, *Herrlichkeit*, 1:409.

118. Cf. von Balthasar, *Le chrétien Bernanos*, trans. Maurice de Gandillac (Paris: Editions du Seuil, 1956), p. 41.

119. [Where the shades of the ancestors cling to the walls, / where previously there had been a solitary tree, a blue deer in the shrubs, / there the white mortal walks on golden steps, / Helian descends into the sighing darkness.] 423.

120. "O, the condescension!", an exclamation common in Byzantine hymns to the Incarnation and the Passion, which here corresponds directly to Helian's *Hinabsteigen*.

121. Gerhard van der Leeuw, *Einführung in die Phänomenologie der Religion* (Gütersloh: Gerd Mohn Verlag, 1933), p. 94.

122. [In the springtime; a delicate corpse, / resplendent in its grave; / under the wild elder-bushes of childhood.] 431.

123. [All growing things seem to be so sick! / A feverish haze circles round a hamlet. / Yet

from the boughs a gentle spirit beckons / to open wide the saddened heart. // So painfully good and true is all that lives; / lightly an old stone touches you: / Verily I will always be with you. / O mouth which trembles through the silver willow!] *Heiterer Frühling,* 2d version, 50 (LG 51–53).

124. [Out of black decay / there step forth God's radiant angels.] *Am Hügel,* 390.

125. "The atonement, which is the deepest expression of the repetition." Kierkegaard, *Papirer,* ed. P. A. Heiberg and V. Kuhr (Copenhagen: Gyldendalske Boghandel, 1912), IVB, 117, p. 293.

126. Muschg, *Von Trakl,* p. 114.

127. Lachmann, *Kreuz,* p. 14.

128. Schier, *Sprache,* pp. 89–90.

129. Ebner, *Schriften,* 1:79.

130. [It was most moving because of its interior distances. It is constructed on its pauses, and the lines play the role of a few railings that enclose the boundless and the unutterable. Like fences on a flat land beyond which that which is fenced in continually extends as a great, unpossessible plain.] Szklenar, *Erinnerung,* p. 8.

131. Langgässer, *Das Chrisliche,* p. 36.

132. No one has expressed this "muteness of God" after Christ's incarnation better than St. John of the Cross, the doctor of the "dark night of the soul": "Dios ha quedado como mudo y no tiene más qué hablar, porque lo que hablaba antes en partes a los profetas, ya lo ha hablado en [Cristo] todo, dándonos al Todo, que es su Hijo." *Subida del Monte Carmelo,* II, 22, 4: *Vida y Obras de San Juan de la Cruz,* ed. Crisógono de Jesús et al. (Madrid: Biblioteca de Autores Cristianos, 1960), p. 522.

133. Søren Kierkegaard, *Repetition: An Essay in Experimental Psychology,* trans. Walter Lowrie (Princeton: Princeton University Press, 1941), pp. 3–4.

134. Sölle, *Realisation,* p. 54.

135. Langgässer, *Das Christliche,* p. 42.

136. Durrwell, *Resurrection,* p. 225.

137. Berdyaev, *Meaning,* p. 112.

138. Kierkegaard, *Papirer,* IVB, 118, 1, p. 301. My translation.

139. Kierkegaard, *Repetition,* p. 18.

140. "You must change your life." *Sämtliche Werke* (Frankfurt/Main: Insel Verlag, 1955), 1:557.

141. [A tapestry in which the suffering landscape turns pale, / perhaps Genezareth, in the storm a boat, / out of the stormclouds there tumble down golden things, / madness which seizes the gentle person. / The old waters gurgle a blue laughter. // And often a dark shaft opens up. / The possessed mirror themselves in cold metals, / drops of blood fall on glowing platters, / and a face disintegrates in the black night. / Flags that stammer in gloomy vaults. // Other things remind one of the birds' flight, / over the gallows the crows' mystical signs, / in pointed grassblades copper lizards slide, / in cushions of incense a smile, whorish and clever. // Good Friday's children stand at the fences, blind, / in the mirror of dark gutters full of decay / the dying people's moanful healing / and angels that walk through white eyes, / from eyelids golden redemption shines forth darkly.] 301.

142. Killy-Szklenar, 2:389.

143. Ibid.

144. Kierkegaard, *Postscript,* p. 517.

145. Berdyaev, *Meaning,* p. 110.

146. Van Esbroeck, *Herméneutique,* p. 194.

147. [Over the Sleeper's face the white-haired Father leans, / the bearded face of the Good One, that had gone far / into the dark.] 422.

148. [Silently, over the Place of the Skull, there open up God's golden eyes.] 56.

149. [The silent God lowers his blue eyelids over him.] 73.
150. [God, into your meek hands / man lays the dark ending, / all guilt and red pain.] *Herbstseele,* 2d version, 107.
151. [Tell how long it is we have been dead.] *Entlang,* 106.
152. *Abendland,* 2d version, 405.

Bibliography

Trakl's Writings

Killy, Walter and Hans Szklenar, eds. *Georg Trakl: Dichtungen und Briefe. Historisch-kritische Ausgabe.* Salzburg: Otto Müller Verlag, 1969.

Getsi, Lucia, trans. *Georg Trakl: Poems.* Athens, Ohio: Mundus Artium Press, 1973.

Scripture and Liturgical Books

Biblia Sacra juxta Vulgatam Clementinam. Tournai: Desclée et Socii, 1956.

Die Bibel nach der Übersetzung Martin Luthers. Stuttgart: Württembergische Bibelanstalt, 1972.

The Holy Bible. Revised Standard Version. New York: Thomas Nelson & Sons, 1952.

Novum Testamentum graece et latine. Edited by Augustinus Merk. Rome: Sumptibus Pontificii Instituti Biblici, 1951.

Αι Ιεραί Ακολουθίαι της Μ. Ἑβδομάδος καί του Πάγχα. Edited by George L. Papadeas. New York, 1971.

Ιερά Σύνοψις των Προσευχων. Edited by Emmanouel G. Mytilenaiou. Athens: N. Alikiotes, 1952.

Missale Romanum, ex decreto sacrosancti Concilii Tridentini restitutum, Pii V. Pont. Max. jussu editum, etc. Various editions.

Other Works

Auerbach, Erich. *Neue Dantestudien.* Istanbul: Ibrahim Horoz Basımevi, 1944.

———. *Mimesis: The Representation of Reality in Western Literature.* Translated by Willard R. Trask. Princeton: Princeton University Press, 1953.

Augustinus, Aurelius. *Confessionum libri XIII.* Edited by Martinus Skutella. In aedibus B. G. Teubneri, 1969.

Avery, Catherine B., ed. *The New Century Classical Handbook.* New York: Appleton-Century-Crofts, Inc., 1962.

Bahr, Hans-Eckehard. *Poiesis: Theologische Untersuchung der Kunst.* Stuttgart: Evangelisches Verlagswerk, 1960.

Balthasar, Hans Urs von. *Apokalypse der deutschen Seele: Studien zu einer Lehre von letzten Haltungen.* 3 vols. Salzburg: Verlag Anton Pustet, 1939.

———. *Le chrétien Bernanos,* trans. Maurice de Gandillac. Paris: Editions du Seuil, 1956.

————. *Herrlichkeit: eine theologische Ästhetik. I: Schau der Gestalt. II/1: Klerikale Stile. III/1: Im Raum der Metaphysik.* Einsiedeln: Johannes Verlag, 1961–69.

Barber, Richard and Ann Riches, eds. *A Dictionary of Fabulous Beasts.* New York: Walker & Co., 1971.

Basil, Otto. *Georg Trakl in Selbstzeugnissen und Bilddokumenten.* Reinbek bei Hamburg: Rowohlt Verlag, 1965.

Berdyaev, Nikolai. *The Meaning of the Creative Act.* Translated by Donald A. Lowrie. London: Victor Gollancz, Ltd., 1955.

Bernanos, Georges. *Oeuvres romanesques, suivies de "Dialogues des carmélites."* Edited by Albert Béguin. Paris: Bibliothèque de la Pléiade, 1961.

Böschenstein, Bernhard. "Wirkungen des französischen Symbolismus auf die deutsche Literatur der Jahrhundertwende." *Euphorion* 58 (1964): pp. 375–95.

Casey, T. J. *Manshape That Shone: An Interpretation of Trakl.* Oxford: Basil Blackwell, 1964.

Chiari, Joseph. *"Symbolisme" from Poe to Mallarmé: The Growth of a Myth.* London: Rockliff Publishing Corp., 1956.

Commodianus. *Carmina.* Edited by Bernhardus Dembart. Vienna: Apud C. Geroldi Filium, 1887.

Croce, Benedetto. *Poesia antica e moderna.* Bari: Gius. Lateza e Figli, 1966.

Cysarz, Herbert, ed. *Barocklyrik. I: Vor- und Frühbarock. II: Hoch- und Spätbarock. III: Schwund- und Kirchenbarock.* 2d ed. Hildesheim: Georg Olms Verlagsbuchhandlung, 1964.

Dante Alighieri. *La divina commedia.* Translated and commentary by Charles S. Singleton. Princeton: Princeton University Press, 1973.

Dolei, Giuseppe. *L'arte come espiazione imperfetta: Saggio su Trakl.* Stuttgart: Akademischer Verlag Hans-Dieter Heinz, 1978.

Durrwell, F. X. *The Resurrection.* London: Sheed & Ward, 1961.

Ebner, Ferdinand. *Schriften, I: Fragmente, Aufsätze, Aphorismen: Zu einer Phänomenologie des Wortes.* Munich: Kösel Verlag, 1963.

Esbroeck, Michel van. *Herméneutique, structuralisme et exégèse: Essai de logique kérygmatique.* Paris: Desclée de Brouwer, 1968.

Eusebius Pamphilus. *The Ecclesiastical History,* trans. C. F. Crusé. London: Bell & Daldy, 1866.

Falk, Walter. *Leid und Verwandlung: Rilke, Kafka, Trakl und der Epochenstil des Impressionismus und Expressionismus.* Salzburg: Otto Müller Verlag, 1961.

Fiedler, Theodore. Review of H. Lindenberger's *Georg Trakl,* in *Comparative Literature* 26, no. 1 (Winter 1974): 82–84.

Focke, Alfred. *Georg Trakl: Liebe und Tod.* Vienna: Buchreihe "Wissenschaft und Weltbild," 1955.

Guardini, Romano. *Die Sinne und die religiöse Erkenntnis: Zwei Versuche über die christliche Gewisserung.* Würzburg: Werkbund-Verlag, 1950.

Günther, Johann Christian. *Gedichte.* Edited by Hannsludwig Geiger. Berlin: Erich Schmidt Verlag, 1947.

Hamburger, Michael. *The Truth of Poetry: Tensions in Modern Poetry from Baudelaire to the 1960's.* London: Weidenfeld & Nicolson, 1969.

————. *Contraries: Studies in German Literature.* New York: E. P. Dutton, 1970.

Hammer, Karl. *W. A. Mozart—eine theologische Deutung: Ein Beitrag zur theologischen Anthropologie.* Zürich: EVZ-Verlag, 1964.

Heidegger, Martin. *Holzwege.* Frankfurt/Main: Vittorio Klostermann Verlag, 1950.

————. "Georg Trakl: Eine Erörterung seines Gedichtes." *Merkur* 61 (1953): pp. 226–58.

Hoffmann, Norbert. "Atonement and the Ontological Coherence between the Trinity and the Cross." In *Towards a Civilization of Love: A Symposium on the Scriptural and Theological Foundations of the Devotion to the Heart of Jesus.* San Francisco: Ignatius Press, 1985.

Isidori Hispaliensis Episcopi. *Etymologiarum sive originum libri XX.* Edited by W. M. Lindsay. Oxford: E Typographeo Clarendoniano, 1911.

Jacob, Max. *Art poétique.* Paris: Emile Paul Frères, 1922.

James, G. Ingli. "The Autonomy of the Work of Art: Modern Criticism and the Christian Tradition." *Sewanee Review* 70 (1962): 298 ff.

John of the Cross, St. *Vida y obras de San Juan de la Cruz.* Edited by Crisógono de Jesús, et al. Madrid: Biblioteca de Autores Cristianos, 1960.

Johnston, William M. *The Austrian Mind: An Intellectual and Social History 1848–1938.* Berkeley: University of California Press, 1972.

Kierkegaard, Søren. *Papirer.* Edited by P. A. Heiberg and V. Kuhr. Copenhagen: Gyldendalske Boghandel, 1912.

————. *Samlede Vaerker.* Edited by A. B. Drachmann, J. L. Heiberg, H. O. Lange. Copenhagen: Gyldendalske Boghandel, 1963.

————. *Concluding Unscientific Postscript,* trans. David F. Swenson and Walter Lowrie. Princeton: Princeton University Press, 1941.

————. *Repetition: An Essay in Experimental Psychology,* trans. Walter Lowrie. Princeton: Princeton University Press, 1941.

Killy, Walter. *Über Georg Trakl.* 3d ed. Göttingen: Vandenhoeck & Ruprecht, 1967.

Kirschbaum, Englebert, ed. *Lexikon der christlichen Ikonographie,* vol. 2. Freiburg: Herder Verlag, 1970.

Klein, Johannes. *Geschichte der deutschen Lyrik von Luther bis zum Ausgang des zweiten Weltkrieges.* Wiesbaden: Franz Steiner Verlag, 1957.

Kurrik, Maire Jaanus, *Georg Trakl.* New York: Columbia University Press, 1974.

Lachmann, Eduard. *Kreuz und Abend: eine Interpretation der Dichtungen Georg Trakls.* Salzburg: Otto Müller Verlag, 1954.

Langer, Susanne K. *Feeling and Form: A Theory of Art.* New York: Charles Scribner's Sons, 1953.

Langgässer, Elisabeth. *Märkische Argonautenfahrt.* Hamburg: Claassen Verlag, 1950.

————. *Das Christliche der christlichen Dichtung.* Edited by Wilhelm Hoffmann. Olten: Walter-Verlag, 1961.

Leach, Maria, ed. *Standard Dictionary of Folklore, Mythology, and Legend.* New York: Funk & Wagnalls, 1972.

Leclercq, Jean. *L'Amour des lettres et le désir de Dieu: Initiation aux auteurs monastiques du Moyen Age.* Paris: Editions du Cerf, 1957.

Leeuw, Gerhard van der. *Einführung in die Phänomenologie der Religion.* Gütersloh: Gerd Mohn Verlag, 1933.

Lindenberger, Herbert. *Georg Trakl.* New York: Twayne Publishers, 1971.

Lorca, Federico Garcia. *Obras completas.* Edited by Arturo del Hoyo. Madrid: Aguilar, 1969.

Lubac, Henri de. *Exégèse médiévale: Les quatre sens de l'Ecriture.* Paris: Aubier, 1959.

Luther, Gisela. *Barocker Expressionismus? Zur Problematik der Beziehung zwischen der Bildlichkeit expressionistischer und barocker Lyrik.* The Hague: Mouton & Co., 1969.

Mann, Thomas. *Doktor Faustus: Das Leben des deutschen Tonsetzers Adrian Leverkühn, erzählt von einem Freunde.* Stockholm: Bermann-Fischer Verlag, 1947.

————. *Doctor Faustus.* Translated by H. T. Lowe-Porter. New York: Alfred A. Knopf, 1948.

Marcel, Gabriel. *Du refus à l'invocation.* Paris: Gallimard, 1940.

Maritain, Jacques. *Art et scolastique.* Paris: Librairie de l'Art Catholique, 1947.

————. *Creative Intuition in Art and Poetry.* New York: Meridian Books, 1954.

Meyers Enzyklopädisches Lexikon, X. Mannheim: Bibliographisches Institut, 1974.

Migne, J. P., ed. *Patrologiae Cursus Completus, Series Latina, CXXII: Johannis Scoti Opera.* Paris: Apud Garnier Fratres, 1879.

Muschg, Walter. *Die Zerstörung der deutschen Literatur.* Berne: Francke Verlag, 1956.

————. *Von Trakl zu Brecht: Dichter des Expressionismus.* Munich: R. Piper Verlag, 1961.

Neidhart, Hans Konrad. *Georg Trakls "Helian."* Schleitheim: 1957.

Palmier, Jean-Michel. *Situation de Georg Trakl.* Paris: Editions Pierre Belfond, 1972.

Pascal, Blaise. *Oeuvres complètes.* Edited by Jacques Chevalier. Paris: Bibliothèque de la Pléiade, 1954.

Plato. *The Collected Dialogues of Plato.* Edited by Edith Hamilton and Huntington Cairns. Princeton: Princeton University Press, 1961.

Rahner, Karl. *Theological Investigations.* Translated by Karl-H. and Boniface Kruger. Baltimore: Helicon Press, 1969.

Ricoeur, Paul. *Finitude et culpabilité.* Vol. 2: *La symbolique du mal.* Paris: Editions Montaigne, 1960.

————. *De l'interprétation: Essai sur Freud.* Paris: Editions du Seuil, 1965.

Rilke, Rainer Maria. *Sämtliche Werke.* Frankfurt/Main: Insel Verlag, 1955.

Roberts, Alexander and James Donaldson, eds. *Ante-Nicene Christian Library. Vol. 14: The Writings of Methodius of Olympus, Alexander of Lycopolis, Peter of Alexandria, and Several Fragments.* Edinburgh: T. & T. Clark, 1869.

————. *The Ante-Nicene Fathers. Vol. 3: Latin Christianity: Its Founder, Tertullian.* Buffalo: Christian Literature Publishing Co., 1885.

Rothe, Wolfgang, ed. *Expressionismus als Literatur.* Berne: Francke Verlag, 1969.

Salmond, S. D. F., ed. and trans. *The Works of Gregory Thaumaturgus, Dionysius of Alexandria, and Archelaus. Ante-Nicene Christian Library,* vol. 20. Edinburgh: T. & T. Clark, 1871.

Schier, Rudolf D. *"Nur dem, der das Glück verachtet, wird Erkenntnis": A Study of Georg Trakl's "Helian."* Ph.D. dissertation, Cornell University, 1965.

———. *Die Sprache Georg Trakls.* Heidelberg: Carl Winter Verlag, 1970.

Schupp, Franz. *Glaube—Kultur—Symbol: Versuch einer kritischen Theorie sakramentaler Praxis.* Düsseldorf: Patmos Verlag, 1974.

Sharp, Francis M. *The Poet's Madness: A Reading of Georg Trakl.* Ithaca: Cornell University Press, 1981.

Sölle, Dorothee. *Realisation: Studien zum Verhältnis von Theologie und Dichtung nach der Aufklärung.* Darmstad: Hermann Luchterhand Verlag, 1973.

Steffens, Henrich. *Caricaturen des Heiligsten.* Pt. 1. Leipzig: 1819.

Szklenar, Hans, ed. *Erinnerung an Georg Trakl: Zeugnisse und Briefe,* 3d ed. Salzburg: Otto Müller Verlag, 1966.

Thomas Aquinas, Saint. *Summa theologiae.* Cambridge: Blackfriars Press, 1964.

Tillich, Paul. *Systematic Theology,* vol. 1. Chicago: University of Chicago Press, 1951.

———. *Theology of Culture.* London: Oxford University Press, 1959.

Trethowan, Illtyd. *The Absolute and the Atonement.* London: George Allen & Unwin, 1971.

Wahrig, Gerhard. *Deutsches Wörterbuch.* Gütersloh: Bertelsmann Lexikon-Verlag, 1968.

Wetzel, Heinz. *Konkordanz zu den Dichtungen Georg Trakls.* Salzburg: Otto Müller Verlag, 1971.

Wiesen, David S. *St. Jerome as Satirist: A Study in Christian Latin Thought and Letters.* Ithaca: Cornell University Press, 1964.

Wilder, Amos N. *The Language of the Gospel: Early Christian Rhetoric.* New York: Harper & Row, 1964.

Index of Persons and Titles

Where no author's name is given in parentheses, the title is that of a poem by Trakl. Asterisks designate poems discussed at some length.

General Index

Abstractionism, poetic, 130–32, 159
Aestheticism, 13, 80, 112
Anagnōrisis ("recognition," poetic and spiritual), 36, 38, 41–42, 114, 118, 122–24, 139
Anamnēsis ("remembering," liturgical and mystical), 69, 137, 139
Anonymity of the Christ-form, 13, 36, 47, 99, 101, 108–9, 127, 136–37, 157
Apocalypticism, 19, 45–47, 113; early Christian, 47–49, 77
Apophatic mysticism, 145, 160
Art as "habit" of the soul, 30
Atonement, 14, 18–19, 40–41, 43, 110–12; and redemption, 111; stages of, 121–22; *Sühne*, 122
Ausgesetztheit, 35, 46
Austro-Hungarian Empire and culture, 42, 48–49, 82
Autexousiōs, 104–6, 120, 135

Baroque poetry and imagery, 19, 47, 54; apocalyptic, 59–61; of the Passion, 65–67, 87, 127
Brenner, Der, and the *Brenner* circle, 14, 41
Byzantine style, 131–32

Christ. *See* Jesus Christ and the Christ-form
Christian art, 30–31, 34, 88, 96, 116
Christian faith and poetry, 14, 19, 29–30, 34, 39, 69, 74, 92, 112
Christianity and the Christian tradition, 17, 19, 23, 26, 96, 151
Contemporaneity with Christ-event, 108, 135, 153, 155
Correspondences, Baudelaire's theory of, 80
Cross, aesthetics of the, 54–55, 58, 68, 92, 159

Darkness and light, 11, 37, 39, 65, 93, 105, 131, 135

Decay, physical and metaphysical, 13, 15, 24, 38–39, 45–46, 49, 52, 59, 73, 123
Demonism, 42–43, 73, 90, 124, 126, 129, 140, 156–57
Despair, 13, 37, 73, 99, 103, 107, 117, 126–27, 135, 159; and the repetition, 154
Dialectical theology, 19, 47, 72–74, 113
Disjunctio mystica, 119

Ekstasis (transcendence of self), 43, 132
Expressionism and Expressionists, 13–14, 19, 42, 47, 59, 64, 74–75, 78–80, 85–86, 112

Fathers of the Church, 84–86, 102, 104
Figura and figural language, 16–17, 19, 26–29, 35, 38, 41, 46, 53, 58, 62, 72, 78, 89, 95–96, 98, 100, 111–12, 116, 145, 151
Form (poetic and existential *Gestalt*), 11, 18–19, 23–24, 27–28, 31–34, 78, 90, 99, 126, 136–37, 146

Gnosticism, 115, 136, 143
Golgotha (Calvary), 106, 143, 145–46, 148, 156, 160
Good and evil, 11, 15, 35, 48, 73, 76, 98, 101, 103, 114, 125–26, 133, 145, 147, 156, 159
Greek liturgy, 102–3
Griffin (as christological symbol), 106–7
Guilt and sin, 16–19, 40, 42–43, 59, 73–74, 110–15, 127, 145, 147, 161; and grace, 122; and the transcendence of despair, 148

Harrowing of Hell, 105, 149
Hebraic tradition and dispensation, 27, 29, 35, 89, 93–94
Hekousiōs, 102–3, 105, 135
Hermeticism, Trakl's alleged, 12, 16, 19, 77, 86

190